Rudolph Ihlee
The Road to Collioure

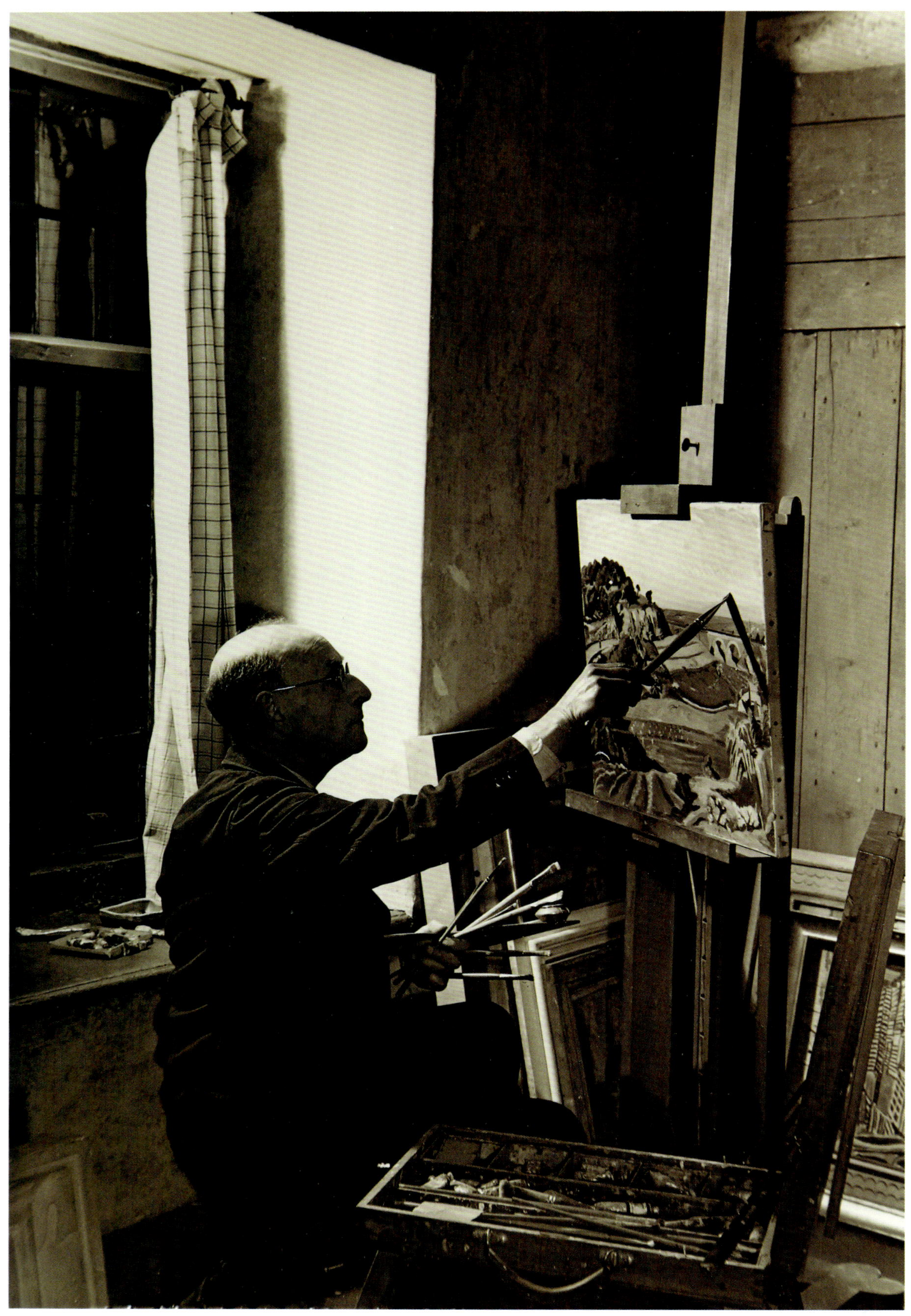

James Trollope

Rudolph Ihlee

The Road to Collioure

LUND
HUMPHRIES

First published in 2022 by Lund Humphries

Lund Humphries
Office 3, Book House
261A City Road
London EC1V 1JX
UK
www.lundhumphries.com

Rudolph Ihlee: The Road to Collioure

ISBN 978-1-84822-482-7

A Cataloguing-in-Publication record for this book is available from the British Library.

Cover image: Rudolph Ihlee, *My Window, Collioure* (detail), 1925, private collection
Frontispiece: Rudolph Ihlee in his studio at West Deeping, 1951, private collection

Copy edited by Eleanor Rees
Designed by Mark Thomson
Set in Bauer Grotesk
Printed in Slovenia

Lines from *The Catalans* by Patrick O'Brian: Reprinted by permission of HarperCollins Publishers Ltd © Patrick O'Brian 1953

Contents

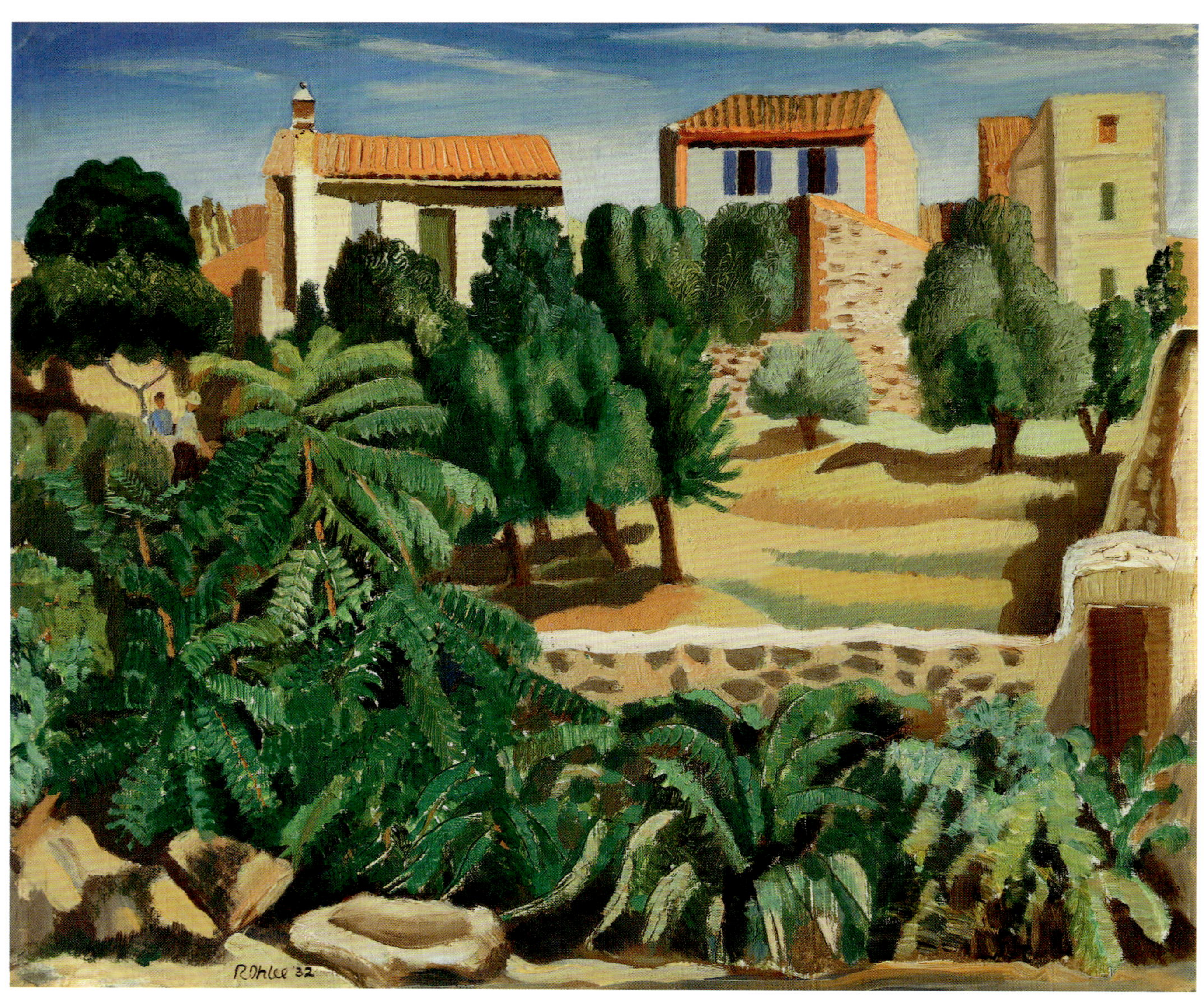

1
Petites Maisons, Faubourg, Collioure, 1932
Oil on canvas
38.1 × 45.7 cm (15 × 18 in)
Author's collection

Preface

On a rainy English afternoon nothing cheers me more than a small painting by Rudolph Ihlee (1883–1968) of a sun-drenched scene in the south of France. Not just any part of France but the department which borders Spain, between the mountains and the Mediterranean, called the Pyrénées-Orientales (Eastern Pyrenees). I feel an affinity with the artist as both he and I chose to live in that delightful corner of the country in our late thirties, some 70 years apart.

Between 1922 and 1940 Ihlee settled in the fishing port of Collioure, rediscovering his love of life but risking his reputation as a painter. As a jaded journalist, I had less to lose when, from 1994, I was happy to spend five years in the foothills of the Pyrenees about half an hour from Ihlee's adopted home. When I returned to England, having rather late in life become a father, I wanted something to remind me of those carefree days in northern Catalonia. A painting caught my eye at an auction. Called *Petites Maisons, Faubourg, Collioure* (fig.1), it shows a small group of houses with a couple, almost hidden, sheltering from the midday sun beneath some trees. While far from Ihlee's most imposing work, it has what I have come to recognise as his trademark charm.

When I bought the picture I had barely heard of its creator but, once it was on my wall, I was curious to find out more. Thanks in part to an organisation which collects money for the heirs of artists, I eventually managed to contact some people who knew him, including a family with a large collection of Ihlees, many of which were inspired by places I knew from my temporary, and much less productive, exile. Then I came across a notebook in which Ihlee had listed nearly all the paintings he produced in Collioure. This enabled me to compile a comprehensive record of all his known work, which is published here for the first time. Thus began my search to discover more about Ihlee's life and, in particular, to find out what, a century ago, had set him on the road to Collioure.

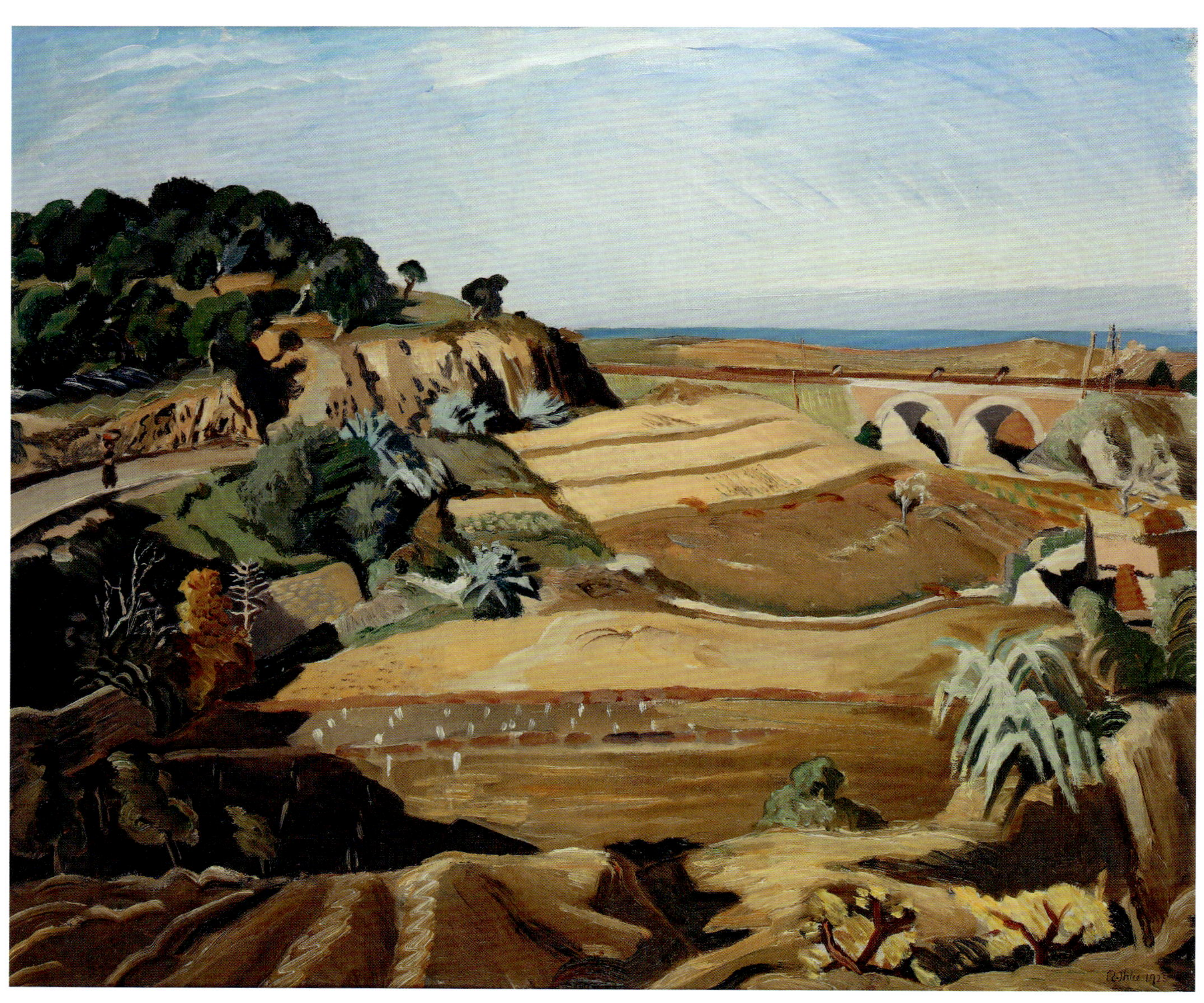

2
The Clear Road (between Argelès and Collioure), 1925
Oil on canvas
50.8 × 60.96 cm (20 × 24 in)
Private collection

Introduction

While the road to Collioure led Rudolph Ihlee to artistic freedom and personal contentment, it also marked a slide into obscurity. An outstanding student at the Slade, he had three one-man shows in London before turning his back on a promising career and heading towards the Mediterranean sun.

In 1922 when he arrived in the small French fishing town, a few miles from the Spanish border, he was nearly 40 and seeking a fresh start. Abandoned by his glamorous wife, he was trying to put the past behind him. He chose to travel with his closest friend, fellow artist Edgar Hereford (1886–1953), who had his own reasons for escape. Exceptionally short in stature, Hereford had long been the victim of cruel jibes, and the death of both his parents gave him the means to start a new life. Both men had cars and private incomes. They were ready for exile.

After a painting holiday in Algeria earlier in the year, the pair sailed to Port Vendres, on the Roussillon coast and took lodgings in neighbouring Collioure (see map, p.78). Ihlee liked it so much he outstayed his welcome, fleeing in haste in 1940 after France's surrender to Germany.

They were not the first artists to draw inspiration from the sun-soaked port magnificently sited beneath mountains that dip into the sea.

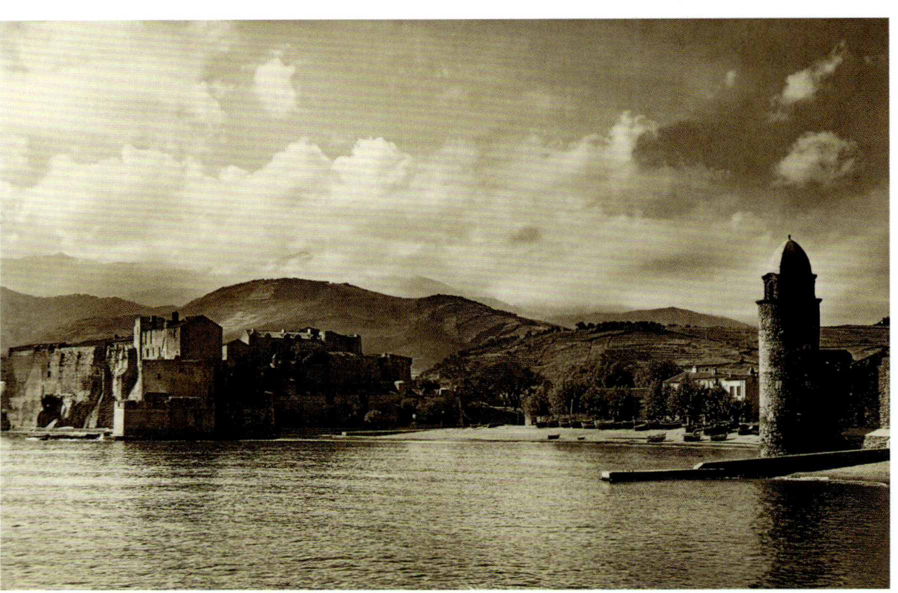

3
Collioure
Postcard

Most notably, in the summer of 1905 Matisse and Derain produced an astonishing series of pictures whose combination of explosive colours and bold brushstrokes led to them being dubbed *Les Fauves* ('the savages'). Nor were Ihlee and Hereford the first artists with a British background to fall under Collioure's spell. James Dickson Innes (1887–1914) and Derwent Lees (1885–1931),[1] Slade contemporaries of Ihlee and Hereford, painted in the French port before the First World War (see Appendix). But none embraced the community in the same way as Ihlee, who married a local girl and probably would never have left had it not been for the German occupation of France in the Second World War.

Soon after his arrival, Ihlee encouraged Charles Rennie Mackintosh (1868–1928) and his wife Margaret to settle nearby. The Scottish architect painted a series of watercolours of the region. Letters from Mackintosh frequently mention Ihlee and Hereford and provide a valuable, at times comic, account of their lives in exile. When, after four years in France, Mackintosh showed signs of a fatal cancer, it was Ihlee who accompanied him back to Britain.

During his long stay in Collioure, Ihlee produced more than 200 paintings, the majority landscapes inspired by the town and surrounding countryside which he and Hereford enjoyed exploring. They often motored to remote mountain settlements or across the border to Spain, where in 1936 Ihlee became caught up in the Spanish Civil War (see Chapter 6).

Governed by the seasons, the 3000 or so locals looked to nature for their livelihoods, fishing for sardines and anchovies in spring and summer and working the vineyards on the mountain slopes for the rest of the year.

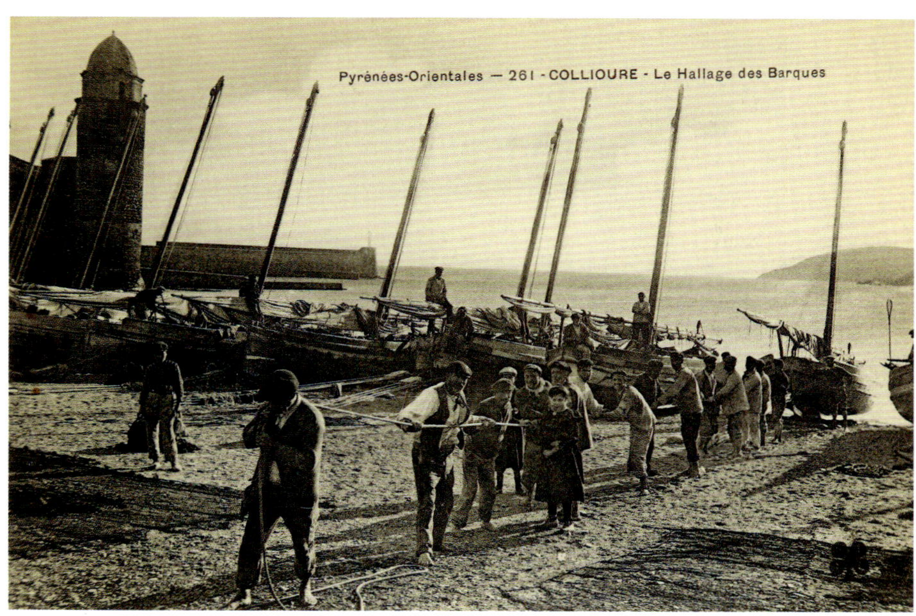

4
Fishermen, Collioure, c.1920
Postcard

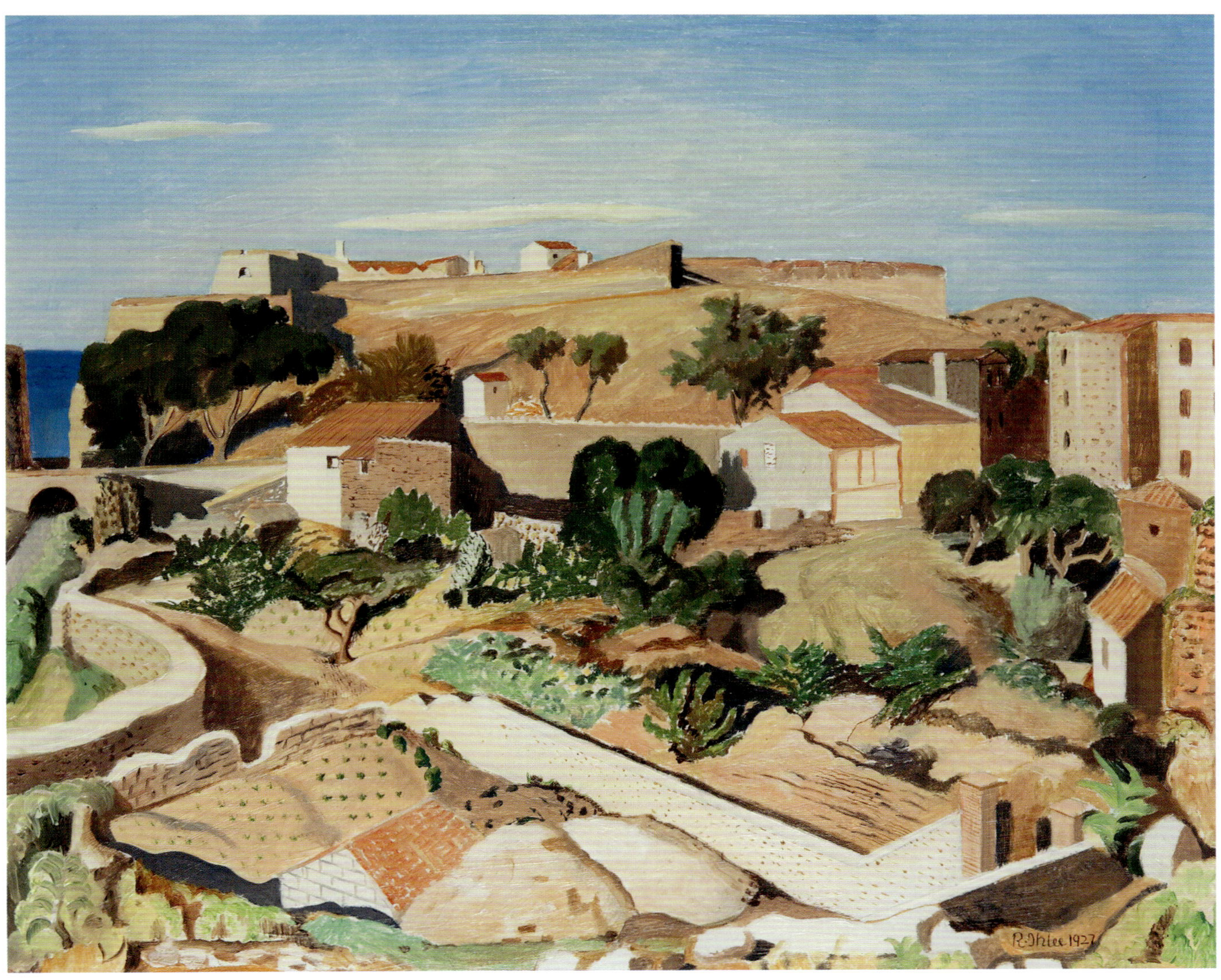

5
Fort Miradou Precincts, Collioure, 1927
Oil on board
38.1 × 45.72 cm (15 × 18 in)
Hunterian Art Gallery,
University of Glasgow

Ihlee, who met his second wife grape-picking, relished this slower rhythm of life under the nourishing, at times unforgiving, sun. He enjoyed the beach and cafés and nights out but also continued to exhibit sporadically in London as well as in Perpignan and Paris, where he had a dealer.[2]

In his student days Ihlee had rubbed shoulders with C.R.W. Nevinson (1889–1946), Mark Gertler (1891–1939), Edward Wadsworth (1889–1949), Maxwell Gordon Lightfoot (1886–1911), Stanley Spencer (1891–1959) and Paul Nash (1889–1946). Later, he had been encouraged by Walter Sickert and William Rothenstein and lauded by critics including Frank Rutter and P.G. Konody.[3] Notable collectors such as Sir Edward Marsh[4] and Charles Rutherston had bought his work. He exhibited with Vanessa Bell's Friday Club and at the Carfax and Leicester Galleries. But his arrival in Collioure marked a turning point in his career. He had broken free from the

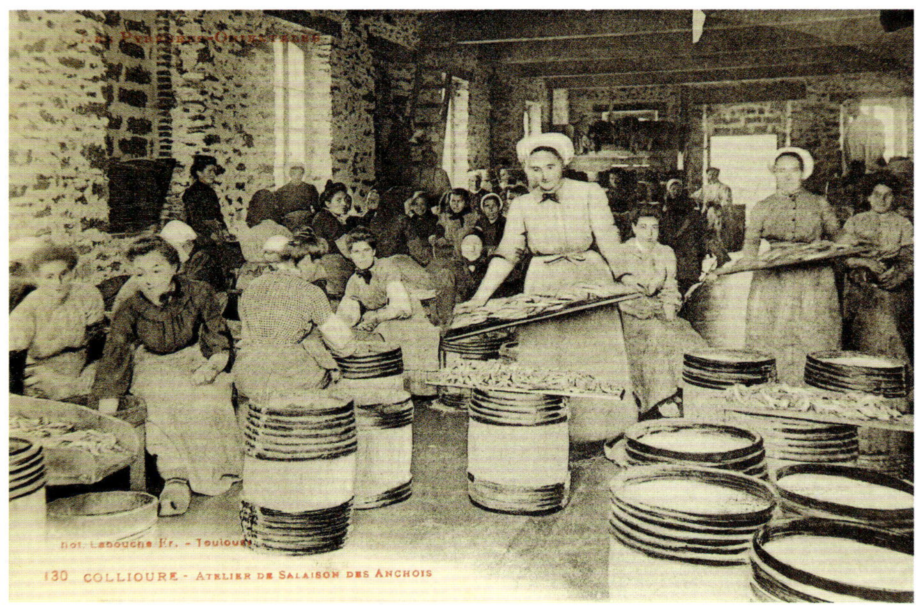

6
Anchovy salting house, Collioure, c.1920
Postcard

demands of the London gallery scene to follow his own path.

In his last one-man show in London in 1926, four years after settling in Collioure, the catalogue notes 'He prefers to associate with the native population of the countryside – with wine-growers and anchovy salters and the ordinary townsfolk rather than with artists, and from whose habits and customs he is enabled to familiarise himself with local conditions and characteristics.'[5]

Ihlee's early reputation was based on his brilliance as a draughtsman. He could draw the human figure better than almost any of his contemporaries. His landscapes were carefully composed and his style compared to that of William Orpen (1878–1931) and Augustus John (1878–1961), both of whom had earlier studied at the Slade.

Collioure brought artistic release. His palette became brighter, his brushstrokes bolder and his compositions more fluid. He concentrated on the structure and form of landscape, becoming intrigued by the patterns of trees, bridges and houses, often being more attracted to quirky views of back alleys, overgrown gardens and crumbling walls than to conventionally 'pretty' subjects.

Throughout his life he was a prolific portraitist and the figures in his landscapes, be they human or animal, are nearly always convincing and occasionally humorous. After buying a painting featuring a dog Sir Edward Marsh enthused: 'It is a delightful and original picture – the way you've fixed the dog's back, in that tense excitement, without any facial expression to help, is the sort of thing that's a miracle to a non-artist who doesn't know how it's done.'[6]

In middle and later life Ihlee painted mainly in oils but also sketched in pencil, pastel and watercolour. As a young man he had experimented with lithography. He had an intensely practical as well as artistic nature. Before the Slade he had trained as an engineer and was often happier talking about machines, cars in particular, than painting. For an exhibition of practical art after the First World War he produced designs for tables, chairs and an electric lamp.[7] He was also methodical, carefully listing his French work up to 1936, noting dimensions, prices, buyers and exhibition history.

In London, Ihlee's German heritage and strange name made him an outsider. His close friendships tended to be with those on the fringes of groups. Apart from Hereford, his closest friend was Maxwell Gordon Lightfoot, a highly strung Northerner who wrote two extraordinary letters to Ihlee shortly before committing suicide in 1911 at the age of 25. In the first he gives unflattering portrayals of fellow members of the Camden Town Group of artists. In the second he reveals surprising depths of feelings towards Ihlee. Written a few months before he killed himself, supposedly because of a broken engagement, they cast a new light on Lightfoot's state of mind before the tragedy.

After the collapse of his own marriage, Ihlee was happy to swap the backbiting London art world for the freedom of France. Exile gave him the opportunity to forget past miseries and shed inhibitions. There was also the possibility of reinventing himself. By adding an accent to his name (Ihlée), which may anyway have originated in Alsace, he made it sound more French, although it never ceased to be a stumbling block. Often misspelt, it is usually mispronounced Ely, like the cathedral, rather than the more correct Ee-lay. 'His reputation I never thought equal to his merits,' mused Sir Edward Marsh, 'perhaps because no one knew how to pronounce him!'[8]

During both wars Ihlee revived his engineering skills by working in factories supporting the Allied forces. By the end of the Second World War he was over 60 and exhausted. Nevertheless, he still managed to restore, almost single-handedly, a house in West Deeping near Peterborough, where Isabelle, his French wife, fought a losing battle with the English language.

Missing the Mediterranean light, warmth and relaxed lifestyle of Collioure, Ihlee abandoned painting for several years before a local draper and amateur artist encouraged him to pick up his brushes once more.[9] From then on he painted right up until his death, returning as often as possible to northern Catalonia where the simple life of the sea and the soil was in marked contrast to his sophisticated Germanic background.

1 A Brilliant Beginning

Both Ihlee's parents came from prosperous families who had flourished for generations in the then Free City of Frankfurt, which was for centuries an independent state within the Holy Roman Empire. 'They were in city government, the universities, the law, commerce, the arts and so on,' recalled James de la Mare,[1] whose grandmother was an Ihlee. 'One can trace a long line of books by, and references in books to, these useful and intelligent people and their descendants.' One of these 'useful and intelligent people' was Rudolph's great-uncle Johann Eduard Ihlée (1812–85), a portrait and history painter who became a professor of art in Kassel, where the museum has a significant collection of his work (fig.7).[2]

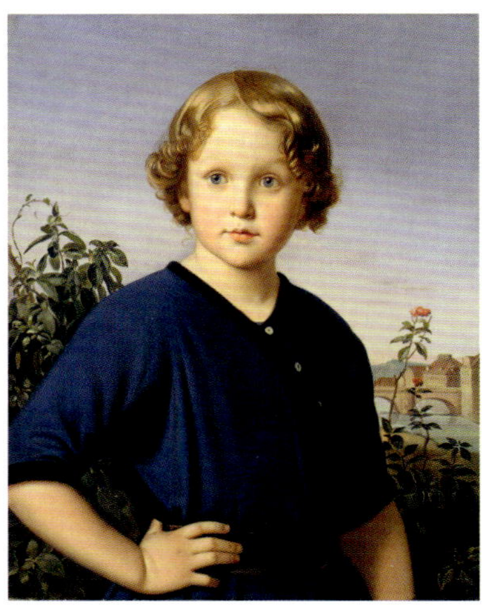

7
Johann Eduard Ihlée
Portrait of a Boy, c.1840
Oil on canvas
64.5 × 53.5 cm (25.5 × 21 in)
Museumslandschaft Hessen Kassel

Unhappy with Bismarck's push for German unification and the prospect of Frankfurt losing its independence, Rudolph's father, Heinrich Ferdinand Ihlee (1844–91), and mother, Victoria (née Hessenberg, 1845–1920), moved to London in the mid 1860s. The family settled in a large house in Wimbledon where the future artist was born on 24 January 1883, the eighth of nine children. It was a comfortable start to life.

Born German, baby Rudolph was naturalised British before his first birthday. There was a Swiss governess to look after him and his younger sister Gertrude. Their father Heinrich, or Henry as he appears on the 1881 census, made a good living importing paper and musical instruments, but his shrewdest move involved exploiting Dr Gustav Jaeger's theory that wool was the best material for clothing. With his wife's sister's husband, Lewis Tomalin, Henry set up the Jaeger company: Dr Jaeger's Sanitary Woollen System Co. Ltd, which grew to become a national brand with a flagship shop on London's Regent Street. Before the First World War George Bernard Shaw and Ernest Shackleton were enthusiastic adherents of their woollen undergarments and later the Jaeger brand progressed from long johns to mainstream fashion, reaching its heyday in the 1950s and 60s when, among others, Audrey Hepburn and Jean Shrimpton modelled its wares.

This was fortunate for Rudolph and his siblings as Jaeger provided them with small but steady private incomes. The Tomalins, who had four children, also lived in Wimbledon and the cousins became firm friends, with Rudolph particularly close to Margaret Tomalin, known as Maggie,

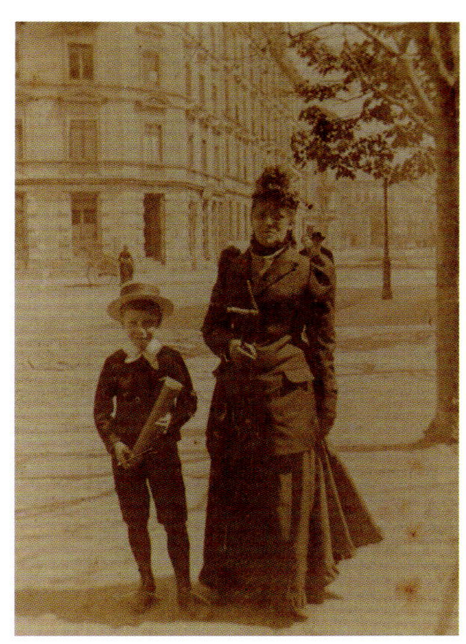

8
Rudolph Ihlee, aged nine, with his aunt, c.1906
Monksgrange Archive

and her elder sister Marie-Charlotte. Unhappily, though, Henry Ihlee died at the age of 47 and his wife Victoria decided to return to Germany with some but not all of her children. Rudolph, though only eight, was one of those left behind, initially in the care of his uncle and aunt, Lewis and Klara Tomalin (fig.8), before his eldest brother Frederick, some 15 years his senior, became a surrogate parent.

Fred Ihlee (1869–1938) was, in some ways, even more dynamic than his father. Although he was for a time chairman of Jaeger, fashion was not really his bag. He was much more suited to running the engineering firm now known as Baker Perkins,[3] whose roots in Germany and London Fred transplanted to Peterborough.

While the factory produced mainly ovens and other baking machinery, Fred had a passion for ships' models and, above all, like his younger brother Rudolph, for cars. His mansion, Paston Hall near Peterborough, housed a world-class collection of models, many of which are now in the Science Museum.[4] For motoring expeditions, he had three Daimlers – one for the family, another for staff and a third for luggage.[5]

In 1906 Fred sank a small fortune into developing a car of his own which he called the Mercial. Unfortunately, most wealthy locals stuck to their horse-drawn carriages and only three were ever built. Undaunted, he next tried a delivery van based on his original car design. Again this failed. Despite his considerable success as a businessman, according to his great-nephew James de la Mare, he 'never quite got over the disappointment'.

Fred was adamant that Rudolph should also embark on an engineering career. To this end in June 1902 he paid a fee of £315, the equivalent of nearly £40,000 today, for Rudolph to enrol on a four-year apprenticeship at Ferranti in Manchester.[6] Rudolph followed his brother's wishes and became a qualified draughtsman, whether reluctantly or not isn't recorded. What is known is that he was already painting seriously. Watercolours of Brighton and Salisbury Plain date from a year before his apprenticeship.[7] One can imagine the brotherly stand-off when, in 1906, Rudolph announced that he was going to the Slade.

Perhaps Rudolph paid the annual college fees of £21 (around £2500 today) from his own pocket, but there can be little doubt that, at the age of 23, he found himself in the right place at the right time. While Frederick Brown was the titular head of the art school, the controlling presence was his assistant Henry Tonks,[8] who, like Ihlee, had switched career, in his case from medicine. Under Tonks' regime, the Slade was all about drawing and it was at drawing that Ihlee excelled.

In his first year he was awarded second prize for figure drawing and two years later won first prize, no mean feat considering the brilliance of some of his fellow students – a roll call which included Adrian Allinson (1890–1959) and John Currie (1884–1914) as well as Spencer, Gertler, Nevinson, Lightfoot and Edward Wadsworth.

Both Nevinson and Allinson described their time at the Slade in memoirs, as did Paul Nash, who started in 1910, Ihlee's final year. Arriving in a suit, stiff collar, bowler hat and spats, Nash remembers it as being 'like a typical English public school seen in a nightmare, with several irrational characters mingled with conventional specimens'.[9] He recalls Nevinson scoffing at 'my rather neat appearance by asking publicly whether I was an engineer. It got a laugh and I felt a pariah.' The real-life engineer Ihlee, around five years older than many of his fellows, probably escaped such barbs although, judging by an early photograph (fig.9), he, like Nash, dressed towards the conventional end of the spectrum. Nevinson himself favoured a 'Quartier Latin tie and a naive hat' but was outdone by John Fothergill, 'an exquisite in dark blue velvet suiting, pale-yellow silk shirt, with a silver pin as large as an egg and patent court shoes with silver buckles'.[10]

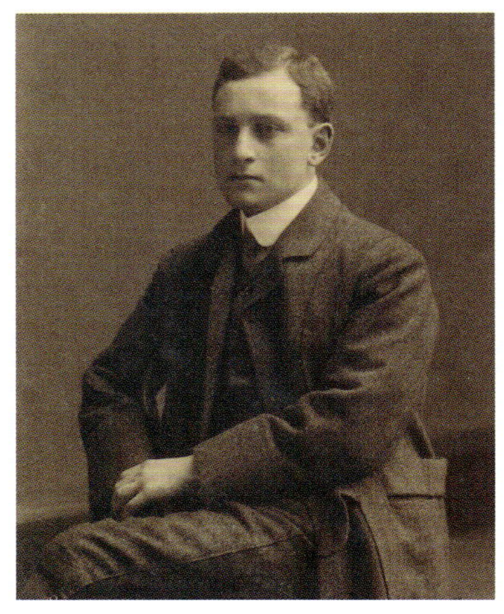

9
Rudolph Ihlee, c.1906
Monksgrange Archive

According to Nevinson there was a different dress code outside working hours. 'Wadsworth, Allinson, Claus, Ihlee, Lightfoot, Curry, Spencer and myself had become a gang, sometimes known in correct Kensington circles as the Slade Coster Gang because we mostly wore black jerseys, scarlet mufflers and black caps or hats.'[11] He goes on to describe how they were 'the terror of Soho and violent participants for the mere love of a row', joining scuffles at anti-vivisection demonstrations and fighting with medical students, which 'often entailed visits to the Tottenham Court Road police station'. Ihlee, in later life, denied belonging to any such gang although he remembered all those mentioned with varying degrees of fondness.

The most important business at the Slade took place in the rooms devoted to drawing from live models. Male students occupied a vast vault-like basement room and, for decency's sake, there was a separate, smaller first-floor room for female students. Adrian Allinson recalled being discomfited by 'the unexpected heat and tobacco fug and the sudden sight of a naked woman enthroned before forty men'.[12]

Tonks encouraged his students to work at speed. The naked models were told to change pose frequently so students could be trained to capture their essential lines quickly. Shading and stippling were frowned upon as a cover for bad draughtsmanship. According to another student, Darsie Japp,[13] Lightfoot and Ihlee were the outstanding draughtsmen of the 1909–10 year, when they were jointly awarded the prestigious Melville Nettleship prize for figure composition. In the previous year Ihlee had come first in figure drawing and Lightfoot second: in figure painting, the positions were reversed.

Thanks, probably, to some networking by the outgoing Nevinson, in February 1911, shortly after leaving the Slade, Lightfoot and Ihlee were both invited to contribute to an exhibition at the Alpine Club Gallery organised by the Friday Club. The club had been founded by Vanessa Bell (1879–1961) in 1905 with an aim to 'create a cultural milieu not unlike that she had observed in certain Parisian cafés'.[14] Among the other artists taking part were Duncan Grant (1885–1978) and Roger Fry (1866–1934), the latter of whom, the previous year, had shaken the London art world by organising the first of two Post-Impressionist exhibitions at the Grafton Galleries.

Most of London was not yet ready to be confronted by the works of Matisse, Cézanne, Gauguin, Picasso and Van Gogh, not least, as Nash reports, the professors at the Slade. 'Tonks made one of his speeches. He could not, he pointed out, prevent our visiting the Grafton Galleries; he could only warn us and say how very much better pleased he would be if we did not risk contamination but stayed away.'[15] It seems unlikely that Ihlee would have been inclined to follow Tonks' advice. Indeed, he came to admire Matisse above all other artists.

After the Friday Club exhibition, Lightfoot was elected to the Camden Town Group, the youngest of 16 original members among whom were Walter Sickert (1860–1942), Spencer Gore (1878–1914), Augustus John (1878–1961) and Henry Lamb (1883–1960). The group's first exhibition, in June 1911, was at the Carfax Gallery, which was to launch Ihlee's career the following year. Writing to Ihlee, Lightfoot is scathing about some of his fellow exhibitors and the group in general.

> It is about the worst show I have ever seen in my life. Lamb has sent two paltry little sketches . . . Gore has got two theatre pieces – they are as pretty as any young lady would wish to see – drawing, none – colour pretty – but not by any means good . . . I suppose you know they drew me in to be a member of this group, without my consent by the way. I have four things there – but I swear on my oath I will never show with the crowd again. It is 19 Fitzroy St to the core.[16] My stuff looks as much out of place and absurd as I do when I go to the Saturday afternoon lying competition at Sickert's. They have had no money from me – and I will take d——d good care they never will.[17]

Despite these disparaging remarks, Lightfoot sold three of his four pictures to the manager of the Carfax, Arthur Clifton (1863–1932), who later took Ihlee under his wing. The letter, written around the time of George V's coronation on 22 June 1911, concludes, 'I intend to belong to no society (except the Friday Club) or clique – I hate them.' His final sentence hints

10
Maxwell Gordon Lightfoot
Male Figure Standing, 1909
Oil on canvas
91.5 × 61 cm (36 × 24 in)
University College London Art Museum

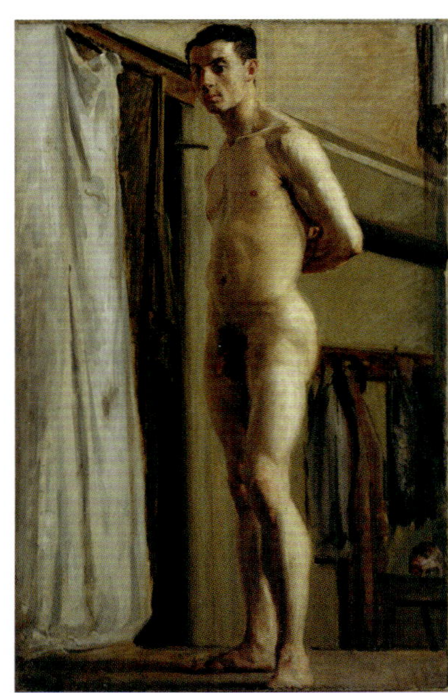

at a troubling loneliness. 'London is quite a trial to me just now everyone you meet seems happy and exciting and I feel exactly the same feeling come over me when I see the flags and decorations everywhere I look.'

Lightfoot was born in Liverpool, one of five children, and grew up in the North West of England in relatively modest circumstances. From the age of 15, he studied first at the Chester School of Art and then at the Sandon Studios under James Herbert MacNair (1868–1955) and Gerard Chowne (1875–1917),[18] who encouraged him to apply to the Slade. Before that, like Ihlee, he had been an apprentice, although with a printing company rather than a firm of engineers. At the Slade they were quick to recognise each other's talent and for a time shared lodgings in Hampstead Road.[19] From Lightfoot's first letter, however, it is clear that by the summer of 1911 they had not seen each other for several months. Although the contents of Ihlee's reply are unknown, Lightfoot responded with an extraordinary emotional outpouring:

> Your letter pleased me beyond words to describe – not because of the flattery it contained, but of what it has made me candidly confess to myself and now to you. For years I have been eating myself up – my heart is choked and suffocated for want of a friend. For the first time in my life I feel it opening. It is as though I have found a friend not only in name but in deed. One may have kind brothers and sisters, a loving mother, good companions and available acquaintances and yet die in solitude. To me friendship is the very essence of life, the only means by which improvement can come by. For there is no greater flatterer than self.

What follows is all the more surprising considering that three months later Lightfoot was due to marry an artist's model called Lilian Thompson:

> I do not at the present time want a wife or mistress and I have plenty of wonderful children companions and yet some days I would give half my heart to remove the load from the other half . . . there is one remedy alone that can relieve the heart and that is a friend. I cannot tell you how pleased I am to have found you [underlined twice]. But I can offer you all I possess – my heart. You know I was never a secret or mysterious person in any way. I hate secrets. When you come back to London I feel that if we could see a little more of each other it would be a good thing for both of us.

It seems one factor underlying Lightfoot's yearning for Ihlee's company was his belief in their special understanding of each other's work:

You must have often felt that the way we have moved along together for the last 15 months solving difficulties and problems of nature almost at the same moment and yet miles apart from each other has been more than just mere coincidence . . . I had begun to realise what the difference was between good and pretty colour and to come to your rooms . . . and to find you had moved along in exactly the same road . . . was one of the greatest pleasures I have yet felt.

It is not known whether Ihlee responded to this, previously unpublished, second letter nor whether the two young artists ever saw each other again. It is possible Ihlee recoiled from Lightfoot's intensity, which reached a pitch in the letter's final words. 'I think it was Bacon who wrote that friendship has two contrary effects: for it "redoubles joys and cutteth grief in half." I am dying to have you back.'

While the circumstances of Lightfoot's suicide are clear, the reasons behind it are not. On 27 September 1911 he cut his throat with a razor blade in his lodgings at 13 Fitzroy Road, Primrose Hill, where he had written the two letters a few months earlier. The coroner's verdict was 'suicide whilst of unsound mind'. The accepted version is that his planned marriage to Lilian Thompson was in some way to blame.

According to Japp, 'when his family refused to become reconciled to the idea of his marrying the girl, he cut his throat the day before what was to have been his wedding day.'[20] Nevinson believed 23-year-old Lilian did not return Lightfoot's feelings. 'Unrequited love for a model' was his verdict.[21] Allinson had another theory. 'It was not until the eve of the marriage did he learn that he had set his heart upon a woman notoriously promiscuous and the discovery drove him to suicide.'[22]

11
Arthur Clifton, c.1905
Tate Archive

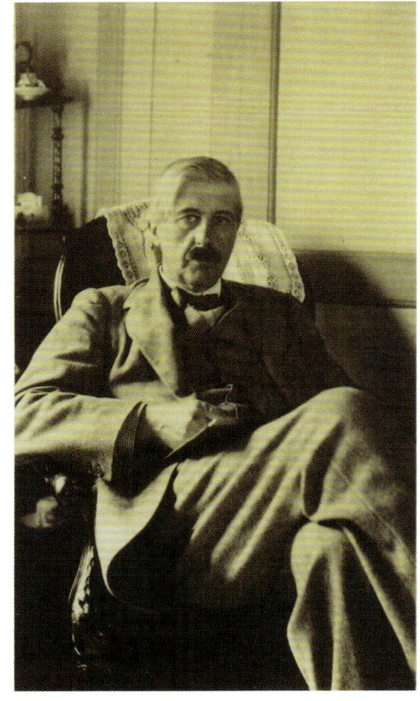

Lightfoot's last letter to Ihlee saying he did not 'want a wife or mistress' only adds to the confusion. Whatever the truth, of all Lightfoot's Slade contemporaries, Ihlee would have felt the loss most keenly and, perhaps, wondered whether he could have done anything to prevent it.

Very little of Lightfoot's work remains. It is thought he destroyed much of it before his death. One particularly beautiful canvas of a mother and child was acquired by Lewis Tomalin, Ihlee's uncle and co-founder of Jaeger. When it was displayed at the Salon Triennial de Liège in 1921, 'the Belgian press generally acclaimed the painting as the masterpiece of the exhibition.'[23]

Lightfoot was said to be planning a solo exhibition at the Carfax Gallery and it may be his place was taken by Ihlee, who, thanks to the gallery's manager Arthur Clifton (fig.11), held his first one-man show there in March 1912.

By coincidence, that same year Paul Nash had persuaded Clifton to give him his debut. 'I knew this was an opportunity in a million. The Carfax was probably the most distinguished and exclusive gallery in London,' wrote Nash, who presents a paradoxical portrait of the gallery manager.

> Clifton was a big man rather inclined to be stout. He was eminently flatfooted but always conveyed a dignified presence crowned by a rather distinguished head . . . he was well known for his shrewd and even generous treatment of artists but could seem on occasion more discouraging and cold-hearted than any man I ever met.[24]

Nash's exhibition was a modest success, although he was a little disappointed that only six or seven drawings were sold, 'mostly to family and friends'. Ihlee did rather better, showing 38 drawings and garnering some impressive reviews. Sir Claude Phillips in the *Daily Telegraph* praised his 'quite remarkable technical skill'.[25] Under the headline 'A New Draughtsman' the *Morning Post* declared, 'since A.E. [Augustus] John . . . several young men of promise from the Slade have attracted attention. The late Mr Lightfoot was of the number . . . R. Ihlee, whose work is in the main akin to his, sails into our ken with a remarkable series of drawings.'[26] Ihlee's drawings also caught the eye of John Middleton Murry (1889–1957), the editor of *Rhythm* magazine, which featured the work of several leading contemporary artists including Jessica Dismorr (1885–1939), Henri Gaudier-Brzeska (1891–1915), S.J. Peploe (1871–1935) and J.D. Fergusson (1874–1961), the journal's art editor. 'I think that Ihlee is extraordinarily good – now that

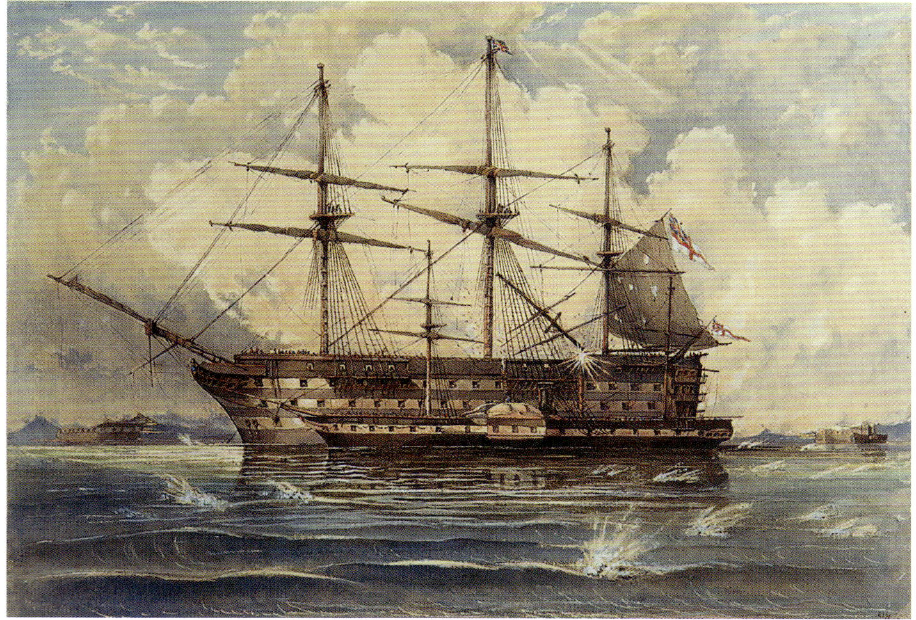

12
Edward Hereford
The Bombardment of Sebastopol, 1854
Watercolour on paper
29 × 44 cm (11.4 × 17.5 in)
Private collection

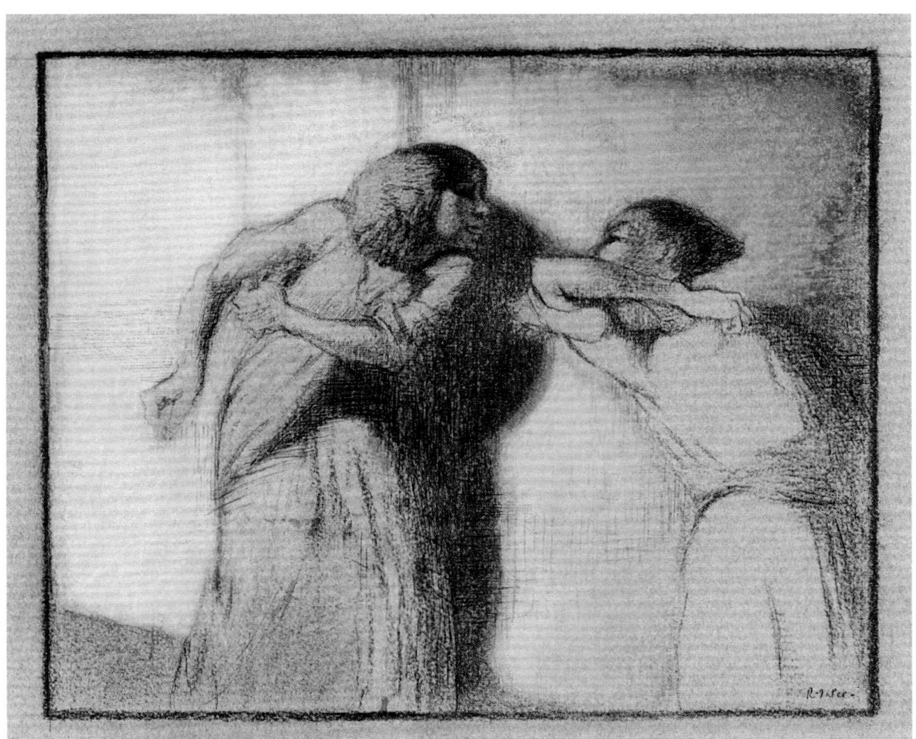

13
The Quarrel, 1912
Pencil, ink, chalk
20 x 24.7 cm (8 x 10 in)
The Higgins Bedford

I have seen more of his work,' wrote Murry to Sir Edward Marsh, who had no doubt brought Ihlee to his attention.[27] *The Quarrel* (fig.13) was one of Ihlee's *Rhythm* images.

With an eye to a second exhibition, and probably with Clifton's encouragement, Ihlee decided to seek new subject matter by taking a trip to France with his friend Edgar Hereford. The pair travelled to Brittany, the first of many adventures together which would ultimately lead to Collioure.

Hereford had started at the Slade a year before Ihlee and was a talented musician as well as an artist. The 1912 census describes him as a music student, although a year before, like Ihlee and Lightfoot, he had exhibited at the Friday Club. Born in Scotland, he was the son of a former naval captain who became Superintendent of the Board of Trade at Greenock on the Clyde.

During his time in the navy Captain Edward Hereford had seen action all over the world. On HMS *Trafalgar* he took part in the bombardment of Sebastopol in 1854 during the Crimean War (fig.12). A few years later he was celebrating victory over the Chinese at the Battle of Canton before helping to suppress the slave trade on the west coast of Africa. Intriguingly, he was also a fine amateur artist, illustrating log books of his travels, some of which are now at the National Maritime Museum in Greenwich. During his lifetime he exhibited 68 pictures, mostly at the Dudley Gallery.[28]

Edgar was born when his father was 50 and it soon became clear that his growth would be restricted. He was teased mercilessly as a child. One of the titles in Ihlee's 1912 Carfax show is *Woman Deriding a Dwarf*, which may be a reference to the abuse suffered by his lifelong companion. When Edgar was a teenager the family moved to St Albans before settling in Surrey. It was at St Albans Art School that he started to develop the artistic talent that was in his genes. From their first meeting at the Slade, Hereford and Ihlee recognised each other as kindred spirits. In their different ways they were both outsiders.

Before settling in Collioure, the pair made several visits to Brittany, where Hereford met a girl who was eventually to become his wife. On their first trip, around the summer of 1912, Ihlee was very much focused on work. Determined to consolidate the promising start to his career, he made numerous sketches, some of which, like *The Two Maids*, he worked up into paintings (fig.14).

The exceptional reaction to his second exhibition, in March 1914, fully justified his efforts. There were 35 pictures in total and he could not have wished for a better response. Everyone seemed to speak of him in the highest possible terms, including three members of the influential Rothenstein family. William Rothenstein (1872–1945)[29] was later to become Principal of the Royal College of Art, his brother Albert (1881–1953),[30] who anglicised his surname to Rutherston, was a painter and prolific networker, and a third brother, Charles (Rutherston, 1866–1927), was a wealthy businessman and passionate art collector. On 6 March Albert Rutherston wrote to the 30-year-old artist.

> My Dear Ihlee,
> I must write a few lines of congratulations on your Carfax show, it is hard for me to tell you how much real pleasure your work gives me. In these days of short cuts to notoriety and sensationalism it is good to find people like yourself with something real to give. My brother Charles is the happy buyer of three of the pictures and I think he has chosen well. I am particularly keen on the Well picture . . . all the drawings are good and there is a particularly good nude. There is no need to wish you success, my dear Ihlee, that has come to you in the instant and I am very happy at it. I want you to keep up with the Friday Club which is now giving a really good show. I am getting new people including William R. [Rothenstein].
>
> We must meet soon . . . again all my congratulations,
> Albert R.[31]

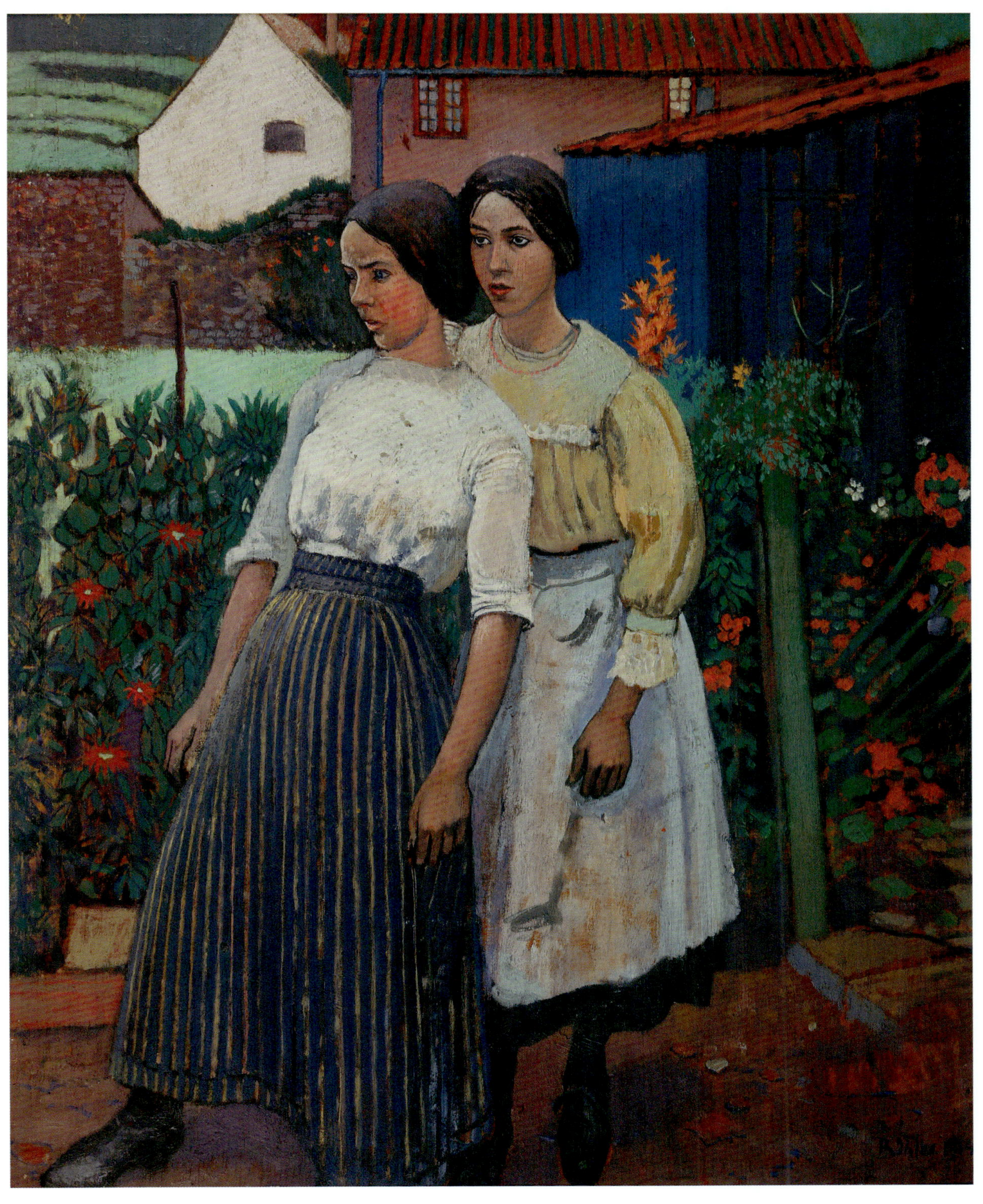

14
The Two Maids, 1914
Oil on board
61 × 50.9 cm (24 × 20 in)
Private collection

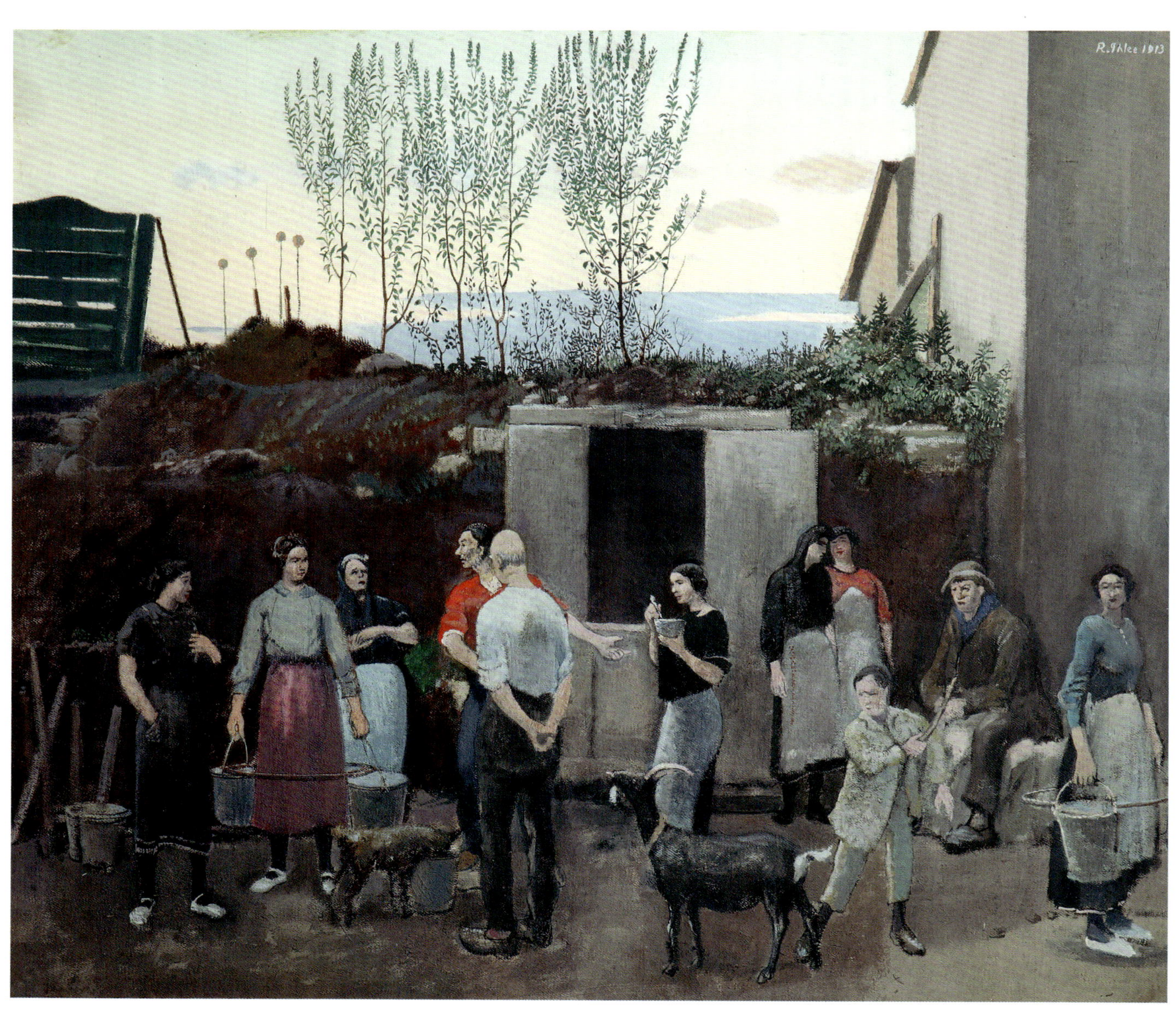

15
The Well, 1913
Oil on canvas
50.9 × 61 cm (20 × 24 in)
Manchester City Art Gallery

Charles Rutherston, whose textile business was based in Bradford, gifted *The Well* (fig.15) to Manchester City Art gallery in 1925, two years before his death. The painting shows a group of eleven Breton villagers of various ages gathered for their daily get-together in front of a well. Painted in a formal, figurative style characteristic of the Slade, it demonstrates Ihlee's considerable powers of observation. A tall balding man with his back to us appears to be listening patiently to a group of five chattering women. An unruly boy is about to whack a goat with a stick while an old man sitting nearby looks thoroughly fed up. To the far right a woman carrying a bucket appears to stare directly at the artist. Other titles in the exhibition such as *Breton Women Washing* and *In the Fields* suggest Ihlee was using his talents to examine the hardship and fleeting pleasures of peasant life. Sir Edward Marsh purchased a sepia pen-and-ink drawing on a similar theme called *Pounding the Bait* (fig.16).[32] Around this time Marsh, who had edited several anthologies of English poetry in the early years of George V's reign, had an idea to produce a companion book of 'Georgian Drawings' including work by Ihlee, Nevinson, Currie, Spencer and Paul and John Nash.[33]

Another new admirer, Walter Sickert, picked out an interior shop scene for special praise. 'Ihlee's *Bootshop* (fig.17) comes in honourable sequence to the work of Degas,' he announced.[34] It is certainly a well-balanced and sympathetic composition which, particularly in his depiction of hands, shows considerable technical skill.

Such was the success of the show that £210 was raised from sales before it even opened to the public, about seven times as much as Paul Nash received from his Carfax exhibition. Perhaps most gratifying to Ihlee was the message he received from Arthur Clifton:

> You know how much I personally admire your pictures; this exhibition seems to me quite splendid and I sincerely hope will be the beginning of great prosperity for you. It will always be a great pleasure to me to think that I have played a humble part in the early days of your career.[35]

After such an auspicious start, what could possibly go wrong? Two things, as it turned out: war and heartbreak.

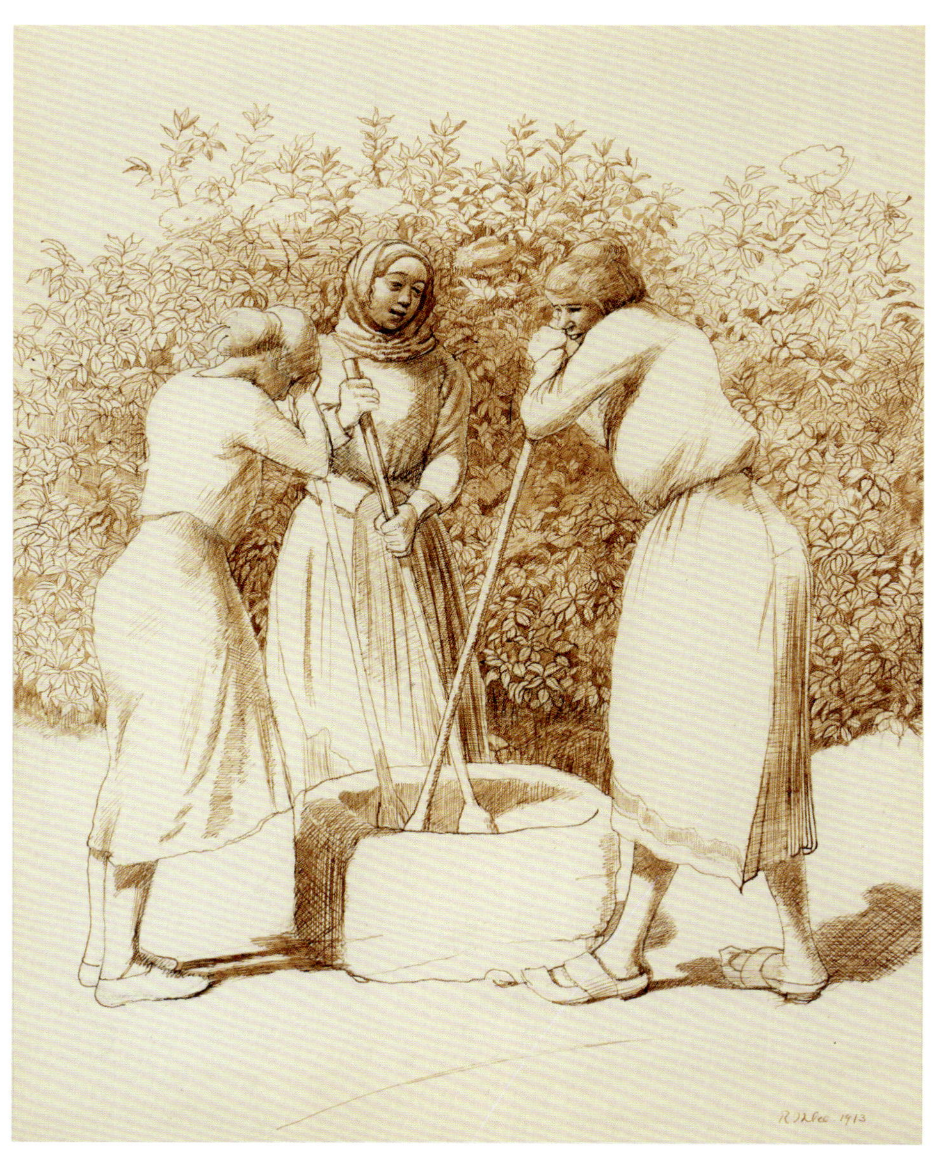

16
Pounding the Bait, 1913
Sepia pen and ink on paper
32.1 × 26.9 cm (12.6 × 10.6 in)
Aberdeen Art Gallery

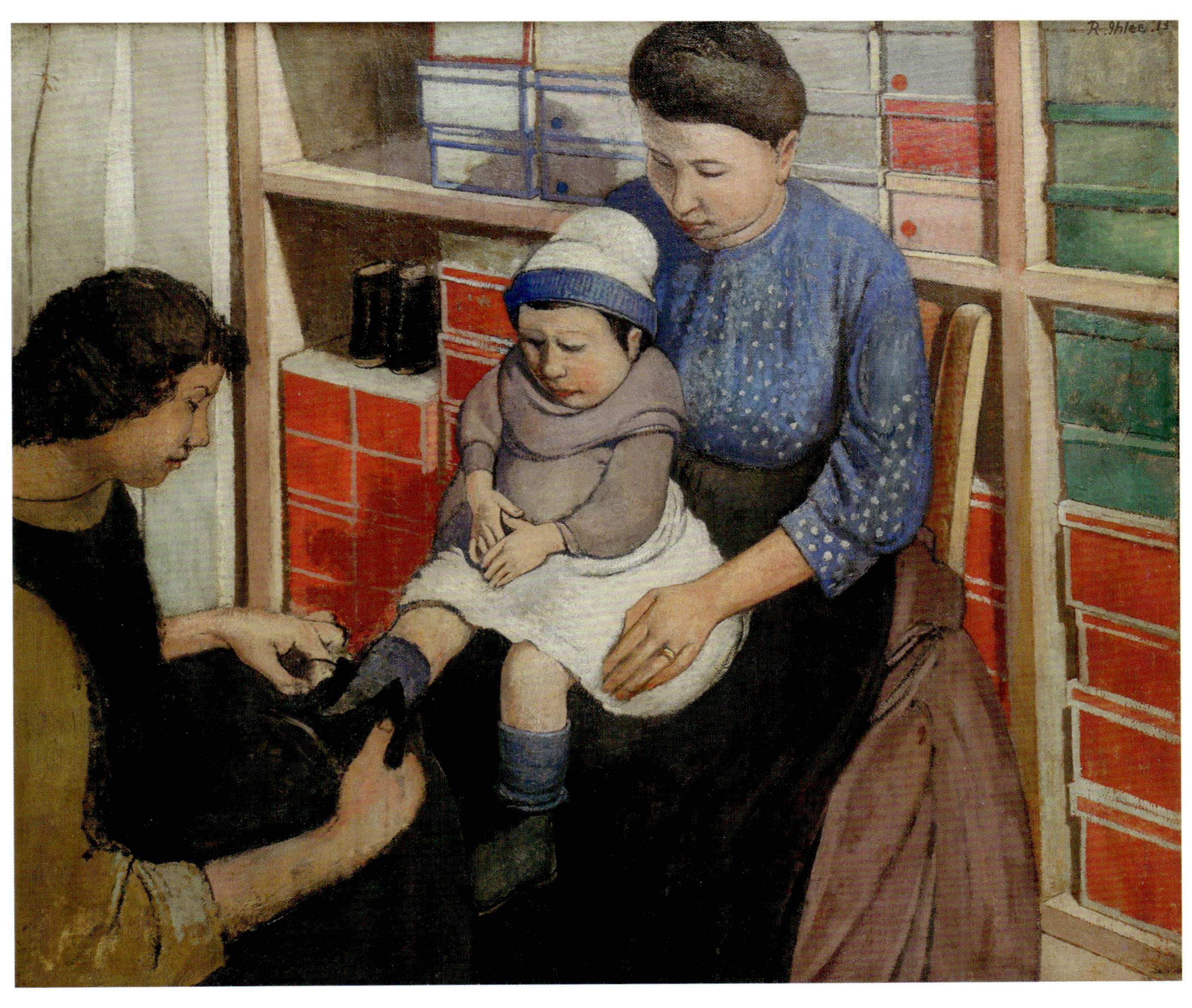

17
New Boots, aka *Bootshop*, 1913
Oil on canvas
50.8 × 61 cm (20 × 24 in)
Private collection

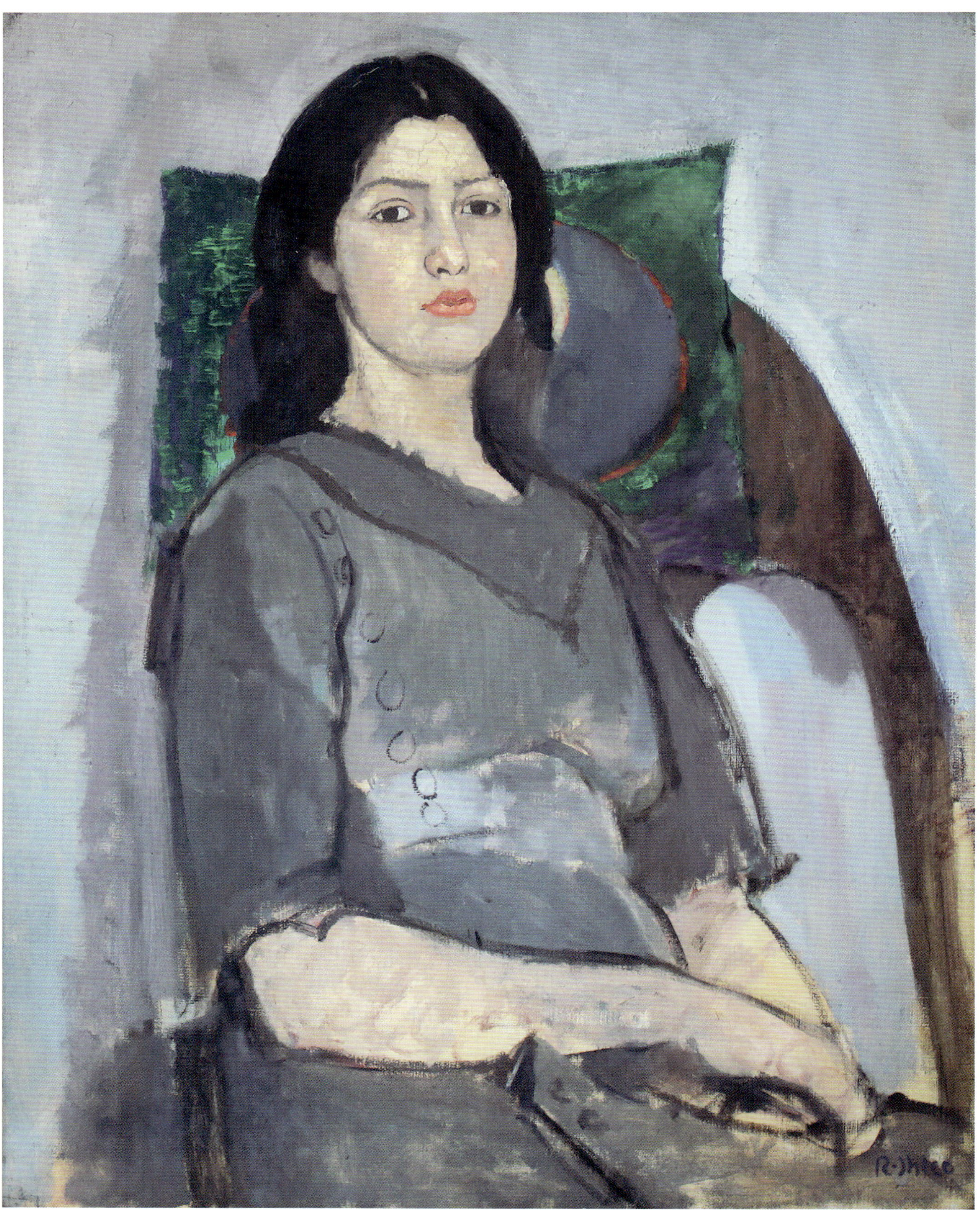

2 War and Divorce

Ihlee called the portrait *The Young Jewess* (fig.18). His new wife, Sophia, was indeed young, just 21 years old. Although he never referred to their failed relationship in later life, the records show that Ernst Rudolph Karl Ihlee, aged 30, married Sophia Roith at Fulham Register Office on 22 March 1913. There were just two witnesses, Edgar Lionel Hereford for the groom and Nancy Gold for the bride. Their respective families either were not invited or chose not to come.

The portrait was painted that same year in the couple's new home at 12 Castletown Road in West Kensington. Physically, they seem an unlikely match: Rudolph short, bespectacled and going prematurely bald, Sophia an outstanding beauty. Her parents, Reuben and Jane, had fled Belarus, then part of the Russian empire, and by 1911 her father was working for a London tobacco business. Sophia had already left the family home and one can only speculate how she met Rudolph. Her self-confident pose suggests she could have been an artist's model, perhaps, like Lilian Thompson, in the life rooms of the Slade. But it could be that tobacco was the link. Rudolph had been lodging in Hampstead Road with someone called Morris Weisberg who, like Reuben Roith, was in the cigarette trade. He had two daughters around Sophia's age and was also Jewish.

Whatever the circumstances of their meeting, it seems likely that Sophia was impressed by Rudolph's growing reputation. He was preparing for his second one-man show and even if some critics struggled with his name they were unanimous in their praise. An intimate drawing of his *Sleeping Bride* (fig.19) is a poignant reminder of their brief marriage. The First World War could not have come at a worse time, both for the couple's relationship and for Rudolph's blossoming career.

The conflict was the making of Nevinson and Nash, and some of his other student contemporaries, but for Ihlee it was a return to the drawing board. His brother's factory needed his draughtsman's skills. Some of the rising anti-German feeling in Peterborough was being directed against the factory, which was then trading under the name of Werner, Pfleiderer and Perkins.[1] It is not clear whether the Germanic background of the Ihlee brothers was identified but Fred's decision to turn the company over to war production seems to have calmed local sentiment. Whatever hostility

18
The Young Jewess, 1913
Oil on canvas
50.8 × 60.96 cm (20 × 24 in)
Private collection

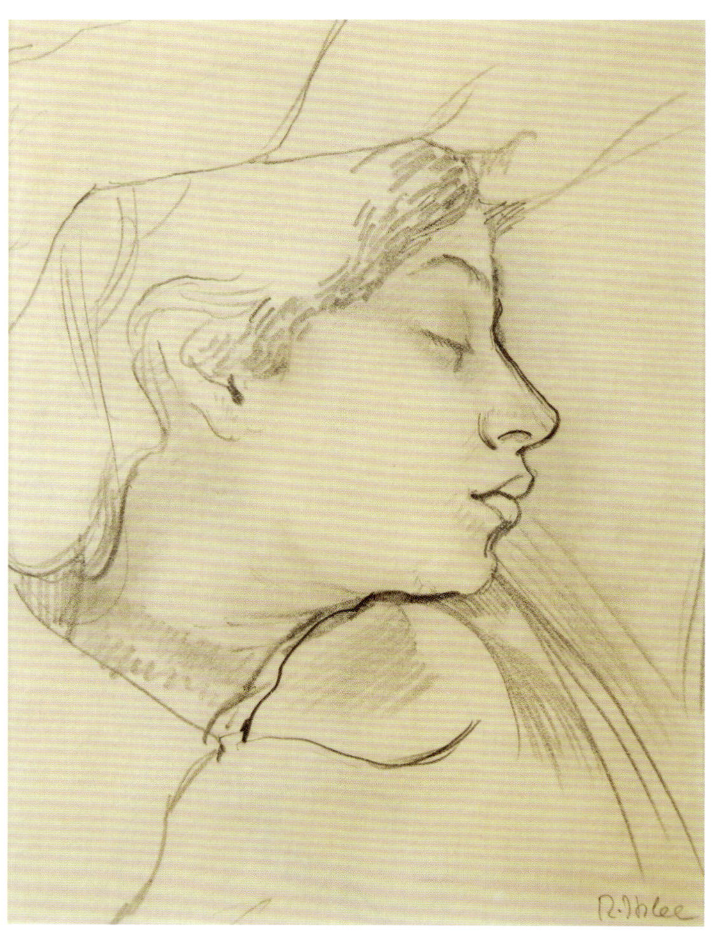

19
Sleeping Bride, c.1913
Pencil on paper
30 × 20 cm (12 × 8 in)
Private collection

20
Complete Six-Inch Howitzer in Erecting Shop Being Removed for Despatch, 1918
Lithograph, edition of 50
38.7 × 27.3 cm (15 × 10 in)
Imperial War Museum

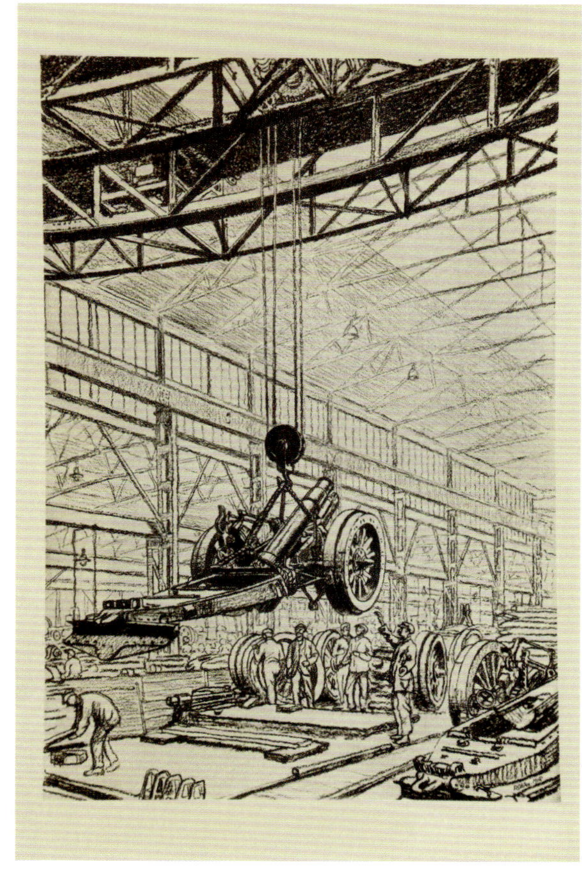

there may have been towards the Ihlee family soon evaporated, and Fred's contribution to the city is now marked by a street called Ihlee Drive.

The plant, under a new name, was soon making tractors, tank parts and howitzers. In 1918 Ihlee produced 12 line drawings illustrating these changes, including one entitled *Complete Six-Inch Howitzer in Erecting Shop Being Removed for Despatch* (fig.20).[2] Another, showing the production of field ovens, was enlarged into a 10-by-14-foot mural decorating one of the firm's buildings.[3] In 1966 Ihlee recalled that 'each drawing would take two or three sittings on the spot of two hours each'.[4] They were later made into lithographs. He also remembered drawing at other factories linked to Baker Perkins, including a chocolate factory in Bristol.

While Ihlee was holed up in digs in Peterborough, his wife was entertaining a naval lieutenant in the marital home in Kensington. It was a cruel betrayal. On 8 July 1918, some four months before the end of the war, Rudolph, then living at 84 Aldermans Drive in Peterborough, filed for divorce against Sophia on the grounds that she 'frequently committed adultery with Algernon William Farnsworth Smith'.[5]

Farnsworth Smith was four years younger than Ihlee and in 1916 had been carrying out inspection duties as a lieutenant in the Royal Naval Volunteer Reserve. How long he had been carrying on an affair with Sophia is not clear but, according to court records, 'From March 1918 . . . they had been cohabiting as man and wife at 27 Rue Jasmin in Paris and habitually committing adultery there.'

Rudolph was not only petitioning for divorce but claiming damages of £500, the equivalent of about £35,000 today. The judge hearing the case was Sir Thomas Gardner Horridge.[6] Two years earlier he had been one of a panel of three judges to pass the death sentence on Roger Casement, the Irish nationalist found guilty of high treason. Although Mr Justice Horridge found Sophia guilty of adultery, he dismissed the claim for damages.

One can imagine Rudolph's distress and bitterness when he discovered that Sophia had fled the country with her lover. Perhaps it brought back memories of his mother abandoning him as a child, but somehow, at his lowest ebb, he had to find the strength to rebuild an artistic career.

Unsurprisingly the art world had moved on in his absence. One observer well placed to comment on the changes was Oliver Brown,[7] who managed the Leicester Galleries:

> The insular tastes of the pre-war years seemed to be on the wane. The visitors at the end of the war were very different in character from those we used to know in 1914. They were much younger and had a more

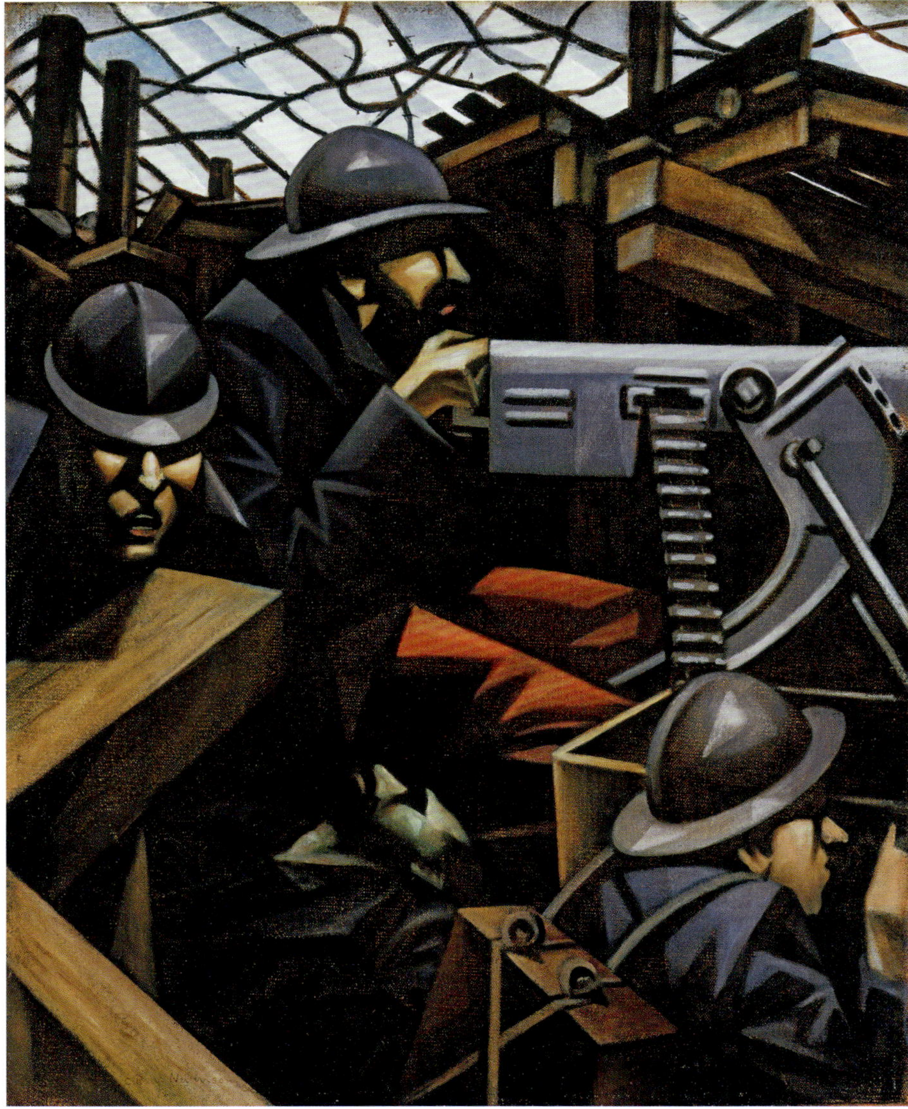

21
C.R.W. Nevinson
La mitrailleuse, 1915
Oil on canvas
61 × 50.8 cm (24 × 20 in)
Tate

adventurous outlook, and they increased in numbers as they began to be released from armies and war work.[8]

In 1916 Nevinson's sensational warfare pictures, including *La mitrailleuse* ('The Machine Gun'; fig.21), were shown at the Leicester Galleries and two years later Paul Nash's landscapes of desolate, shell-ravaged woods made a deep impression. 'Nevinson had as his subject matter the mechanisation of a modern army – the engines of war, the wire and the shells; Paul Nash, the tragic devastation and disfigurement of a beautiful landscape.'[9] Ihlee's drawings of the inside of a Peterborough factory paled in comparison.

Nevertheless, having found new lodgings with Edgar Hereford in Drayton Gardens off the Fulham Road in London (fig.25), he managed to pick himself up and start exhibiting again. In the spring of 1919 he showed

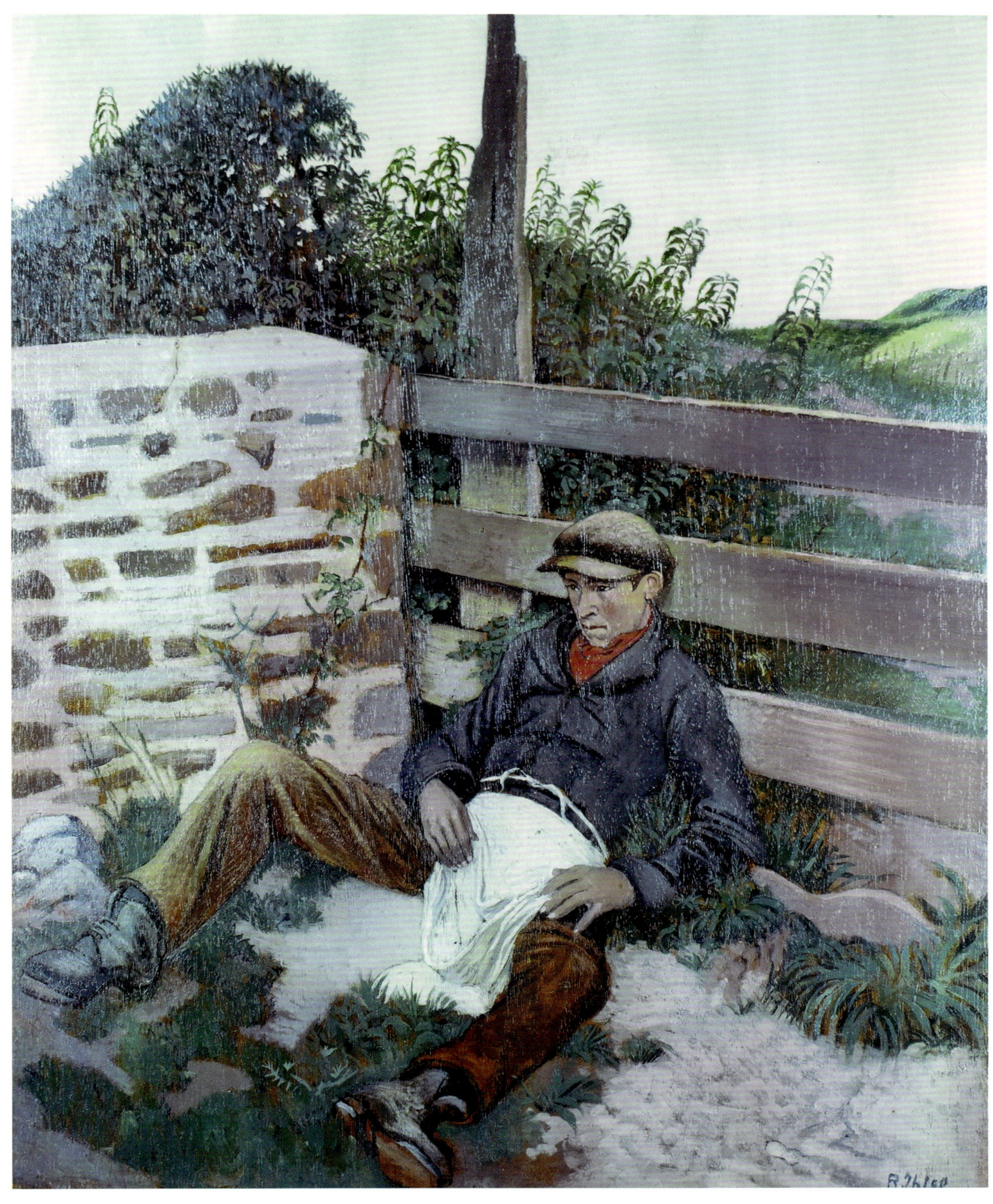

22
Peapicker Resting, 1914
Oil on board
46 × 38 cm (18 × 15 in)
Private collection

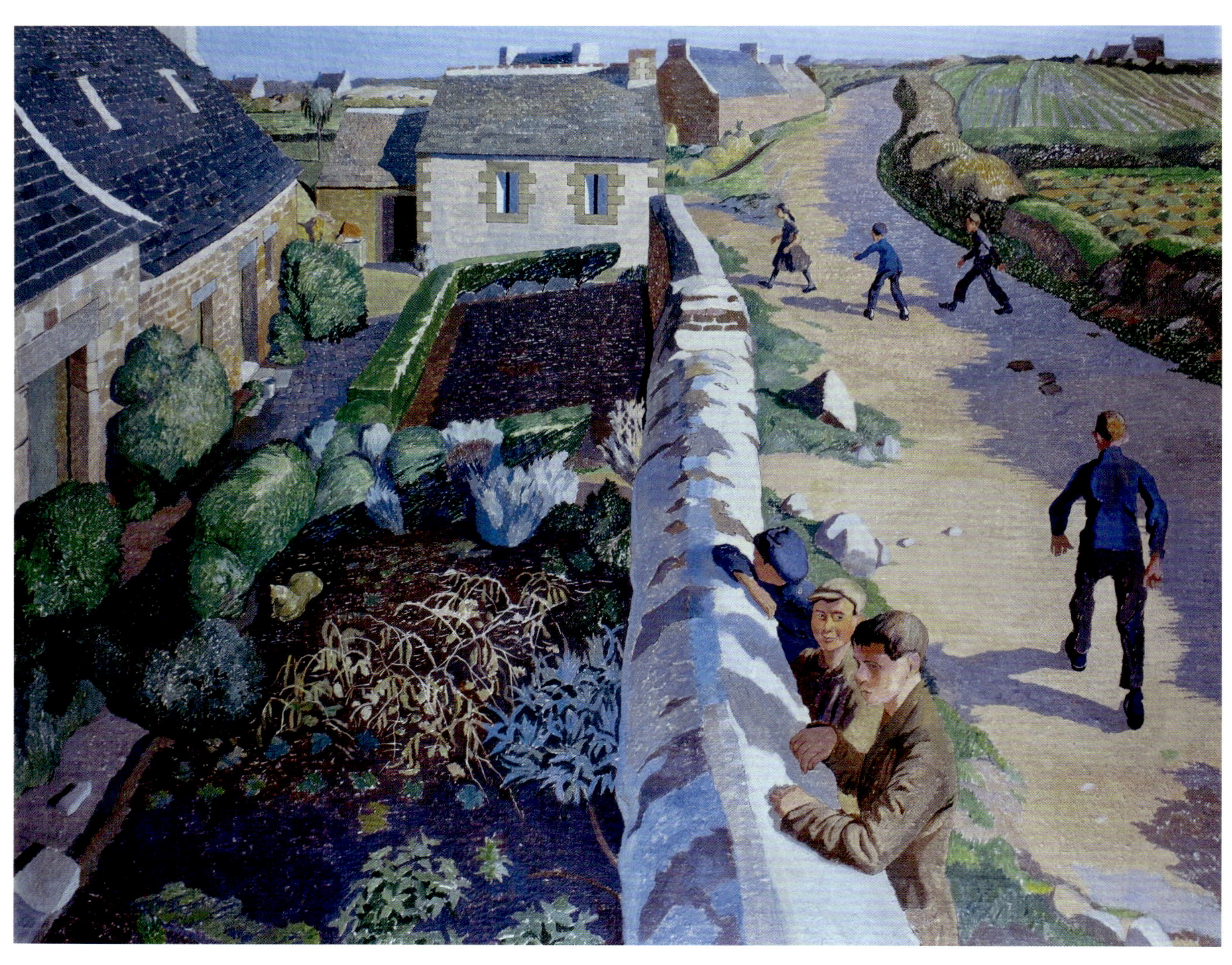

23
Gosses, 1921
Oil on canvas
71.12 × 91.44 cm (28 × 36 in)
Private collection

three pictures with the Friday Club, including *Peapicker Resting* (fig.22), a finely observed portrait from before the war. Later in 1919 he participated, with Nevinson, Nash and others, in the inaugural exhibition of the Arts League of Service.[10] The league's motto was 'To bring the arts into everyday life' and its display of practical arts at the Twenty-One Gallery featured an impressive contribution by Ihlee, including designs for a printed textile, a tureen, a coffee pot, miscellaneous china, two tea tables, a bell push, a tea caddy and an electric lamp fitting.

In 1920 he was elected to the New English Art Club (NEAC), where some of his pictures were favourably reviewed. The *Daily Chronicle* commended an image of a French country ball, presumably painted before the war, as a 'first-rate impression full of observation'.[11] Sir Claude Phillips of the *Daily Telegraph* applauded an 'extraordinary' character study of a girl called Mélanie – 'an aggressive little maiden from whom we may momentarily expect an outburst of some kind or another'.[12]

In March 1921 Ihlee received another confidence boost – a one-man show at Oliver Brown's Leicester Galleries featuring 20 drawings and 24 oil paintings.[13] Some, such as *Black Cattle* (see p.114), were inspired by his pre-war trip with Hereford to Brittany. Others, like *Odalisque* (fig.24), reminiscent of Matisse's nudes, were more experimental in colour and style and had been completed after the war at Drayton Gardens. Picasso had exhibited in the same space two months earlier, so Ihlee was in exalted company.[14] Inevitably, though, some of his earlier work looked old-fashioned in comparison. Frank Rutter in the *Sunday Times* described it as being 'modest' in the 'John Orpen' school, while acknowledging its 'solid achievement'.[15] Claude Phillips in the *Daily Telegraph* was more enthusiastic, commending the 'strongly rhythmic, though quite natural movement' of *Black Cattle*, which he thought 'an admirable composition'.[16] A month later the painting appeared in *Vogue* along with *Gosses* (fig.23) another scene from a Breton village.

Financially the show was less successful than his 1914 exhibition at the Carfax: Ihlee's share was a little under £110, about £5000 in today's money. Perhaps it left him feeling rather flat and restless, a mood which may have been reinforced by the loss of both of Edgar Hereford's parents in that same year.

Meanwhile the decree absolute of Ihlee's divorce had come through. Finding themselves free of family ties, the two housemates, both approaching 40, decided to leave their London lodgings in search of sun and adventure.

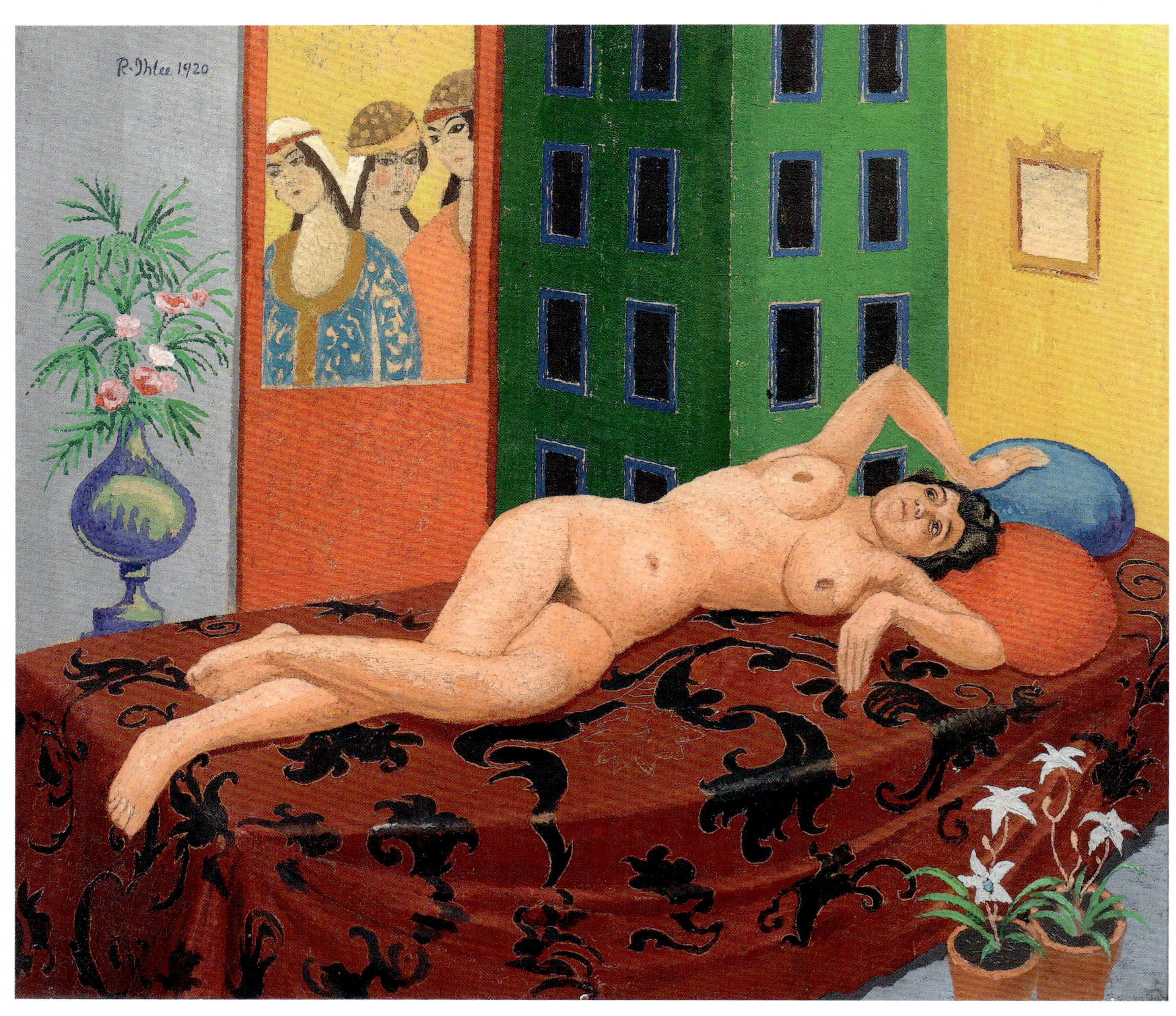

24
Odalisque, 1920
Oil on canvas
50.8 × 60.96 cm (20 × 24 in)
Private collection

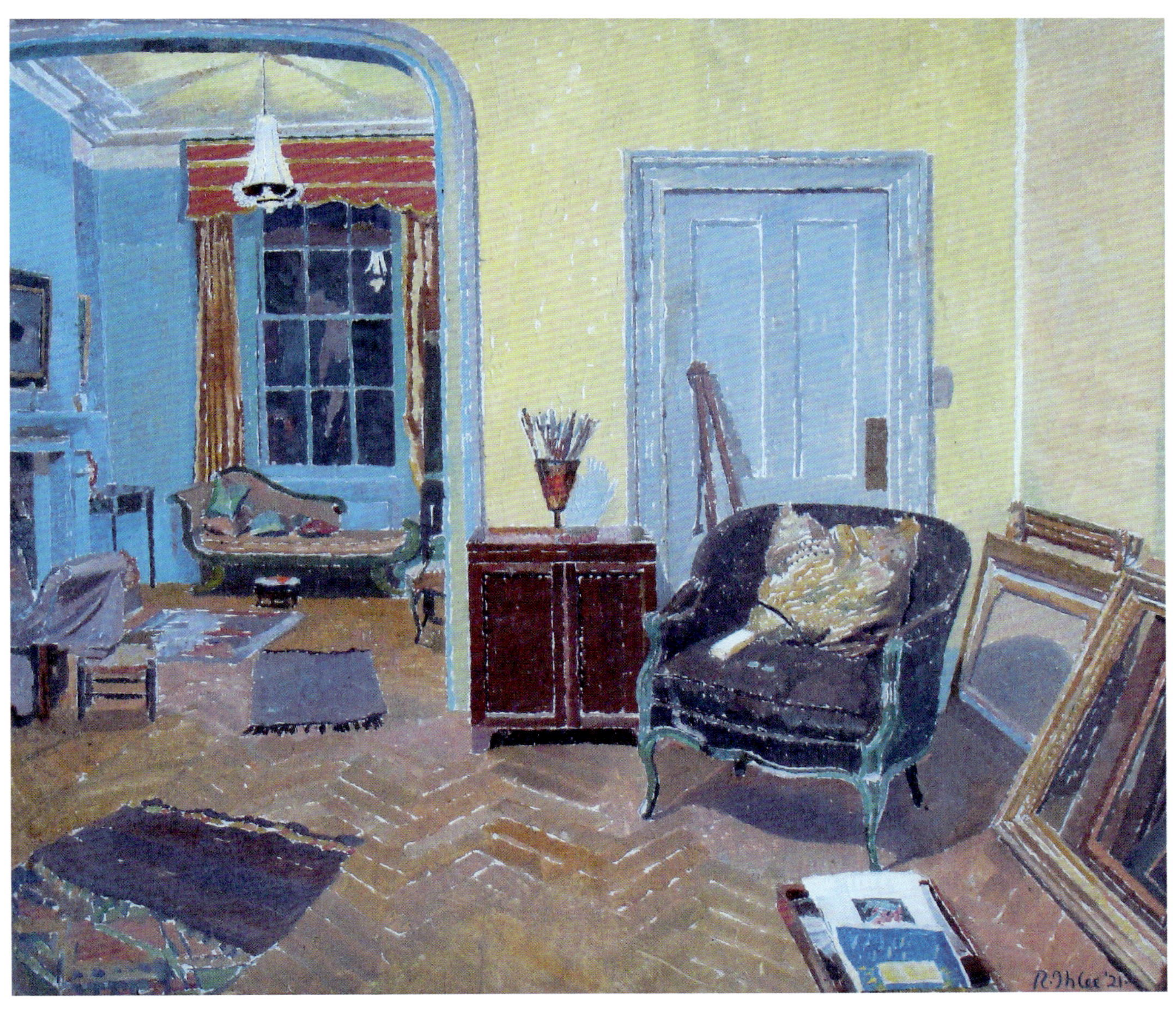

25
Interior, 28 Drayton Gardens, 1921
Oil on canvas
38 × 46 cm (15 × 18 in)
Private collection

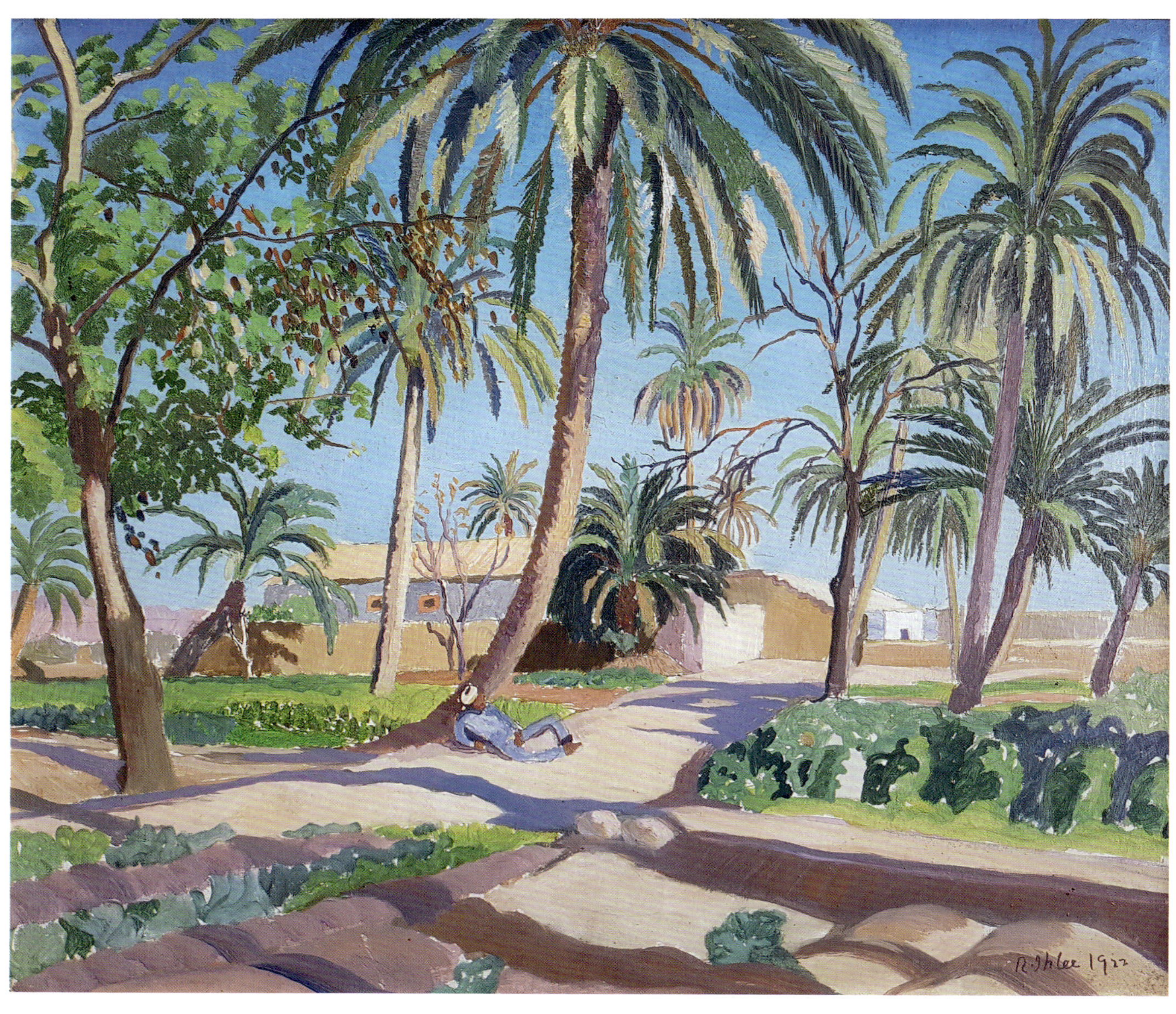

26
Le Jardin militaire, 1922
Oil on canvas
38.1 × 45.72 cm (15 × 18 in)
Private collection

3 Algeria, Collioure and Charles Rennie Mackintosh

While Collioure was their ultimate destination, Ihlee and Hereford decided on an expedition to Algeria before basing themselves in the south of France. It is possible they sailed from Port Vendres to Algiers, a voyage of some 22 hours. In the 1920s around 100,000 passengers a year used the boat service between the French colony and the busy Catalan harbour, which is two miles from Collioure. However, considering Ihlee produced a painting of Marseilles in 1922, it seems more likely that they set off from there, even though the journey was eight hours longer and through less sheltered waters.

For Ihlee, in particular, it was an exceptionally fertile interlude. In the space of a month or two, he produced 25 oil paintings. The pair based themselves in the oasis town of Biskra on the northern edge of the Sahara desert. It was a far cry from Brittany. The light was dazzling and the choice of subjects almost overwhelming. Rather than Breton peasants there were belly dancers, Arab beggars and carpet merchants. There were mosques, markets and pleasure gardens. And yet the imprint of France was everywhere, from the Senegalese soldiers recruited by Algeria's rulers,[1] to the hotels, banks, post offices and other services under French control; for the country was more than a colony, it had been annexed as part of France.

The oasis with its date palms, freshwater streams and sulphur springs attracted many artists. Matisse had found the light and heat too intense on a visit some 15 years earlier,[2] but the Dutch artist Philippe Zilcken (1857–1930) left a description which could be a commentary on Ihlee's painting *Le Jardin militaire* (fig.26): 'It is delicious to dream in the shade of the palm trees, their greeny-blonde foliage heightened by blue reflections . . . there is nothing to be heard except for running water and rustling palms.'[3]

Standing out from the veiled Arab women were groups of Berber girls from the Ouled Naïl tribe. They came down from the Atlas mountains to work in Biskra, often as dancers or prostitutes, and were famed for their independence and beauty. Captivated by their forthright gazes and colourful clothes, Ihlee produced several portraits of these tribeswomen and their children. One shows a young girl with two facial tattoos (fig.27).

The tattoo on her chin expresses a hope for fertility while the other, applied later on her forehead, indicates 'the potential for motherhood'.[4]

Many of Ihlee's Algerian pictures were shown at various galleries in London and one, *Nocturne in Biskra*, was bought by the artist Samuel Peploe and his wife Margaret at the Scottish Academy.[5] Hereford produced some attractive desert and oasis landscapes without the same commercial success.

During the first half of 1922, the pair made the return journey to Port Vendres and found lodgings in Collioure. Perhaps they intended to stay for a few months. As it turned out, Ihlee stayed for nearly eighteen years and Hereford for even longer. It is easy to see why they fell in love with the place. 'It is the magic of a perpetually blue sky, the enchantment of a climate without winter, it is the intense light – a golden glow which, to someone from the North, evokes a feeling of entering a new world,' wrote Paul Soulier in an early guidebook to Collioure,[6] some 20 years before Ihlee and Hereford made it their home.

A year after their arrival, an American writer, Evelyn Scott, gave a less flattering description to a friend who was coming to stay in her rented villa:

> It is on the Midi railway about an hour from Perpignan. It is very filthy and very beautiful. It is very near the Spanish border, about 75 miles from Barcelona. The Pyrenees have a luxurious severity like the richness of ecclesiastical voluptuousness. The bathing is good. The town is without a WC (our house has one thank God) and there are amorous cats in the streets by the hundreds.[7]

Any misgivings Ihlee and Hereford may have had about marauding felines were outweighed by Collioure's many attractions, not least the relatively low cost of living. Although both had private means, funds were by no means unlimited. Ihlee's *My Window, Collioure* (fig.28),[8] painted in 1925, suggests they certainly were not splashing out on accommodation. The room seems small, the bed monastic and, beneath the shutters, the wallpaper is peeling.

Thankfully, the climate allowed them to spend much of the time outdoors like the peasants and fishermen who formed the bulk of the community. The town's half dozen beaches were at the centre of village life, especially during the summer.[9]

In the morning, after fishing overnight for sardines or anchovies, the men would haul their boats onshore and sell their catch. During the day their women, often with children in tow, would mend the nets. 'In the evening,' according to Paul Soulier, 'most of the men go down to the beach,

27
Tattoo Girl, 1922
Oil on board
38.1 × 45.72 cm (15 × 18 in)
Private collection

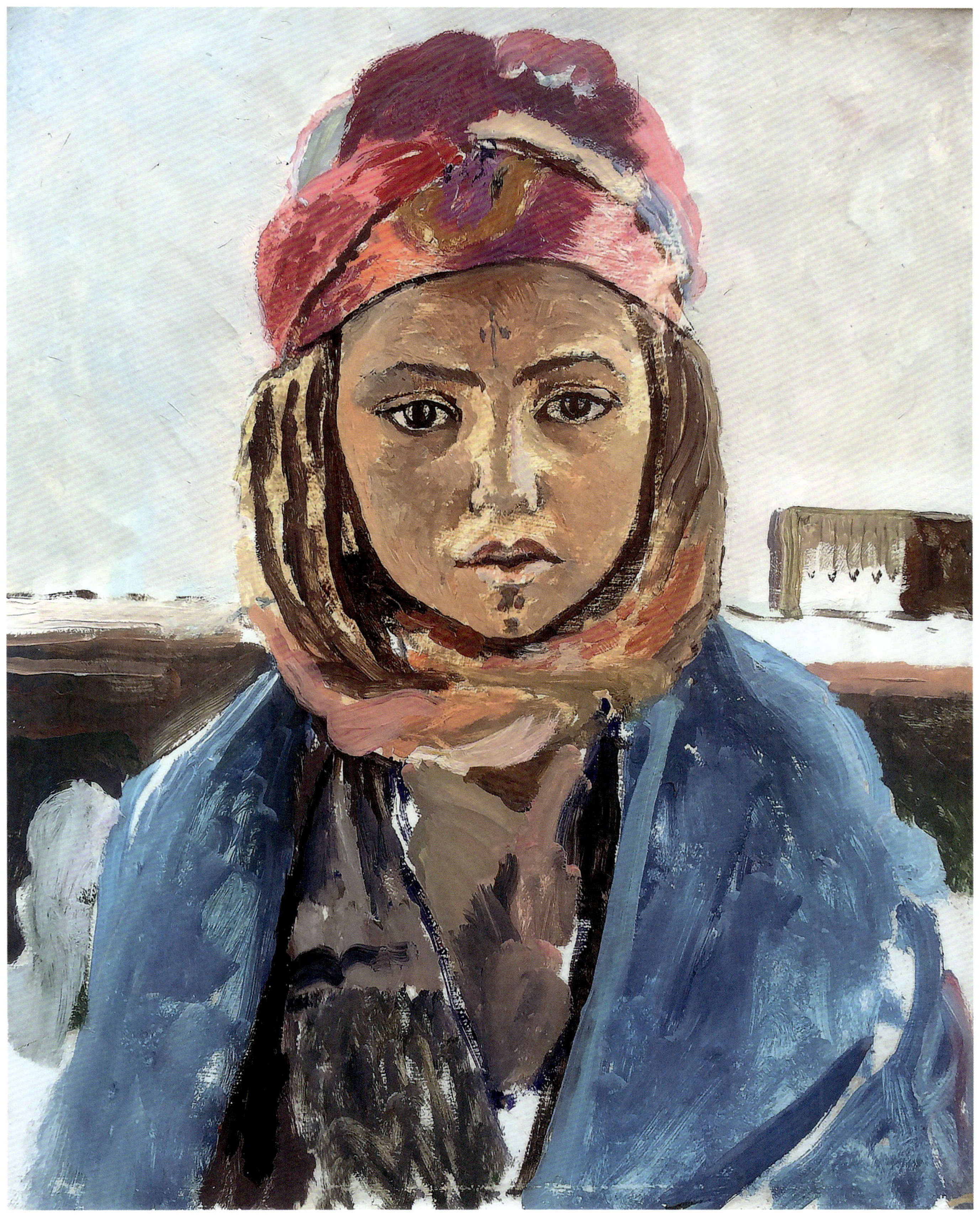

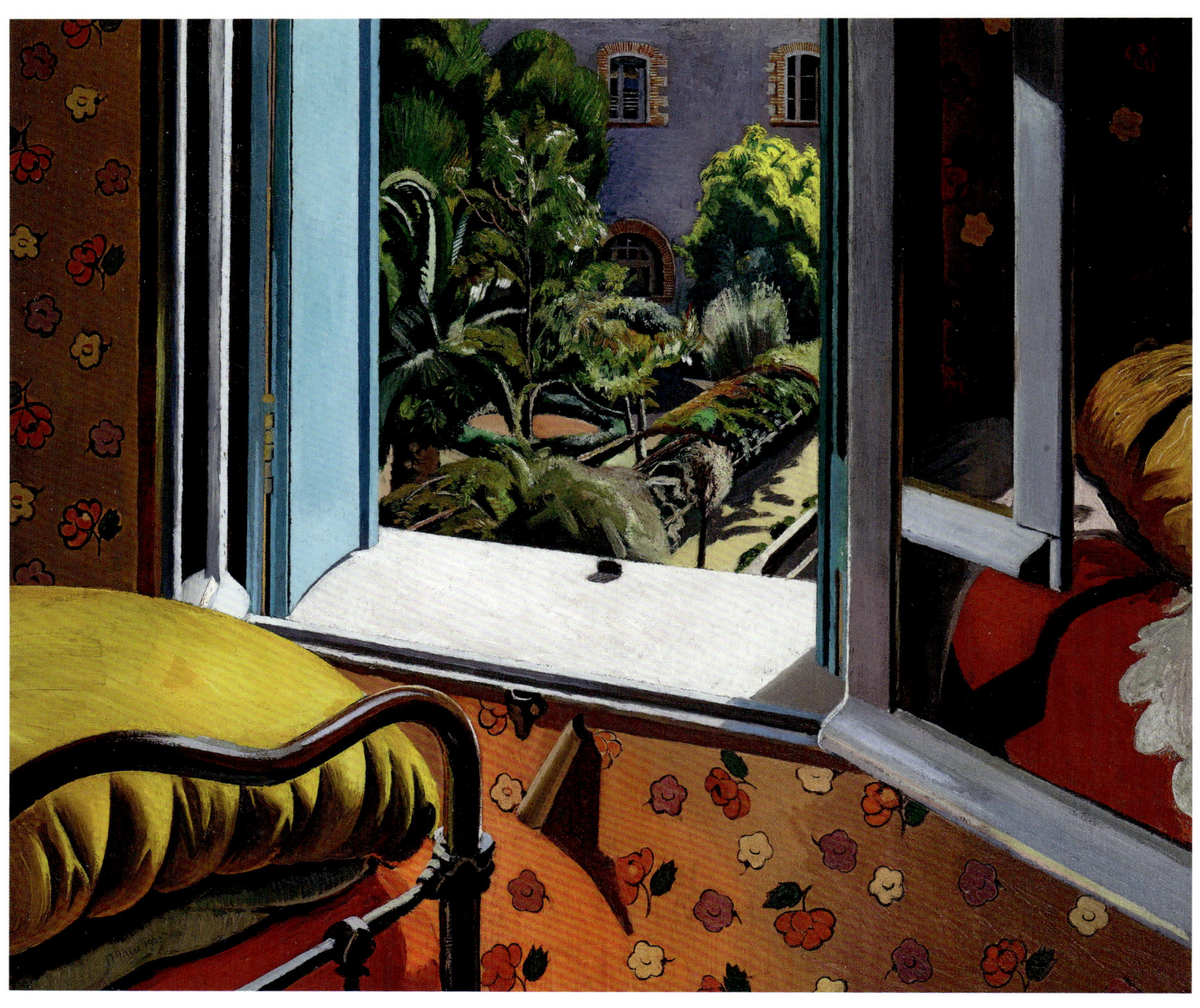

28
My Window, Collioure, 1925
Oil on canvas
63.5 × 76.2 cm (25 × 30 in)
Private collection

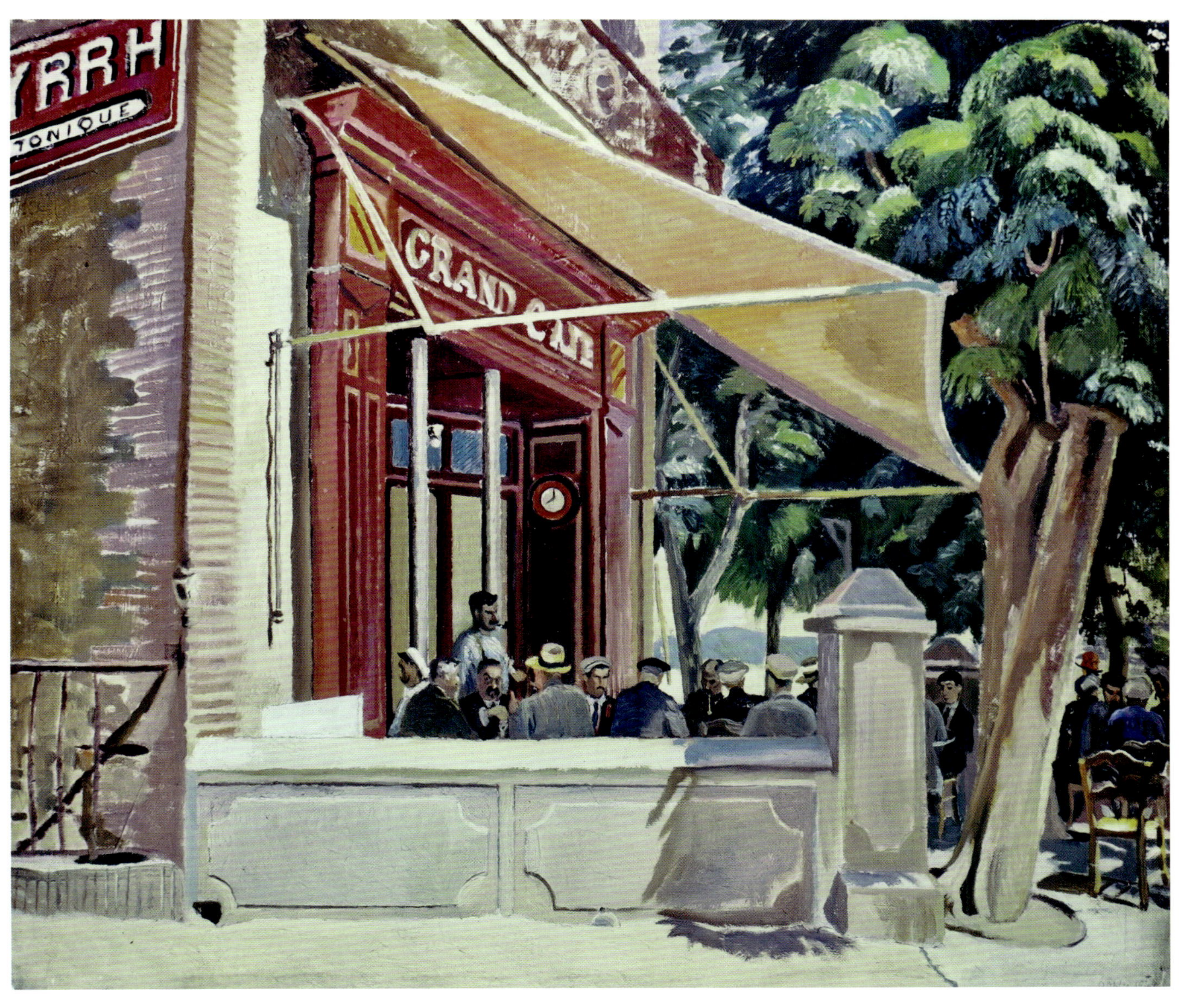

29
Le Grand Café, Collioure, 1924
Oil on canvas
63.5 × 76.2 cm (25 × 30 in)
Private collection

to examine their boats, and then gather in groups to discuss politics or exchange gossip. Later the more sensible ones go back home, while others frequent the cafés.'

Ihlee, who took to café culture more enthusiastically than Hereford, is said to have known all the customers shown in *Le Grand Café, Collioure* (fig.29), now the Hotel Frégate, which he painted in 1924.[10] Overwhelmingly male, the majority, like Ihlee, were smokers. The half-concealed sign on the top left of the painting advertises the local aperitif Byrrh (pronounced 'beer'), which was invented in the nearby town of Thuir by two brothers, Pallade and Simon Violet. Although the aromatic tipple later declined in popularity, Ihlee remained a lifelong devotee.

The local vines were cultivated on the hills overlooking the town. The harvest (*la vendange*), usually in October, followed the end of the fishing season. In his novel *The Catalans* Patrick O'Brian,[11] a later Collioure resident, describes the backbreaking work of picking grapes on the terraced slopes.

> Everywhere on all the unnumbered terraces, there were vines; and among the vines the vendangeurs, moving among the dark green rows; for the grapes were ripe, and now the families were assembled, friends, cousins from as far as Marseilles and Toulouse, relations to the farthest point of kin. For them the vendange was a feast, a ritual, a time of strange excitement, more intense by far than the harvest of the corn in the north, more religious. These hillside vendanges were entirely different from the vendanges in the plains . . . for here the vineyards, cut by the loving hands of the generations, climbed in mad shapes up to the limit of fertility, hand-planted in basketfuls of carried earth, hand-grafted, hand-hoed; the evidence of hands, the uninterrupted generations for how many years?

Cork for bottling the wine came from the *chênes-lièges* (cork oak trees) which grow abundantly in the region. Ihlee's 1925 painting *The Cork Wood* (fig.30) shows some that have recently been stripped of their cork bark, which takes a decade to grow back. Given that *chênes-lièges* live for 200 years, Ihlee's wood may still exist.

Nature supplied most of Collioure's other needs. Paul Soulier, himself a wine grower, compared its outdoor market to the promised land.

> In the cool of the morning, beneath the shade of the big trees there is a profusion of riches one can hardly imagine. Great hampers of cherries, pyramids of pears, tumbled masses of apricots; the sharp red of tomatoes and the pale yellow of cucumbers add their brilliant notes to this pleasing

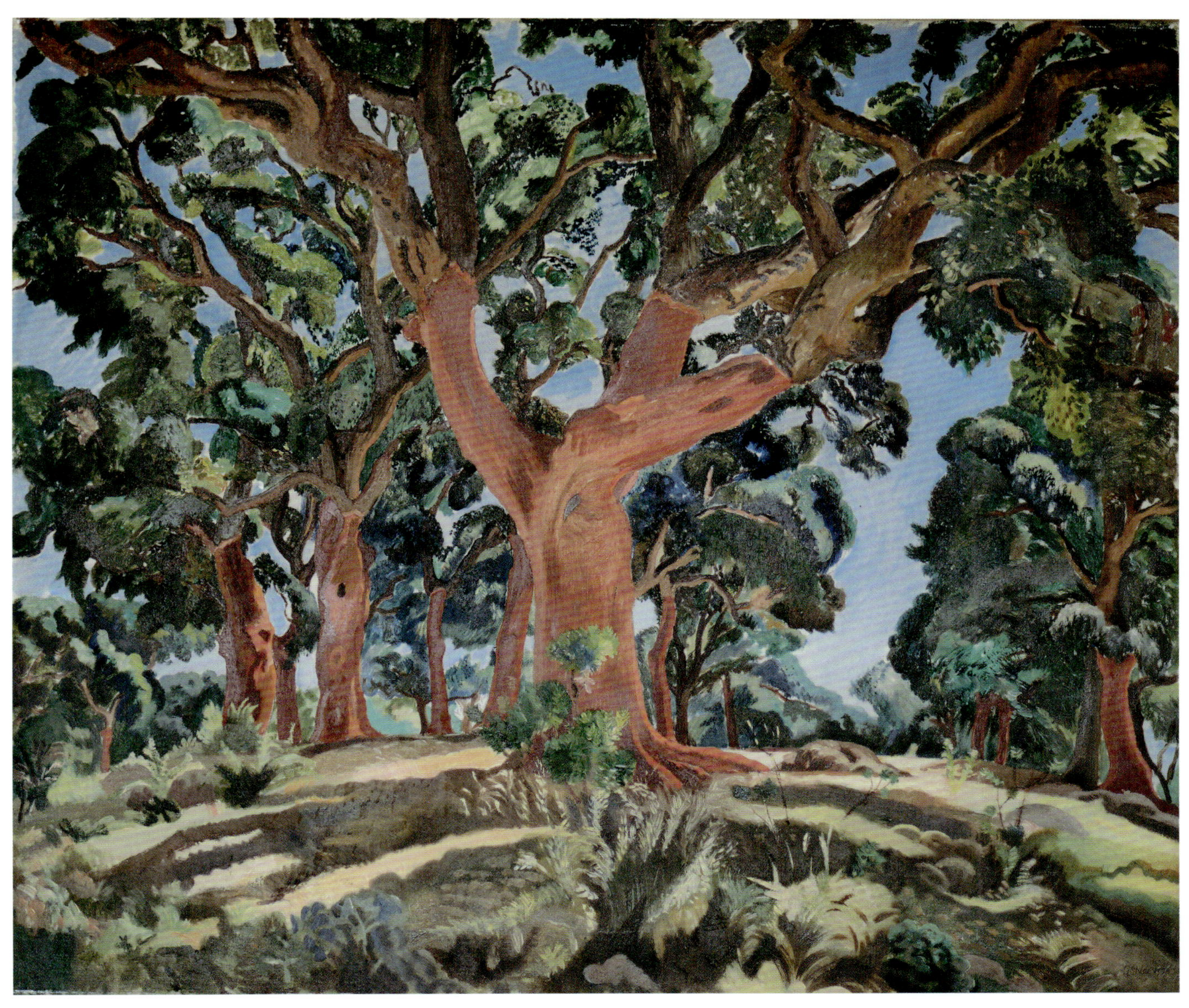

30
The Cork Wood, 1925
Oil on canvas
63.5 × 76.2 cm (25 × 30 in)
Private collection

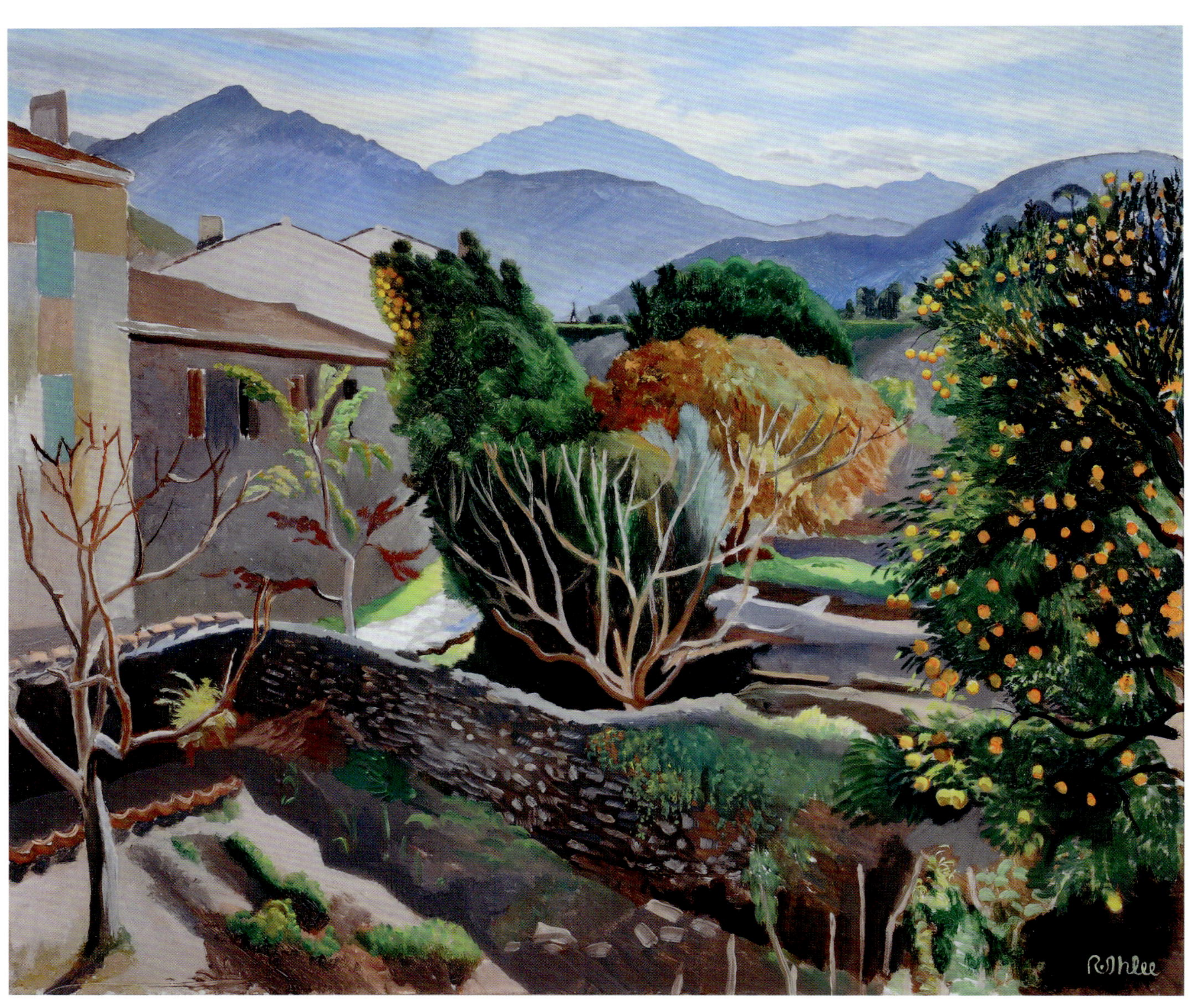

31
Montagnes et orangiers, Collioure, 1933
Oil on canvas
60 × 73 cm (24 × 28 in)
Hull University Art Collection

> picture. Endless strings of garlic . . . next to onions which make their Egyptian counterparts look like pygmies. Carts full of oranges . . . white and purple aubergines . . . visitors who come to Collioure declare unanimously that it is a land of plenty [*un pays de Cocagne*].[12]

The great majority of landowners in the Pyrénées-Orientales (P-O) were peasant farmers with less than five hectares. Nearly all of them had some livestock and grew vines alongside other produce. Soft fruits were cultivated extensively in the plains. Before the Second World War the department supplied, annually, a third of the country's peaches (25,000 tons) and 8,500 tons of apricots.[13] Ihlee's 1933 painting *Montagnes et orangiers, Collioure* (fig.31) shows oranges, and other fruits and vegetables, flourishing domestically.

Many of the artists' neighbours had to work hard to survive, with women bearing an equal burden. As well as repairing nets and tending vines, they made up the bulk of the workforce in the anchovy salting houses. According to Soulier, whose son Honoré was a friend of Ihlee, they also drove carts for builders and gathered fuel for heating and cooking.

> In the mountains one meets long lines of women with enormous loads of brushwood which they gather up to 12 km from their homes. Each load weighs 80 lb, they leave at midnight and don't return until 8 or 10 in the morning.[14]

In Ihlee's *The Red Arch, Collioure* (fig.32),[15] painted in 1926, a heavily laden woman is making her way back from just such an expedition. She is walking along the dry bed of the River Douy, towards Le Pont du Douy alongside what was a tannery. The river, more of a road when it is dry, divides the old town of Collioure, known as Le Faubourg or Port d'Aval, from the northern section, known as Port d'Amont or La Ville. More often than not the older women wore black, giving them, according to Soulier, 'the lugubrious look of a brotherhood of penitents' (*confrérie de pénitentes*).[16]

Soulier is also critical of the town's hygiene. 'Unpleasant smells of all origins are strongly evident to all but the town's inhabitants . . . when it comes to public or private hygiene the Catalans show a profound indifference.'[17] According to Evelyn Scott the situation had not much improved 20 years later. In a letter dated September 1923, she writes:

> Every morning ladies going to market carry, on the left arm, the china slop pail with the offering to the all consuming sea in it. Gentlemen trouble

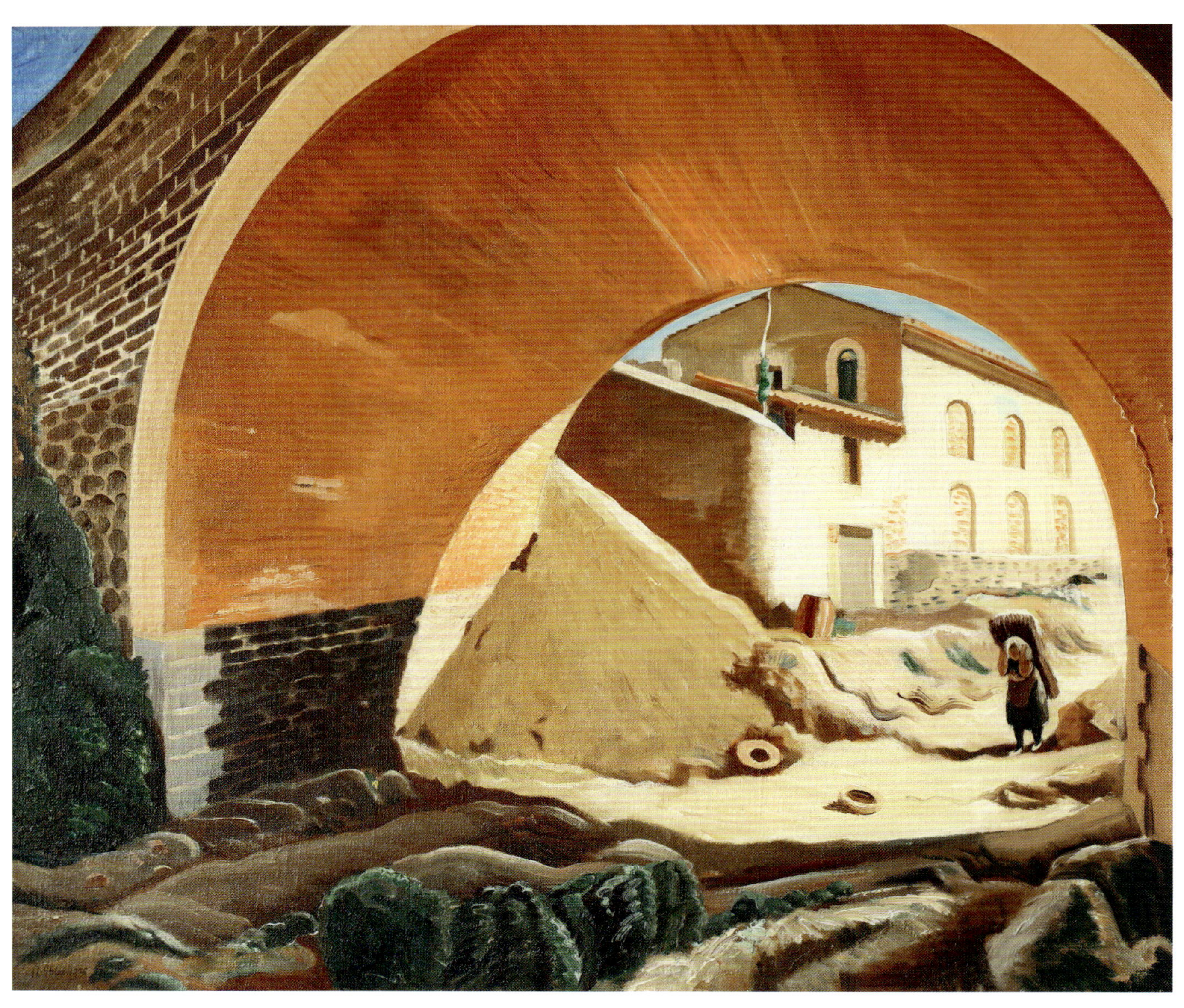

32
The Red Arch, Collioure, 1926
Oil on canvas
63.5 × 76.2 cm (25 × 30 in)
Private collection

themselves less and merely squat. God help me, I shall return to America and light an ikon in the bathroom. The smell of merde is on the breath of the sea and is almost everywhere.[18]

In the same letter she refers to a rather more pleasant spectacle, which Ihlee and Hereford would almost certainly have witnessed. 'There was a fete here two weeks ago and the fishing boats were decorated with paper lanterns and the harbour very lovely in the vague night with floating flat-radiance of the candles.'[19]

The Fête of St Vincent (fig.33) takes place every year around 16 August to celebrate the patron saint of the fishermen of Collioure, who was said to have been burnt alive by the Romans in the fourth century for refusing to recognise their pagan gods. His relics are taken by boat across the bay and paraded around the town. As well as religious formalities there are dancing and fireworks with lanterns lighting up the night sky. The whole town turns out and their numbers are doubled by revellers from across the department and beyond. Most Catalan villages have regular, albeit smaller, communal gatherings with a mix of generations sharing a meal and, perhaps, joining hands to dance the *sardane*, which, as many novices have discovered, is more complicated than it looks. In 1925 Ihlee spent a summer's evening sketching a festival in the neighbouring village of Laroque-des-Albères.[20] Under a night sky there is dancing in the packed square dominated by the Church of St Felix. Some watch from under a plane tree; others, lined along festooned ramparts, look down from above.

In Collioure, that same year, an art lover called René Pous took over

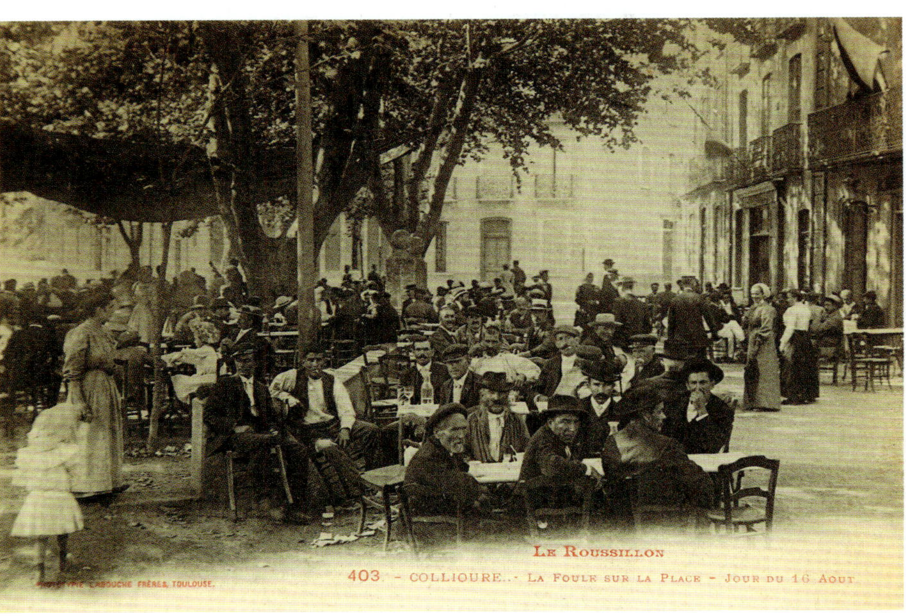

33
Fête de St Vincent at Collioure, 16 August
Postcard

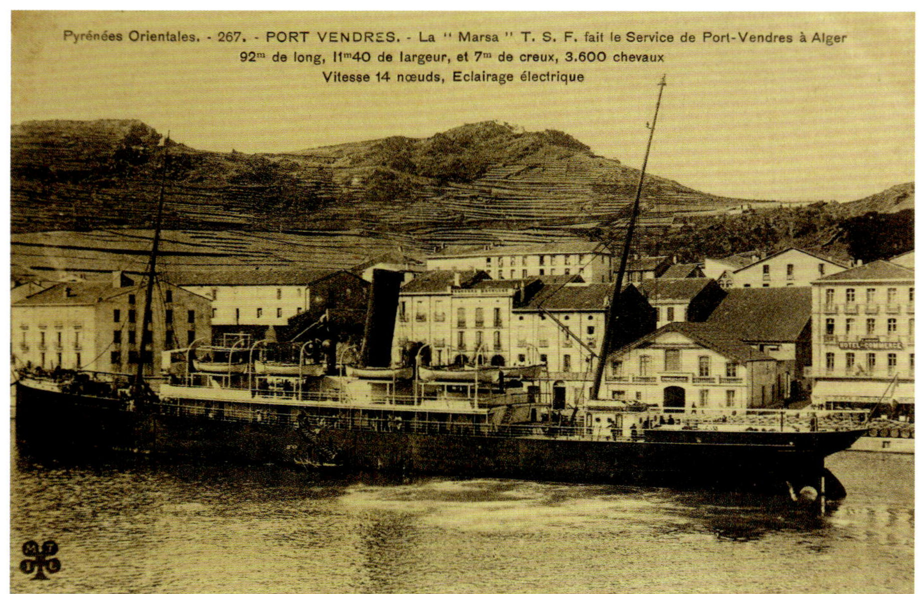

34
Liner at Port Vendres, c.1920
Hotel du Commerce, where the Mackintoshes stayed, on extreme right
Postcard

the management of his mother's small restaurant and hotel opposite the Chateau Royal, which he developed into the Hotel les Templiers.[21] He reserved a special welcome for artists, including Ihlee and his friend Charles Rennie Mackintosh who had recently come to live in neighbouring Port Vendres. 'Mackintosh was always well dressed,' recalled M. Pous in 1986; 'each time he came to Hotel Les Templiers, he had a drink – and he came often . . .'[22]

Ihlee had met Mackintosh and his wife Margaret in London and he helped them settle in Catalonia. By the end of the First World War Mackintosh's architectural commissions were drying up and he was struggling to make a living in the applied arts.[23] In 1921 both he and Ihlee contributed to a Friday Club exhibition at Heal's Mansard Gallery in Tottenham Court Road. Ihlee showed designs for textiles and wallpaper and Mackintosh designs for silks. Like Ihlee, Mackintosh had also been involved with the Arts League of Service.[24] Other points of contact were Mackintosh's brother-in-law James Herbert MacNair,[25] who had taught Ihlee's great friend Maxwell Gordon Lightfoot in Liverpool, and Ihlee's art editor at *Rhythm*, J.D. Fergusson, an artist Mackintosh particularly admired. Mackintosh and Hereford also, of course, shared a Scottish heritage.

In Port Vendres the couple were able to survive on Margaret's meagre private income, allowing 'Toshie', as his friends called him, to concentrate on painting. Between 1923 and 1927 he produced a remarkable series of watercolour landscapes which nowadays can fetch six-figure sums. Sadly, only two sold in his lifetime, for paltry amounts.

Mackintosh and his wife found lodgings at the Hotel du Commerce on the port's busy quayside (fig.34), where they enjoyed looking at ships being loaded and unloaded and the arrival and departure of liners to and from Algeria. 'Four other ships have come in besides the Esperos. One is laden with wood (sweet smelling), one with copper ore, one with what looks like gold dust, I suppose it is sulphur, and one has salted sardines . . . these all seem suitable merchandise to bring into this our beautiful sunlit harbour,' wrote Mackintosh to his wife in 1927.[26] During six weeks in May and June that year Margaret was in London for medical treatment as well as trying to interest galleries in her husband's watercolours. In a series of 23 letters to his absent wife, he refers frequently to Ihlee and Hereford, providing an insight into their way of life.

Margaret may have asked the pair to keep an eye on her husband and Ihlee, in particular, seems to have made a point of dropping by the Hotel du Commerce or inviting him to Collioure. By foot it was a pleasant 40-minute stroll between their respective lodgings, although Ihlee sometimes made the journey by car and, on one memorable occasion, by train:

> Last night when I was sitting quietly in my room Ely [i.e. Ihlee] and Hereford appeared about 6.30 and asked if they could feed with me – of course I was politely delighted. They had gone in their motors and left them at Perpignan for repairs and come here by train – Hereford is having a new hood put on his car but it seems that about a week ago Ely had gone to Perpignan with some of his Collioure friends and after a carouse was coming back about four o'clock in the morning when he ran into the back of a great cart laden with strawberries that were knocked off the cart. He had to compensate the driver for the loss and now he has had to take the car to be repaired and to get all the crushed strawberries picked out of every corner of his car. The steering gear and all the machinery was grinding the strawberries into a pulp all the way back to Collioure so it has to be thoroughly overhauled.[27]

Mackintosh himself was not immune from accidents, one of which involved a painting stool lent to him by Ihlee:

> As I had on my good clothes I took Ely's Paris stool and I had not been sitting on it 5 minutes when down I came, the beautiful leather tore away at one of the nails holding it to one of the wooden legs so there I was sprawling among the cistus with no prying eyes to be amused – but yes before I could get up and see what happened there was my raven circling around and laughing more heartily than most human beings ever could.[28]

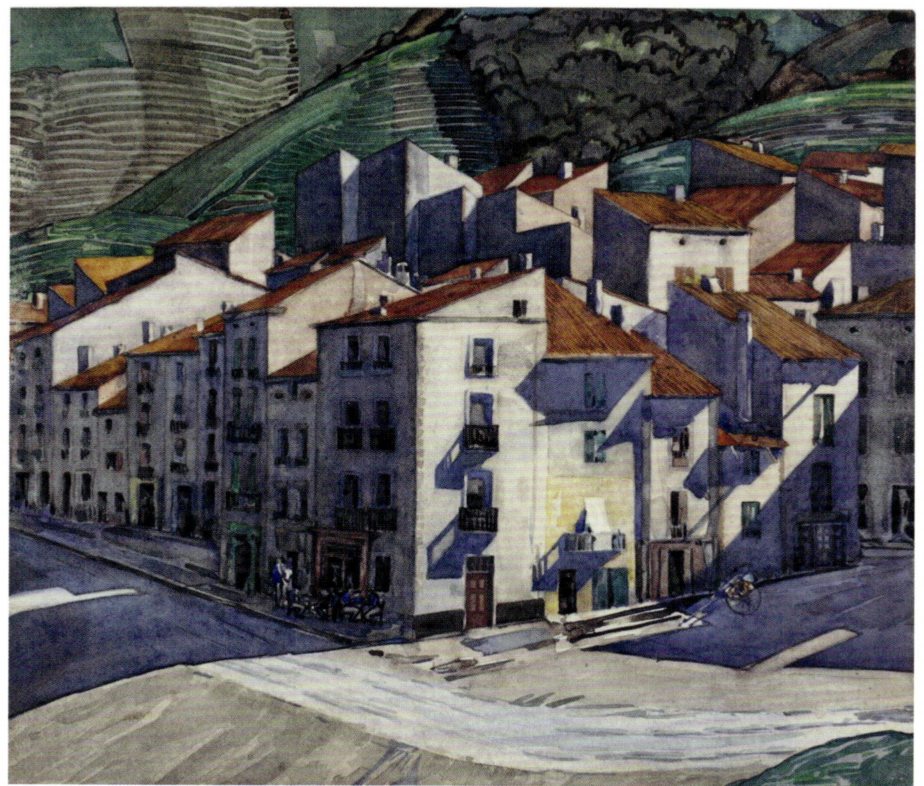

35
Charles Rennie Mackintosh
Corner of Collioure, c.1924
Pencil and watercolour
32.3 × 37.5 cm (12.7 × 14.7 in)
Hunterian Art Gallery,
University of Glasgow

Apart from collapsing stools and regular blasts from the tramontane wind, familiar to all visitors to the region, Mackintosh found insects a constant irritant, particularly the 'incredible' number of flies in Collioure. A slow worker, he produced just 30 pictures during his four years in France. They are as meticulous as the architectural plans which had made his reputation. With the exception of an image of a street corner in Collioure (fig.35), people are usually absent. Mackintosh's palette is cooler than Ihlee's, seldom evoking the region's characteristic brightness and warmth. He himself admits to having an 'insane aptitude for seeing green and putting it down here, there and everywhere'.[29] By this time both artists had developed individual styles largely independent of current trends.

Beautiful though they are, Mackintosh's pictures can seem remote. One of Hereford's few surviving canvases, featuring the church at *Port Vendres* (fig.36), has a similar unworldly quality, although his stylised composition in oils has little of the delicacy or detail of a Mackintosh watercolour.

Despite the disparity in their outlook and ages, the three artists seemed to have rubbed along pretty well. Mackintosh, then approaching 60 and devoted to his wife, was inevitably more set in his ways than Ihlee and Hereford, who were in their early forties and enjoying a bachelor lifestyle.

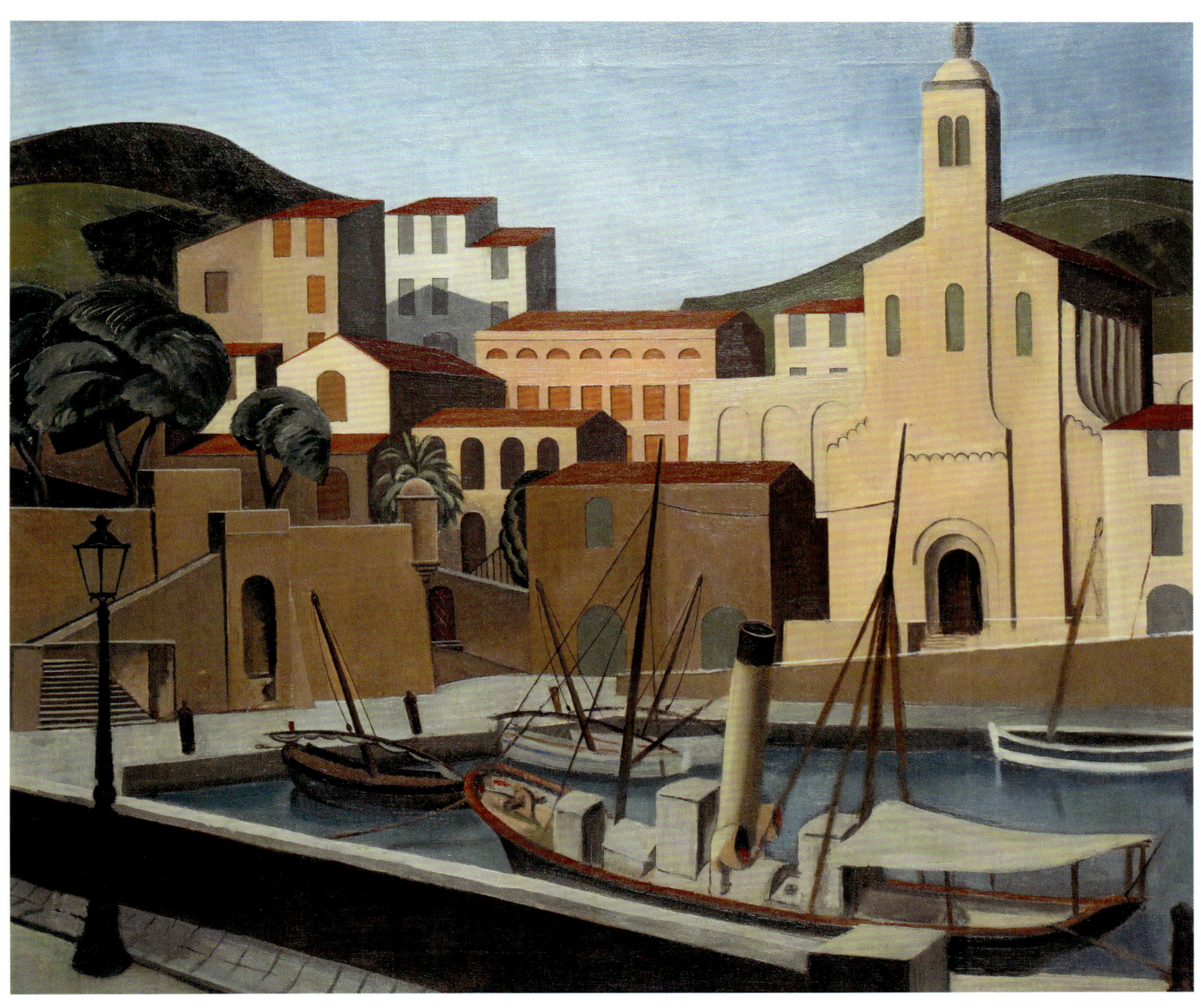

36
Edgar Hereford
Port Vendres, 1925
Oil on canvas
61 × 76 cm (24 × 30 in)
Private collection

Sometimes a bit of a curmudgeon, Toshie did not always appreciate unannounced visits from the pair, although he usually rallied.

> I had just finished my soup when Kim [the hotel waiter] hurried up saying '*voila votres camarades*' and then appeared two youths in blue shirts and blue ties – Ely and Hereford – they had just come along because they hadn't seen me for a week so we had quite a jolly dinner and then some coffee and I have just sent them home with some back numbers of the *News of the World*, *Dispatch* and *Observer*. Ely is delighted with his new studio, Hereford probably likes his quite as much but says less of course.[30]

The letters reveal Ihlee as more outgoing and spontaneous than Hereford, who seems to have been a restraining influence. For instance, when Ihlee suggested they pay for some of Toshie's London friends to visit, Hereford vetoed the plan, saying: 'You don't pay people's fares when they are coming to see you.' Ihlee, according to Mackintosh, was very open about his feelings: 'He shows them all like a young child and that in a way makes him an object of sympathy and attraction,' whereas Hereford was 'little prone to enthusiasms'.[31]

At that time, the pair were lodging with a rather fearsome landlady whom Mackintosh refers to as 'Madame'.[32] In the days before mass tourism there were very few boarding houses in town and 'Madame' may well have been Pauline Bougnol Quintana, who ran a hotel of the same name with help from her son Fernand. On a visit to see his friends Mackintosh refers to 'Madame and Fernando', and Ihlee gave one of his paintings to someone called Pauline. Separated from her husband Antoine, she would have been in her early forties at the time and Fernand about 15.

When Ihlee and Hereford were not out and about, they could retreat to their separate studios near the hotel. Hereford had a gramophone player and when Mackintosh went to Collioure to celebrate his fifty-ninth birthday he may have found himself in need of some calming music.

> I have just got back from Collioure where we had a fairly miserable night – they had the night before a terrible row with Madame and she ordered them out of the house – some girl, I understand they had been seen with or speaking to, I don't know but I was sent down as a sort of decoy to make some sort of peace with Madame – we had a sort of dinner but she had not entirely thawed when we left for the studios to have some gramophone music. The two of them seem to have been drinking like fish for the last three weeks – that is all the impression of my birthday party – I walked home and got in just before midnight.[33]

Whatever Ihlee may have got up to in his spare time, he was not neglecting his work. In 1927, for example, he produced almost as many pictures as Mackintosh managed during his entire stay in France. What's more, in those early years in Collioure, he kept up his contacts with several London galleries including the Goupil, the Chenil and the Whitechapel, who were happy to exhibit his work.

Mackintosh, meanwhile, was struggling to find a market for his watercolours, although it does appear Margaret managed to place a few with the Leicester Galleries despite him failing to sign them:

> I am sorry there were no signatures, I always forget about that, it seems so unimportant but I am sure you can put down my signature on each picture quite easily – do it in pencil and then wet it with clean cold water – you will do it much better than I could have done it.[34]

The letters clearly show how much Mackintosh relied upon his wife. Like Ihlee he was a keen smoker and on a couple of seemingly innocuous occasions he grumbles to her about his swollen tongue, caused, he thought, by a change in the quality of his tobacco. 'Formerly it was light and fragrant now it is sodden, sordid and sickening.'[35] The swelling turned out to be a symptom of a fatal cancer. When his condition deteriorated it was Ihlee who accompanied him back to London. The journey, by car and boat, was distressing. 'Monsieur Mackintosh was overcome. He could not even speak,' said Ihlee's wife many years later.[36]

Ihlee is said to have made a last sketch of his old friend on the ferry home.[37] After painful radiation treatment at Westminster Hospital, Mackintosh died, aged 60, on 10 December 1928. The following year Margaret, who outlived him by four years, returned to the Hotel du Commerce to scatter his ashes near their 'beautiful sunlit harbour'.

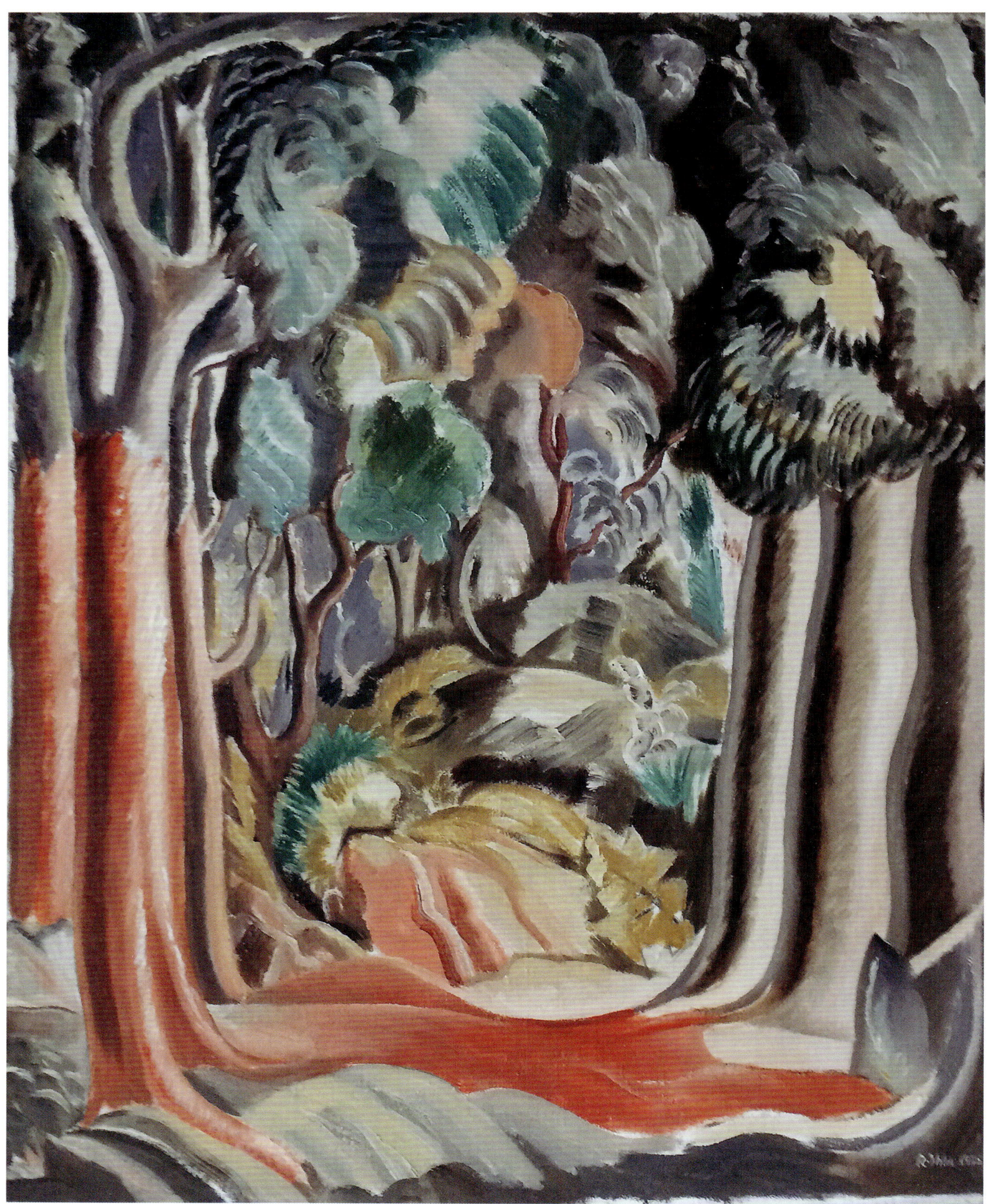

4 Artists about Town

In 1926, the year before Mackintosh's sad departure from France, Ihlee had a one-man show at the Chenil Gallery in London, which was run by William Rothenstein's brother-in-law, Jack Knewstub.[1] It was five years since his last solo exhibition at the Leicester Galleries and critics had noticed the difference. 'In recent years Mr Ihlee has lived much in France and this exhibition shows he has completely emancipated himself from the usual Slade influences,' observed the *Sunday Times* critic.[2] His erstwhile teacher Henry Tonks would, no doubt, have recoiled from the free brushwork of *The Red Wood* (fig.37), which is in marked contrast to the formality of his earlier oils like *The Well* (Fig.15) and bears some similarity to the work of Paul Nash.[3]

In all Ihlee produced 36 pictures for the Chenil show, some dating from the trip to Algeria but most from his early years in Collioure. Many visiting artists tended to set up their easels on the beach in front of the Catholic church, Notre-Dame-des-Anges, whose distinctive pink-domed tower served in medieval times as a lighthouse. In the 1926 exhibition Ihlee chose instead to present an image of the Protestant church, *The Temple, Collioure* (fig.38),[4] with the unusual addition of a naked lady peeping out from a top-floor window. Humour often played a part in his work, which was inspired as much by the mundane as the picturesque. Among his other paintings of the period are *The Tree Stumps, The Gutter, The Cutting* and *The Soapy Stream*.

As well as the Chenil, Ihlee showed at the Redfern and Whitechapel galleries and exhibited 17 pictures at the Goupil Gallery, which was managed by Sickert's dealer William Marchant until his death in 1925.[5] Although his contact with London galleries diminished after 1927, he continued to show with the NEAC throughout his time in Collioure.

After seeing his work at the NEAC in March 1927, P.G. Konody commented in the *Observer*:

> Mr Ihlee does not accept the accidents of nature submissively but in his *Landscape with Cat* (fig.39) and his *Landscape with Jug* shows his habit of imposing his sense of pictorial fitness upon the motif presented to him by nature. These pictures are not so much representations of things seen as reconstructions based on abstract principles of art.[6]

37
The Red Wood, 1925
Oil on canvas
60.96 × 50.8 cm (24 × 20 in)
Private collection

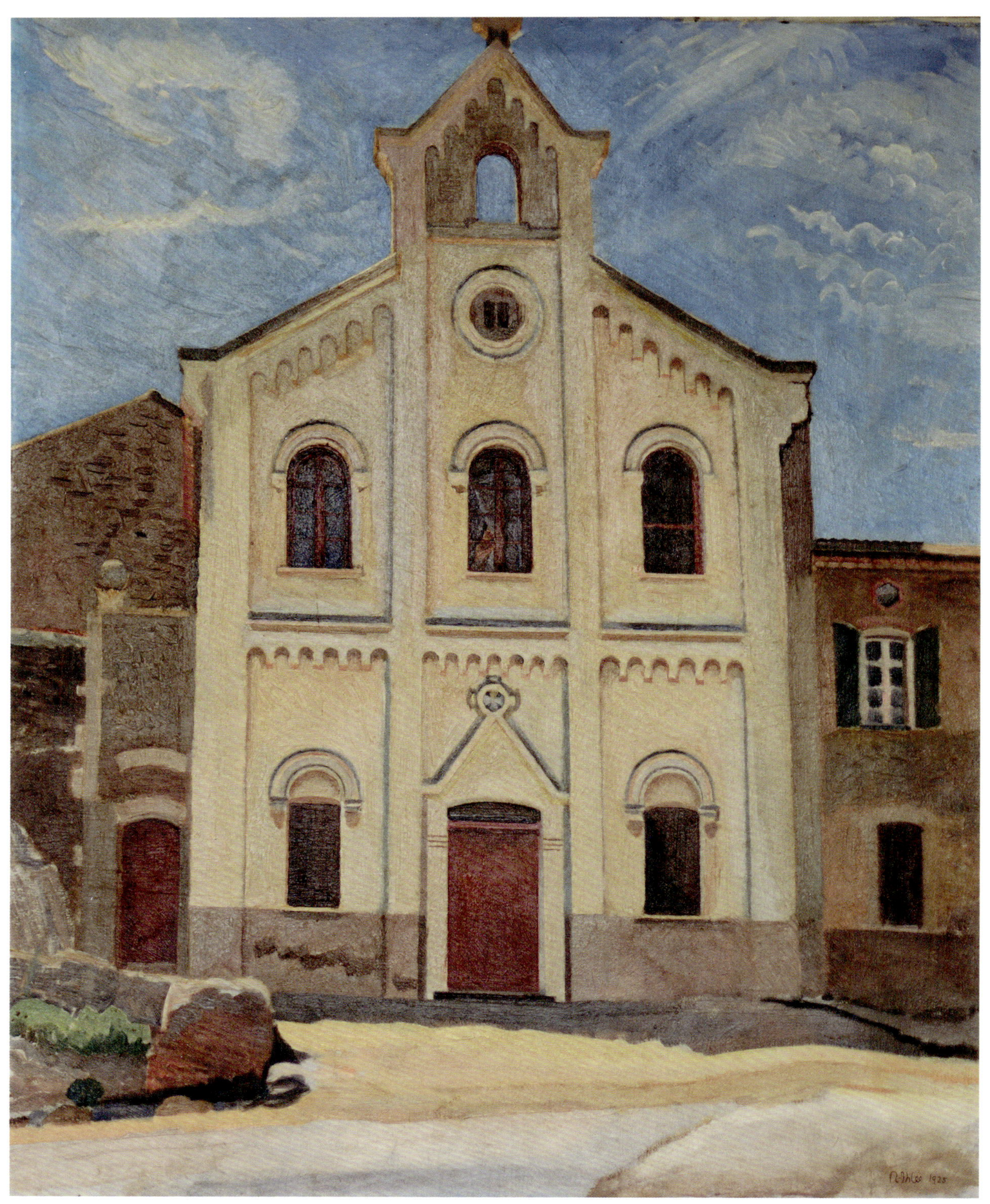

38
The Temple, Collioure, 1925
Oil on canvas
76.2 × 63.5 cm (30 × 25 in)
Private collection

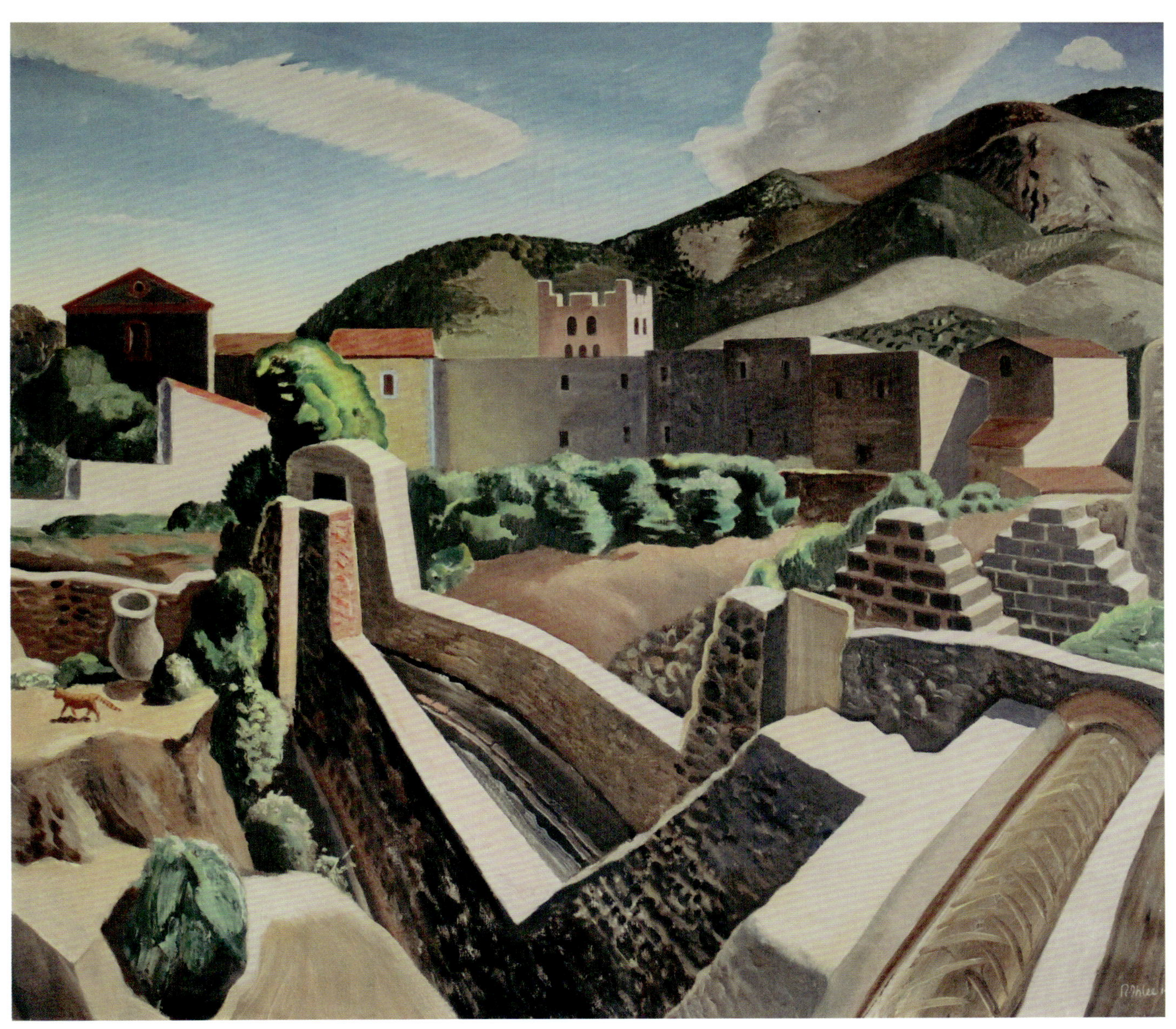

39
Landscape with Cat, 1926
Oil on canvas
81.28 × 96.52 cm (32 × 38 in)
Private collection

Landscape with Cat may well be partly imagined but, despite its dreamlike, almost surreal quality, there is little doubt that the distinctive bell tower belongs to L'Abbaye Sainte-Marie in Arles-sur-Tech (see map, p.78). Other images, such as *L'Heure de la soupe* (fig.40),[7] are more firmly grounded in reality. After painting Senegalese troops in Algeria, Ihlee may have been surprised to have come across them again in Collioure. Some were stationed at the Chateau Royal where we see them at supper time. Many Senegalese riflemen (*tirailleurs*) were trained in southern France, the climate being similar to North Africa which was, of course, readily accessible by boat from Port Vendres. Attached to the French army, they had a reputation for bravery and ruthlessness.

Another familiar sight around Collioure were Paul Soulier's 'lugubrious' ladies in black. Ihlee went up into the hills, a mile or so above the town, to paint one such figure in the shade of two plane trees at the Ermitage de Notre Dame de Consolation (fig.41).[8] The lady is sewing in the courtyard of the seventeenth-century building near a fountain fed by mountain streams. Later a hotel, it was a popular refuge from the heat of the day and also a place of pilgrimage. The twelfth-century chapel attached to the hermitage contains some unusual religious offerings including model ships and a stuffed crocodile.

The canvas is now in the collection of Collioure's Museum of Modern Art, a gift, perhaps, from Ihlee when the museum was started by another foreign artist in 1934. Jean Peské (1870–1949),[9] of Russian descent, had been a regular visitor to the region since the turn of the century and encouraged fellow artists to donate works which were initially shown in a room in the town hall. The collection, which consisted of about 190 works, has since swelled to nearly 1400 works and is now housed in La Maison Pams, the former home of Gaston Pams,[10] a politician and member of the Resistance who became a senator for the department.

Ihlee would have known some of the other artists with works in the museum, including Augustin Hanicotte (1870–1957) and Henri Vergé-Sarrat (1880–1966). Originally from northern France, Hanicotte settled in Collioure with his Dutch wife during the First World War when he was seeking warmer climes to counteract his arthritis. He is best remembered for setting up drawing classes for local children known as '*les gosses* [kids] *de Collioure*'. His largest work, *La Grande Plage*, is more than 15 feet long and teems with activity. What seems like the whole town is gathered on the beach with a variety of costumes and emotions on display. Fishermen in blue, old women in black, young women brightly clothed, children in shorts and everyone either working, gossiping, squabbling, drinking or fighting.

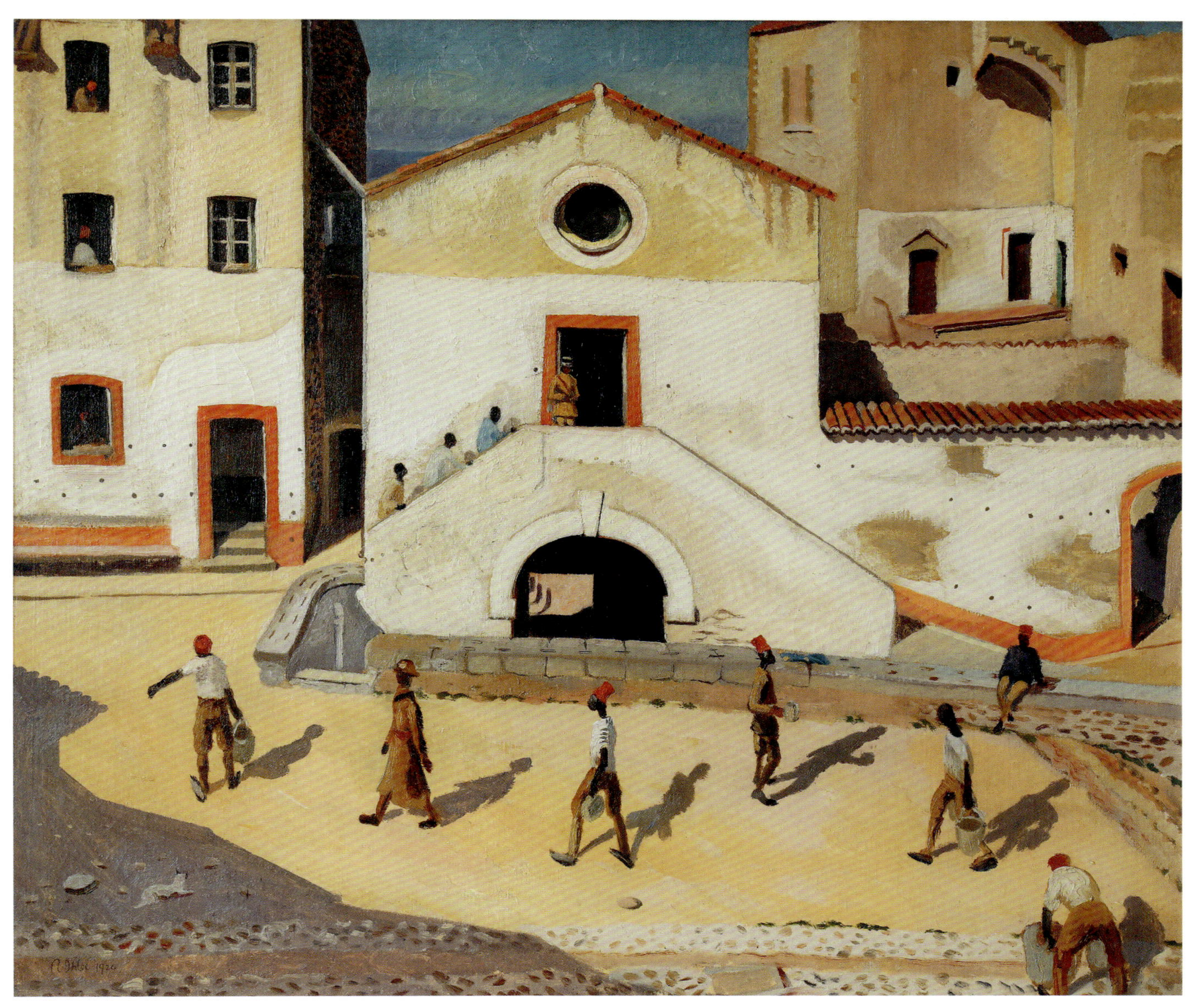

40
L'Heure de la soupe, 1924
Oil on canvas
63.5 × 76.2 cm (25 × 30 in)
Private collection

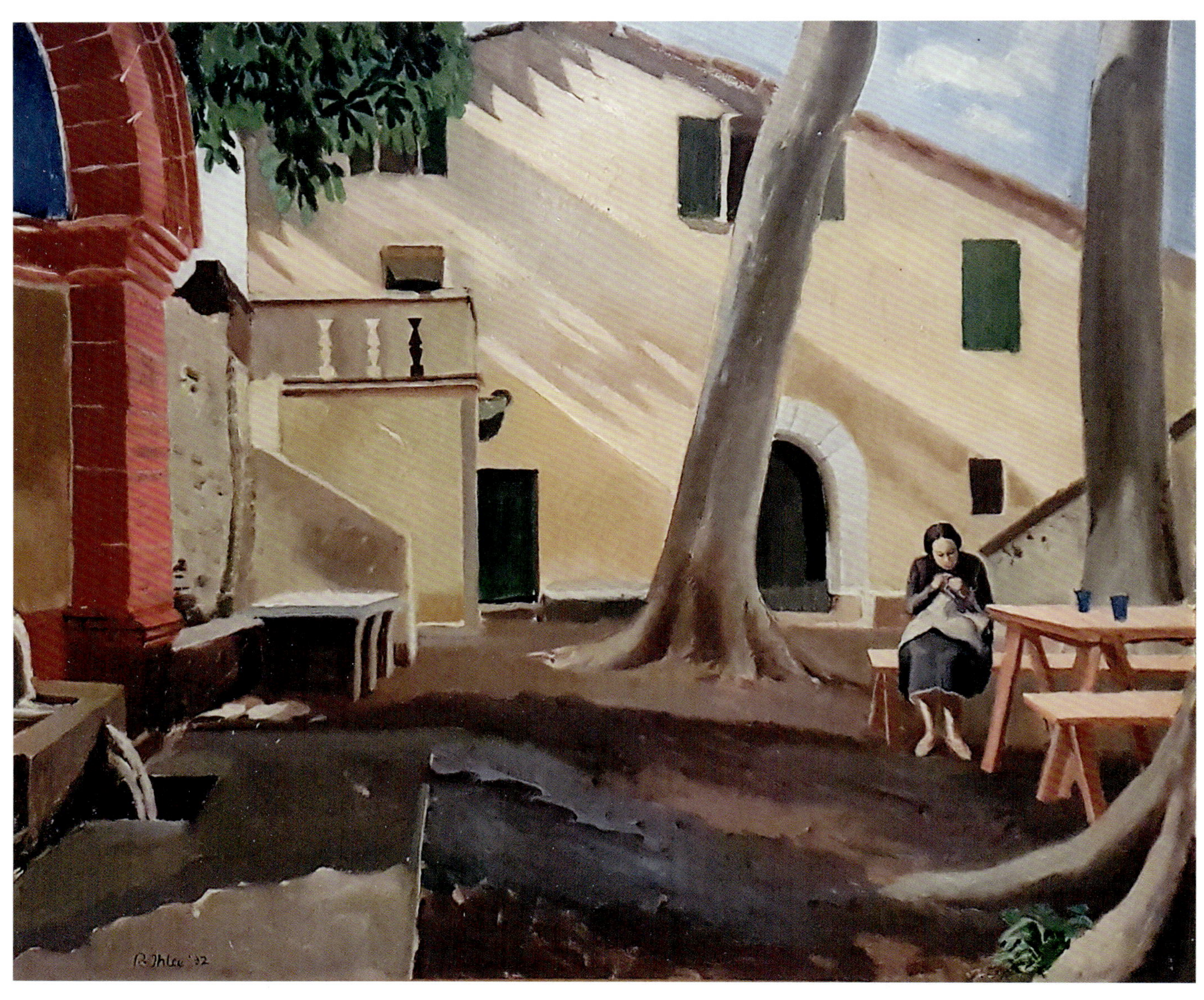

41
Terrace Consolation, 1932
Oil on canvas
50.8 × 60.96 cm (20 × 24 in)
Musée d'Art Moderne, Collioure

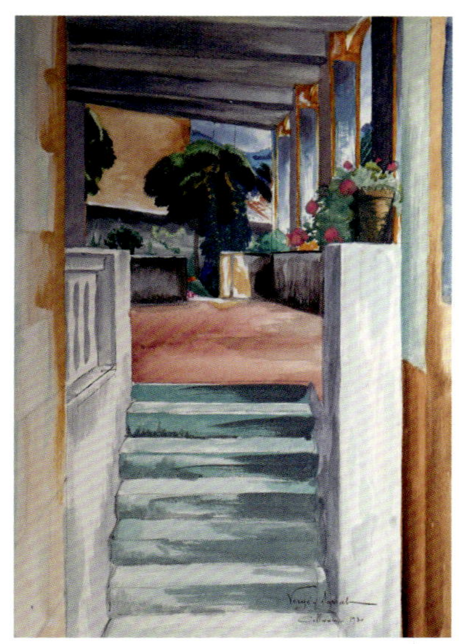

42
Henri Vergé-Sarrat
Villa Les Terrasses, Collioure, 1930
Gouache on paper
45.5 × 32 cm (18 × 12.5 in)
Musée d'Art Moderne, Collioure

During the Second World War when Port Vendres came under Nazi control, Hanicotte became friendly with its German commander.[11] Suspected of collaboration, he was later imprisoned in Perpignan. After the war he was released and left the town, spending much of his later life in Narbonne. Despite this episode, a street has been named after him in Collioure.

Ihlee also came across Henri Vergé-Sarrat, who, although not a permanent resident of Collioure, was a frequent visitor in the 1930s. He and his artist wife, Rolande, a former pupil 18 years his junior, stayed in a villa called Les Terrasses, now the Hotel Triton, overlooking the sea. Vergé-Sarrat was born in Belgium but his father came from the French Pyrenees. The couple's great-niece, Valia Boulay, said they made a striking pair. 'Henri, a poet with his blue eyes and an open outlook, was quite a contrast to Rolande, who was large and sturdy with a deep voice.'

Vergé-Sarrat and Ihlee shared common ground. They were roughly the same age, both were involved with much younger women and both had painted in Biskra.[12] As a mark of friendship, Ihlee gave Vergé-Sarrat a painting of the mountain village of Molitg near Prades.

Another frequent visitor to Collioure was Léopold Survage (1879–1968), who had trained at the Moscow School of Painting before settling in Paris where he had shared a studio with Amedeo Modigliani (1884–1920). Survage first came to the Catalan port in 1925 and, until 1932, often stayed at the Hotel Bougnol-Quintana. Survage was a more experimental artist than Ihlee. Symbolism and Cubism were evident in much of his work although he sometimes painted more conventionally.

The region's most famous living artist was the sculptor Aristide Maillol (1861–1944), who divided his time between the outskirts of Paris and his birthplace in Banyuls-sur-Mer a few miles down the coast from Collioure. Renowned for his monumental statues of curvaceous women, he was very much admired by Ihlee and by Hereford, who lent a book about him to Mackintosh. It is not known whether they actually met the great man but they could not have failed to notice his many public works in the region. Perhaps his finest is *La Méditerranée* (fig.43), which has all the graceful voluptuousness of the sculptor's ideal woman. There are versions of her at the Hôtel de Ville in Perpignan and at Maillol's country house, La Métairie, in Banyuls, which is now a museum.[13] Maillol died in a road accident in 1944 and *La Mediterranée* sits above his tomb in the grounds of his former home.

Since 1913 the 20-mile stretch of coast from Argelès, just north of Collioure, to Cerbère on the Spanish border, just south of Banyuls, has been known as La Côte Vermeille, the vermilion coast. Ihlee captured its

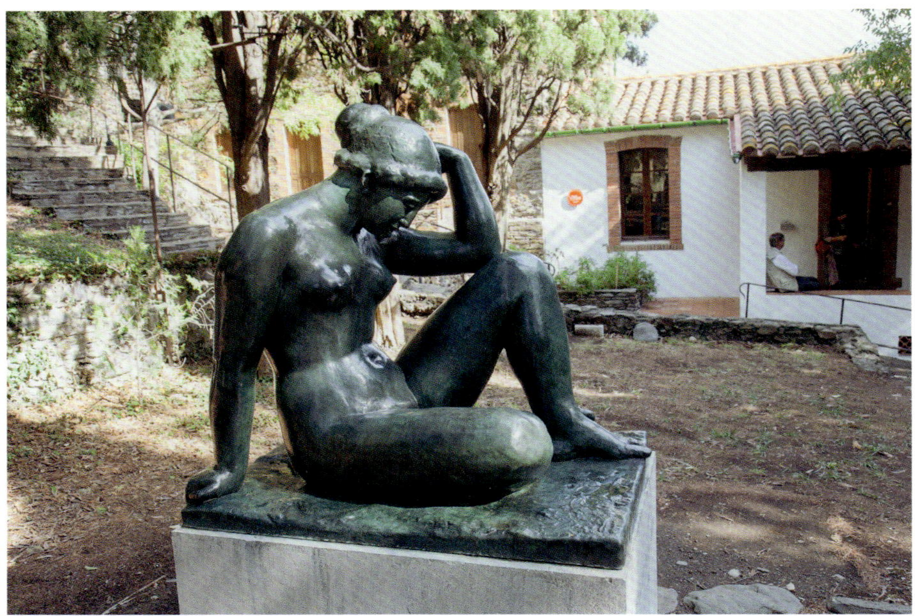

43
Aristide Maillol
La Mediterranée, c.1925
On Maillol's tomb at Banyuls

rugged rocks with a reddish (vermilion) hue in a painting of 1926 called *The Terrace* (fig.44). Although Ihlee had little regard for topographical accuracy, the lighthouse in the top right of the picture may be the one at Cap Béar, just south of Port Vendres. The terrace from which the artist surveys a fleet of fishing barques could have been part of a restaurant or hotel. It was hoped the Côte Vermeille brand name would help the region emulate the success of the Costa Brava and Côte d'Azur, but it was not until the 1930s that a concerted effort was made to attract tourists to the beaches, bays, creeks and coves around Collioure.[14] Although railway posters promoting Collioure as a holiday destination were aimed at a domestic rather than international market, visitor numbers inevitably increased.

While it was nothing like the mass tourism of later years, the character of the port, in summer at least, was subtly changing. Ever since Matisse and Derain had put the town on the artistic map some 20 years earlier, the number of easels around the bay had been multiplying. They sometimes surpassed the number of boats lined up on the shore, although, in the 1920s, the influx of artists did not seem to bring much prosperity either to them or the town. Writing to a friend in September 1923, Evelyn Scott remarks:

> This town is miserably poor and now, at the end of summer, is haunted by devastated artists who are going to get one picture in the Salon before they die, or die at once of a starch diet. Some wear pilgrim father hair and

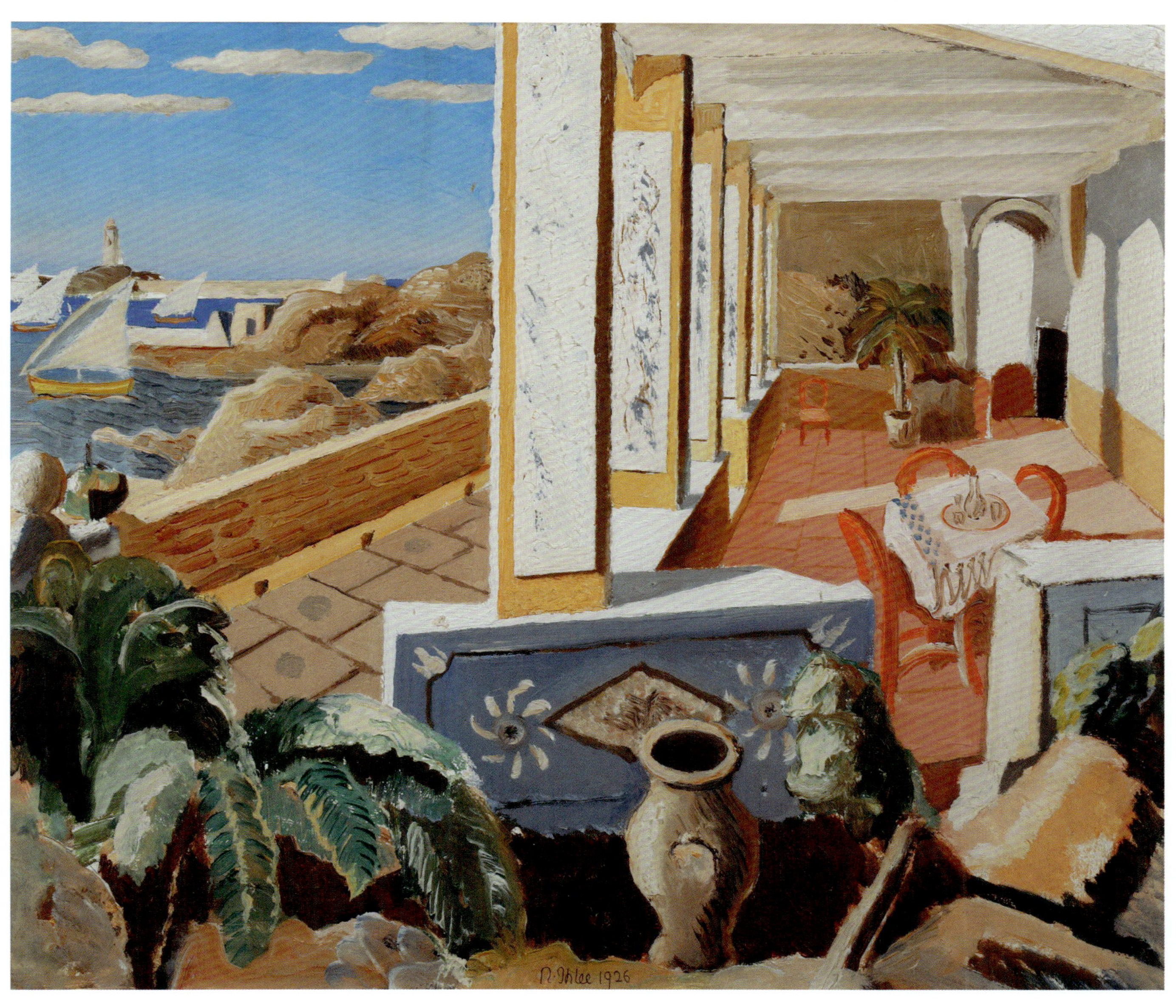

44
The Terrace, 1926
Oil on canvas
38.1 × 45.72 cm (15 × 18 in)
Private collection

blue coats, some fence with their palettes . . . and some trudge to painting armed like Tartarin[15] on his hunting expedition with a meek little wife and three daughters to assist. You never saw so many awful pictures as are being painted in Collioure at the present moment.[16]

Ihlee, by contrast, was having considerable success with the various Paris salons. In 1926, the same year as his Chenil show, he had three landscapes accepted at the Salon d'Automne and for the next dozen or so years he exhibited more in France than in Britain. From 1928 he exhibited at the Salon des Indépendants, and soon afterwards at the Salon des Tuileries.[17] He also started to exhibit in Perpignan, holding two one-man shows at the Galerie Campistro,[18] in 1931 and 1932, and two shows at the Salle d'Arago in the city's handsome municipal building in 1934 and 1935. His list indicates a respectable number of sales.

Most of his exhibits were inspired by the landscape around Collioure but few were the sort of scenes you would find on a tourist's postcard. In his oil sketch *La Placette, étude, Collioure* (fig.45) Ihlee found the market place all but empty, the plane trees shorn of leaf and, under a winter sun, the shadows lengthening across the square.

Hereford was far less prolific but his few known surviving paintings display a distinctive talent. A landscape with a mountain backdrop, possibly based on Le Jardin Naudin in Collioure, is a well-balanced design dating from 1925. Called *Hills, Houses and Garden* (fig.46), it was the last of his ten recorded exhibits with the NEAC. Apart from one Breton portrait, *Jean Remeur*, his work seldom features people but his compositions are neat and tightly structured, chiming with Mackintosh's description of him as a somewhat reserved personality.

Ihlee's most enigmatic picture of the period, painted in 1929, is called *Nocturnal Conversation* and subtitled *The Plot* (fig.47). Perhaps it points to Ihlee and Hereford's uncertain, 'in-between' status in Collioure. Neither tourists nor natives, they could not have expected to be accepted unreservedly by people who would have known each other from cradle to grave. Huddles of men are common sights in Catalan towns and villages but this particular huddle looks as though it might be up to no good. The looming shadow of a figure in priestly garb adds to the menacing scene, which could have been influenced by the symbolism of Léopold Survage. The meaning of this intriguing image, with its hint of Surrealism, is as mysterious as some aspects of Ihlee's life, including his marriage to a peasant girl with whom, on the face of it, he had very little in common.

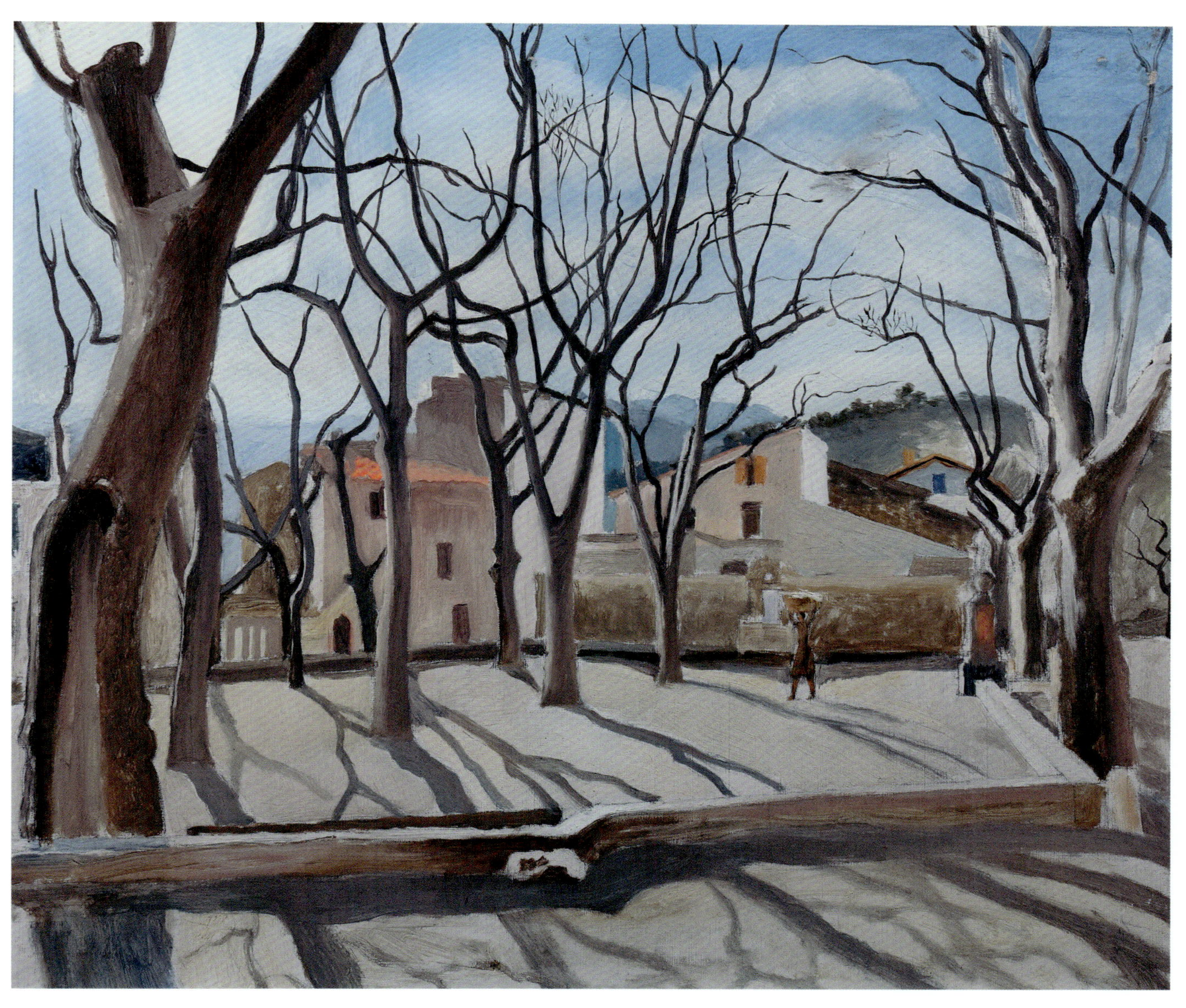

45
La Placette, étude, Collioure, 1933
Oil on canvas
38.1 × 45.72 cm (15 × 18 in)
Private collection

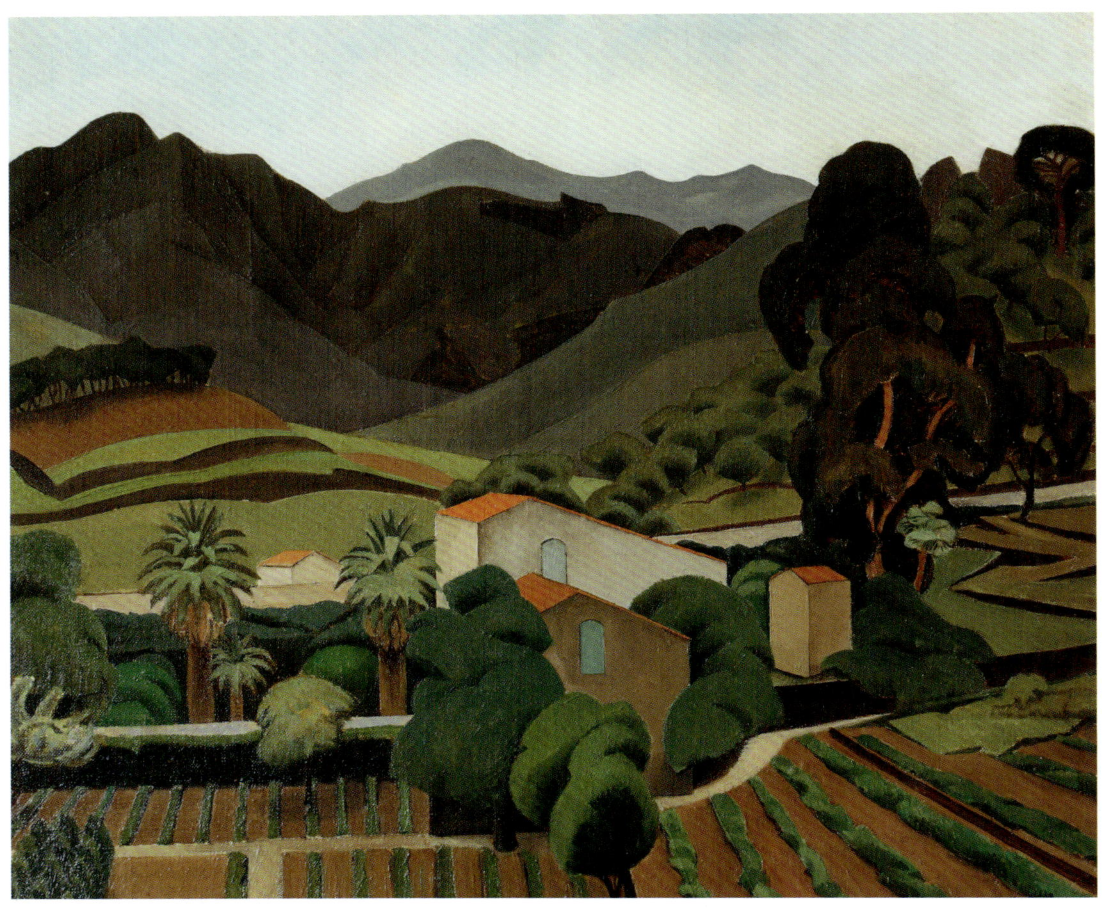

46
Edgar Hereford
Hills, Houses and Garden, 1925
Oil on canvas
51 × 61 cm (20 × 24 inches)
Private collection

47
Nocturnal Conversation (The Plot), 1929
Oil on canvas
100 × 81 cm (39 × 32 in)
Private collection

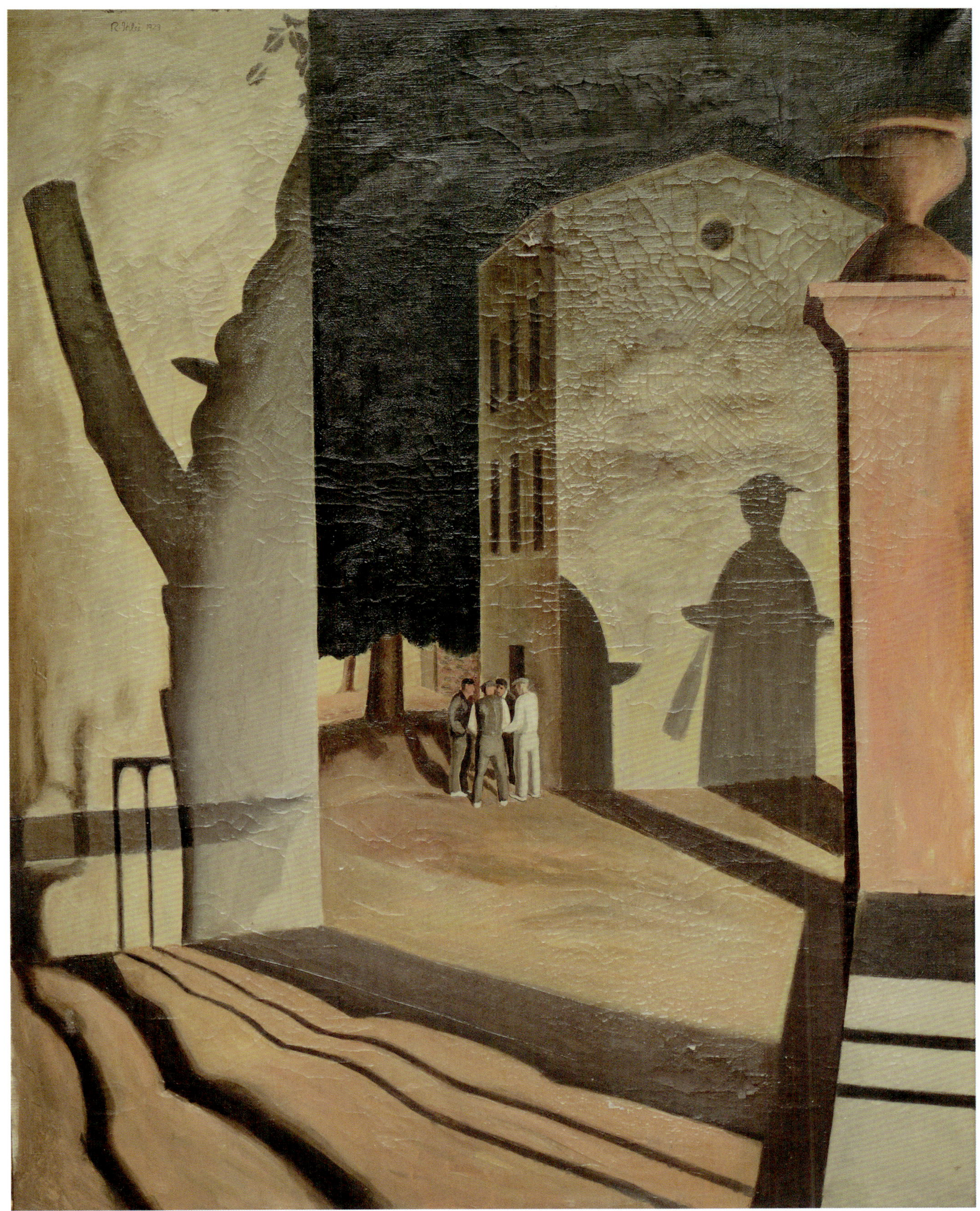

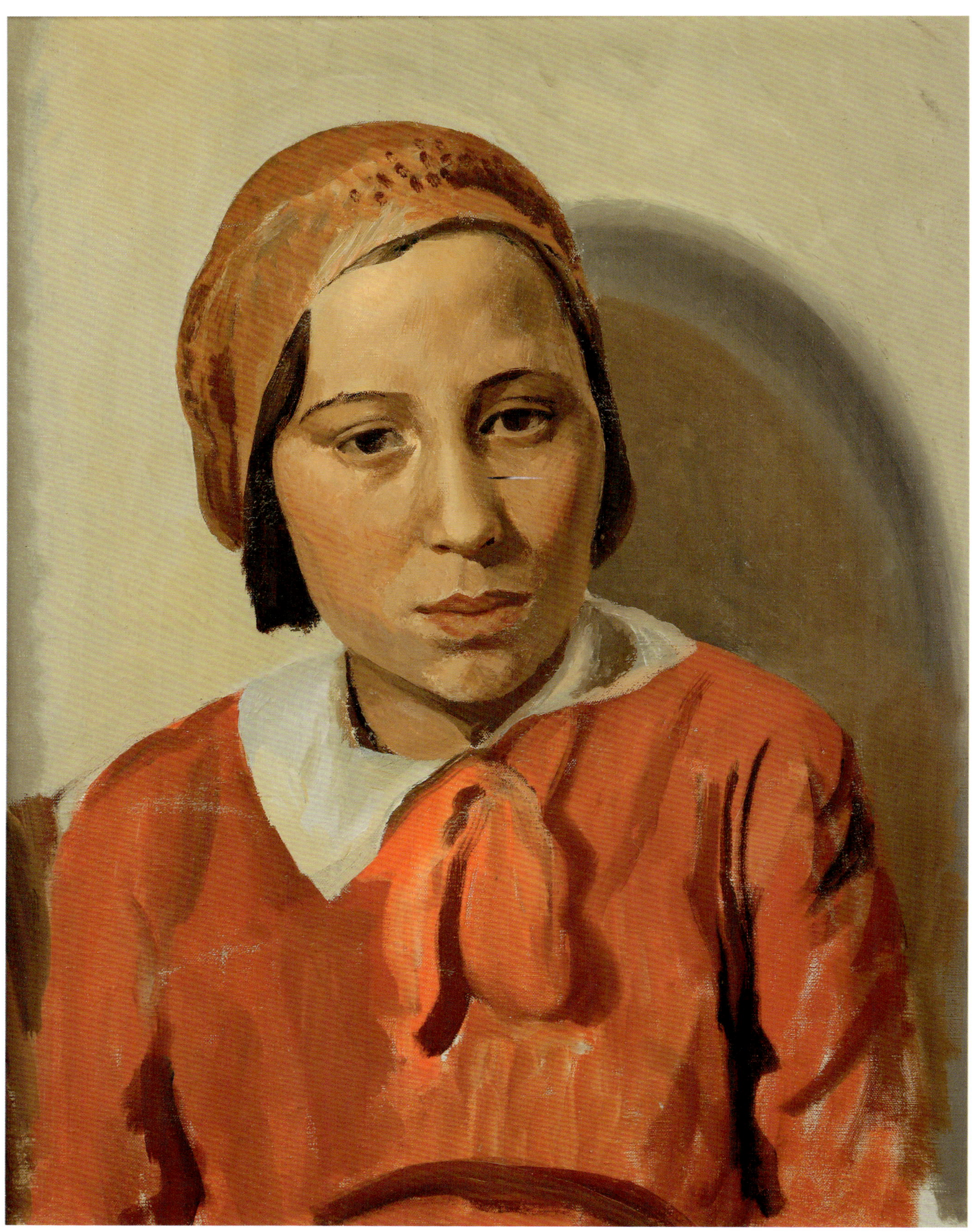

5 Romance in Languedoc-Roussillon and Brittany

Isabelle Mons (1904–99) was 21 years younger than Ihlee and was born in a small village called Payra-sur-l'Hers in the neighbouring department of Aude.[1] Like many in that part of France, her family scratched a living from a modest parcel of land. In the grape-picking season she would help relatives who tended vines in the hills above Banyuls-sur-Mer and it was during one such harvest, possibly in the late summer of 1927, that she came across Rudolph Ihlee.

They made an unlikely pair: the sophisticated European artist and the poorly educated peasant girl. Nevertheless the relationship suited them both well. Ihlee, then 44, with his car and private income, and by this time a dog (fig.49), offered a different way of life. Isabelle, with her youth (she was 23) and culinary skills, had attributes that he lacked. To start with it is probable that Isabelle kept house for Ihlee and Hereford, but the relationship developed and endured for over 40 years despite Isabelle having very little interest in art. Her schooling, part of which coincided with the First World War, would have been patchy at best. Many pupils were kept away from classes to work on the land, replacing their fathers and brothers who had been mobilised.[2] In several villages the education of girls suffered from a widespread view that they were better off learning

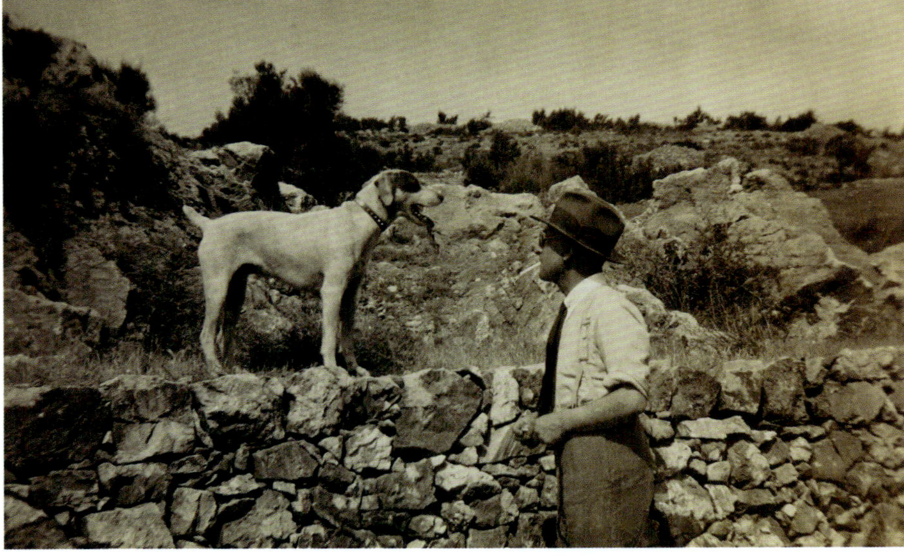

49
The artist with dog
Private collection

left:
48
Isabelle, c.1930
Oil on canvas
61 x 51 cm (24 x 20 in)
Private collection

household skills at home. '*Pourquoi instruire des filles qui peuvent apprendre à conduire un ménage sans frequenter l'école?*' ('Why bother teaching girls when they can learn domestic duties without going to school?')[3]

Ihlee painted a number of portraits of Isabelle (fig.48), whose modest demeanour could hardly have been more different from the self-confident glamour of Sophia. He would have felt on firmer ground with Isabelle, who was loyal, quick-witted and hard-working. He was in no hurry, though, to get married. It was not until 30 March 1938 that Isabelle, in a small ceremony in Collioure, became the second Mrs Ihlee, Hereford apparently having told Ihlee 'it's time you made an honest woman of her!'[4]

Hereford, meanwhile, had become involved with a married woman whom he had met on one of his many trips to Brittany with Ihlee. It is probable that when he first encountered Marguerite Doher, known as Margot, she was unattached but, according to her grandson, she was forced into an arranged marriage to a 'brute of a man' with whom she later had a daughter.[5] Nevertheless, despite long periods of separation, Hereford and Marguerite maintained their relationship, which involved a lot of secrecy and travel.

Partly, perhaps, because of Hereford's emotional entanglement, Ihlee painted more in Brittany than anywhere except Collioure. He found plenty of subjects of interest along its rugged coastline. The Doher family came from the area around Morlaix in northern Finistère. Ihlee's painting *Bathers* (fig.50),[6] exhibited at the Leicester Galleries in 1921, shows a creek called Porz-Louarn at Diben in the bay of Morlaix. Beyond the bathers and their huts stands the house of the local fishmonger, a Monsieur Oulhen, and next to it, the ice store where he conserved his stock.[7] Christian Millet, a Breton historian, was also able to identify the subject of another painting, which shows the old railway station at Primel-Trégastel in the commune of Plougasnou.

On another painting trip, Ihlee and Hereford based themselves in Guilvinec, some 70 miles south of Morlaix. It is not far from Concarneau where, like Collioure, sardine fishing supported much of the population. Concarneau's Fête des Filets Bleus,[8] named after the blue nets in which sardines were caught, takes place in August at the same time as Collioure's Fête de St Vincent.

In contrast to some of their Catalan counterparts, on such ceremonial occasions Breton women pulled out all the stops. Ihlee was particularly taken by their tall lace bonnets which vary in style depending on the locality and age of the wearer. The headdresses worn by Gauguin's women from Pont Aven,[9] for example, differ from those of Ihlee's in Guilvinec, which were called *bigoudens*. Women from this south-westernmost part

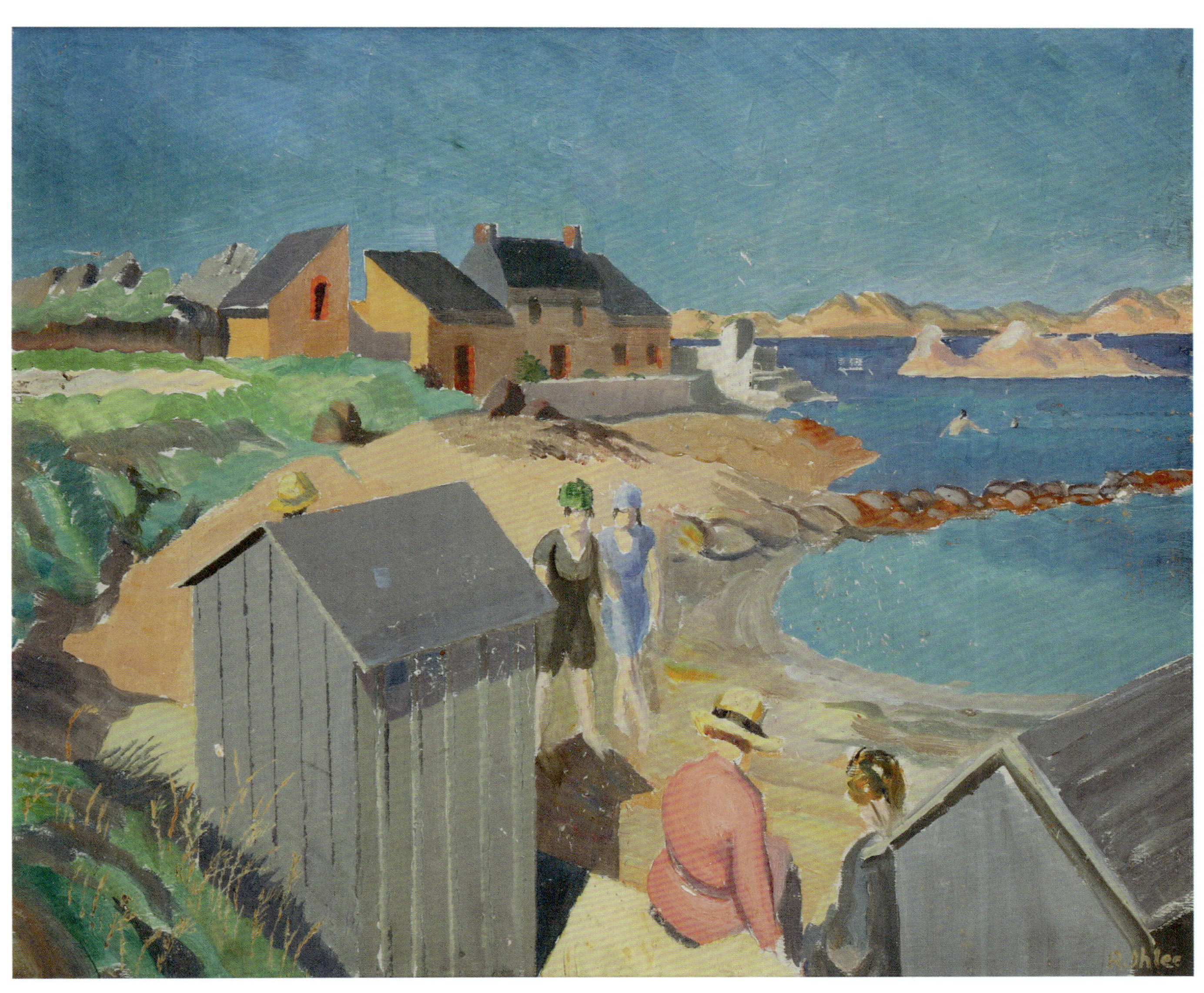

50
Bathers, c.1920
Oil on canvas
38.1 × 45.72 cm (15 × 18 in)
Private collection

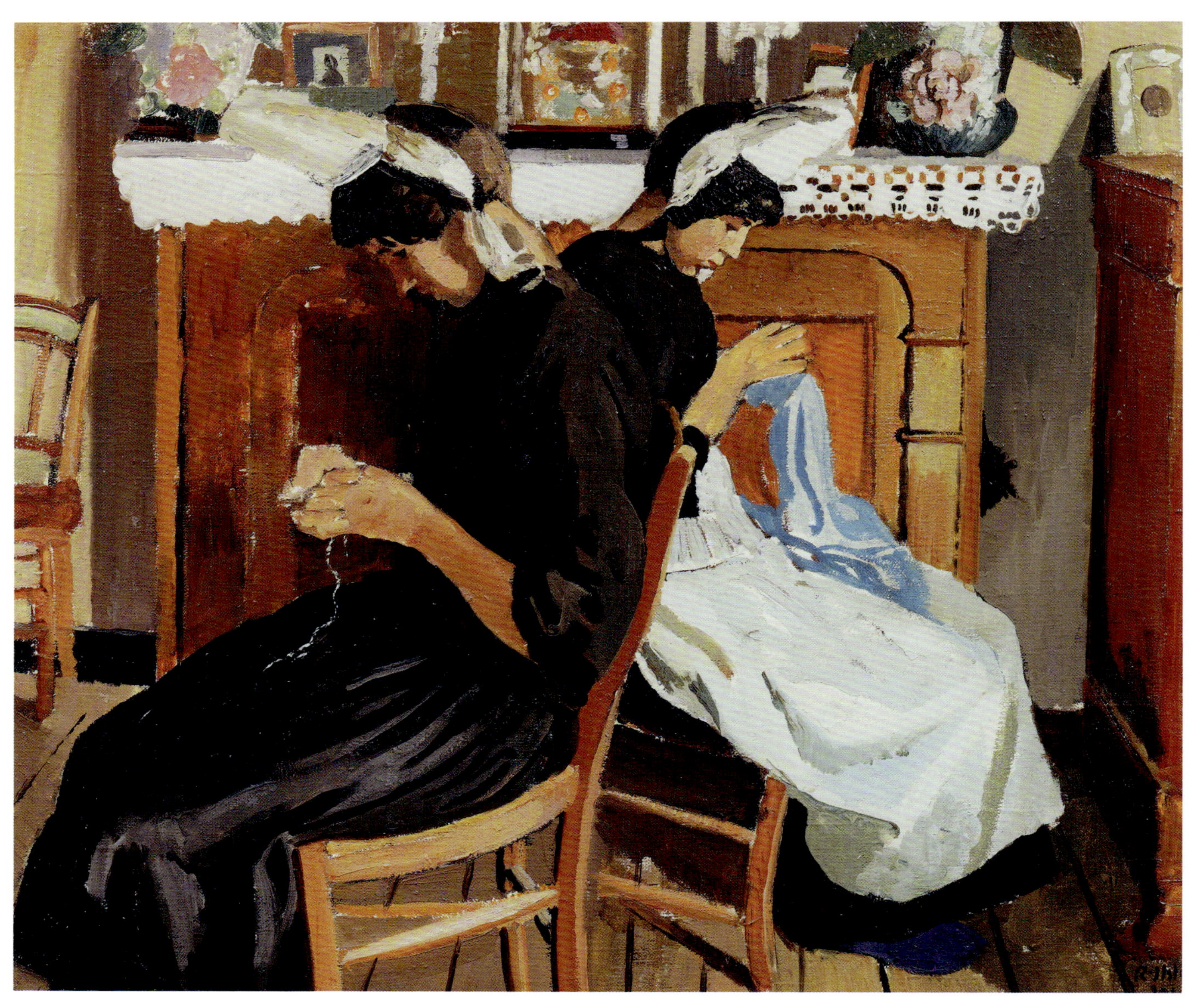

51
Les deux brodeuses, 1921
Oil on canvas
50.8 × 60.96 cm (20 × 24 in)
Liss Llewellyn Fine Art

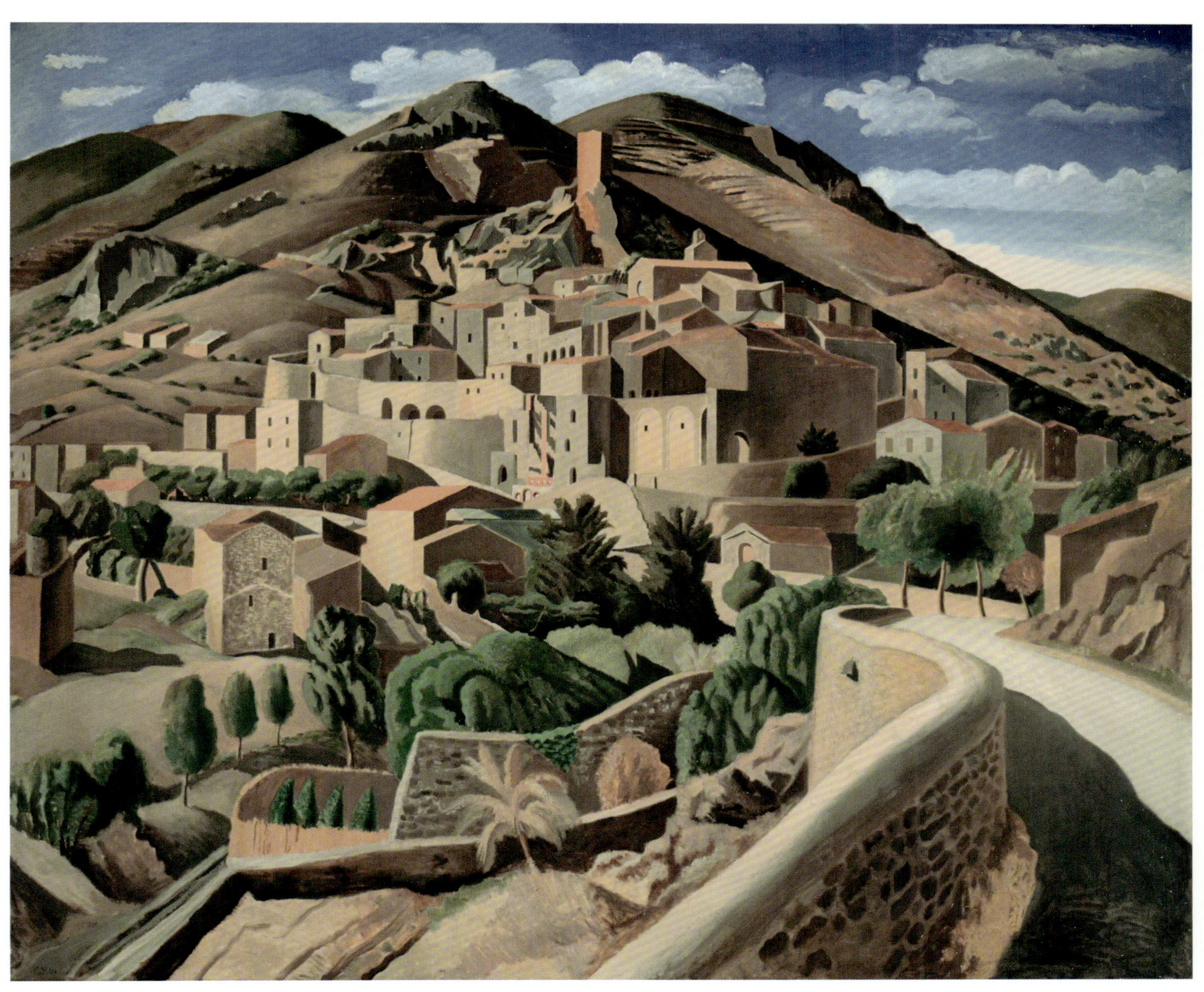

52
Roquebrun, 1930
Oil on canvas
100 × 120 cm (39.3 × 47.2 in)
Private collection

of Finistère were often called *Bigoudènes*. Ihlee's *Les deux brodeuses* (fig.51) ('The Two Embroiderers'), exhibited at the Goupil Gallery in 1921, is perhaps the pick of his Bigoudène portraits but he made several others, including *Augustine en Bigouden*, *Smiling Bigoudène* and *Trois Bigoudènes* (front and back versions).

Ihlee also spent some time in Audierne, another fishing village, about 20 miles north of Guilvinec. Painted in 1923, Ihlee's *The Quay at Audierne* was sold at the Chenil Gallery three years later. The tranquil view was the scene of an explosive battle on 23 August 1944 when three Allied warships sank eight German vessels two days before the liberation of Paris. In 1931 Ihlee was back in Brittany, where he painted two landscapes, one called *Breton Farm* and the other *Winter in Brittany*. The second of these he gave to Albert Doher, presumably one of Margot's relatives.

When Ihlee's relationship with Isabelle became more serious they began visiting the area where she grew up. In 1928 Ihlee and Isabelle made the first of several trips to Félines-Minervois in the Hérault, about an hour's drive from Isabelle's birthplace in the neighbouring department of Aude and close to Laure-Minervois where her father Marc Mons was born. Like parts of the P-O, the landscape is characterised by hills, vineyards and scrub (*garrigue*). Ihlee painted three pictures in Félines-Minervois, one of a gorge, another of some builders and a third called *A Bend in the Road* which was exhibited at the Galerie Campistro in Perpignan in 1932.

He also explored surrounding villages, painting a river in St Chinian, a fir wood in Quarante and two images of Roquebrun, the larger of which was exhibited at the NEAC in 1932 (fig.52). It is a striking composition which, by the look of the shadow on the road and the sun-browned hills, was made in high summer. Magnificently sited 1000 feet above sea level, the village is capped by the Tour de Guep, a restored remnant of a ninth-century castle. Seemingly deserted, *Roquebrun* has some of the otherworldliness of *Landscape with Cat* (fig.39), painted four years earlier. The aridity of the scene is enhanced by Ihlee's decision not to include the River Orb which flows beneath the village and offers swimmers welcome relief from the summer heat.

The vast majority of Ihlee's output during his long stay in northern Catalonia centred on Collioure. Scenes of the town and the surrounding countryside account for more than 200 of his pictures. Since his comprehensive list of works between 1922 and 1936 records where each was painted, it is possible to track his progress and pinpoint his favourite places within easy driving distance of Collioure, mainly within the P-O or just across the departmental border into the Aude.

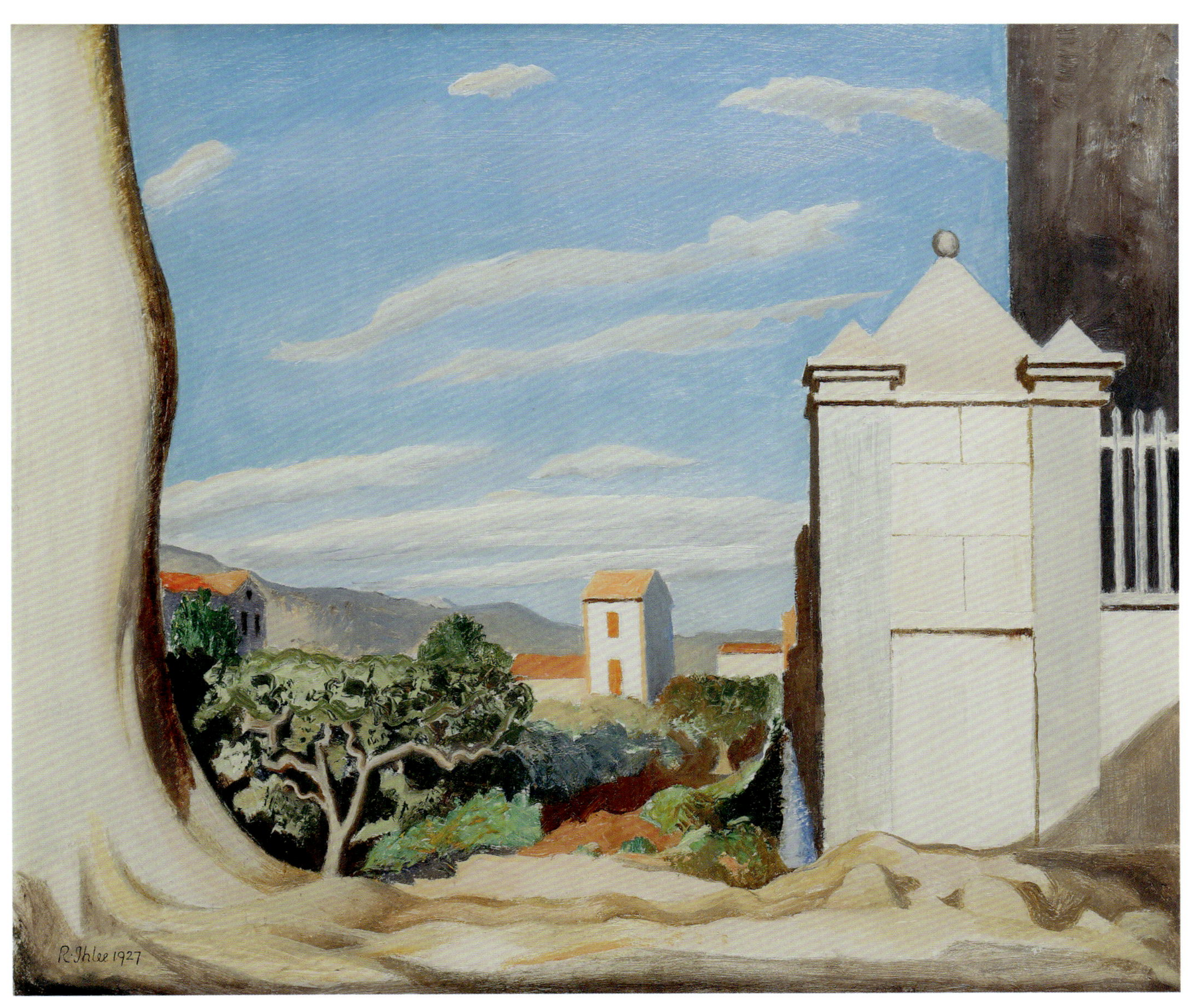

53
The Narrow House, Prades, 1927
Oil on canvas
38.1 × 45.72 cm (15 × 18 in)
Private collection

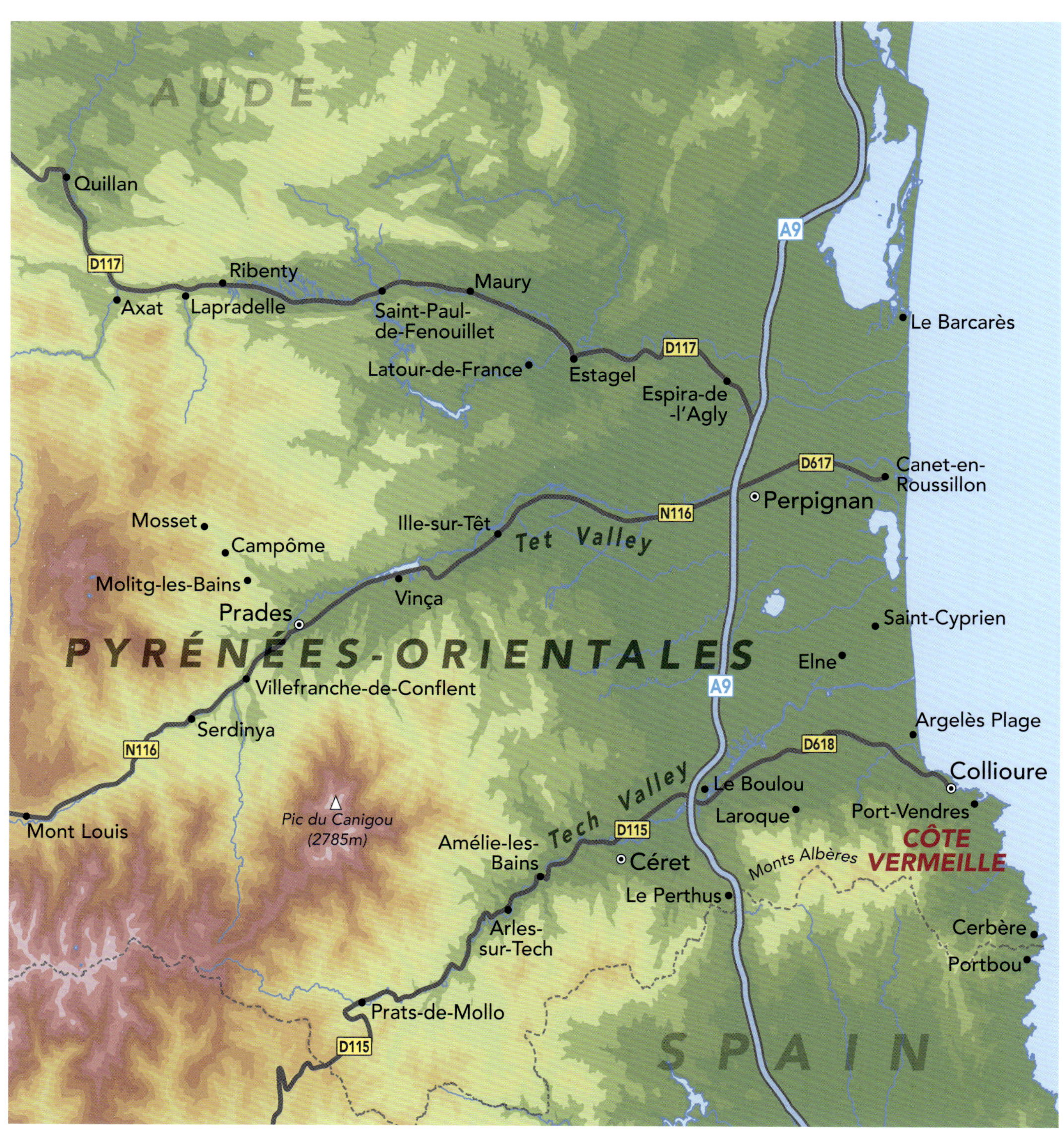

54
Map of where Ihlee painted in the 1920s and 30s

The outstanding feature of the P-O is the Pic du Canigou, Catalonia's own Mount Fuji, whose jagged outline dominates the foothills and plains which lead down to the Mediterranean. Surprisingly, the mountain seems to have been the principal subject of only one of Ihlee's paintings. His *Le Canigou*, produced in 1934, was exhibited at the Salon des Tuileries in Paris and later sold at the NEAC. Nevetheless, it would have formed the backdrop to many of his landscapes and, like anyone who has spent any time in the region, he would have been constantly reminded of its presence.

From the main north–south road (the A9) which runs parallel to the coast and leads into Spain there are three major inland routes heading westwards into the valleys, gorges, hills and mountains. Ihlee and Hereford explored them all. The most southerly route, closest to Collioure, runs through the Tech Valley along the D115, passing through Le Boulou, Ceret, Amélie-les-Bains and Arles-sur-Tech. Several roads intersect at Le Boulou, which is on the main route to Spain. Thousands of Republican refugees converged on the town after fleeing Franco's forces during the Spanish Civil War. Ten years earlier, in 1926, Ihlee produced an image of Le Boulou which was exhibited at the Goupil Gallery.

Ceret, the next town along, had a thriving artistic community. It has a claim to be the birthplace of Cubism based on the works Picasso and Braque painted together there in 1911. Picasso made several visits in the following years, along with other notable artists such as the Catalan Surrealist Joan Miró. Ceret's Musée d'Art Moderne has a fine collection of works by these and other artists.[10] Although Picasso's visits to Ceret did not coincide with Ihlee's stay in Collioure, it is probable their paths crossed at some time before the Second World War.[11]

Continuing through the Tech Valley, also known as Vallespir, the next place of significance is the spa town of Amélie-les-Bains where Mackintosh and his wife, Margaret, stayed for a month or so in December 1923 before heading down to Port Vendres. Writing to a friend, Margaret describes the town as a beautiful spot. 'We get the snow wind off Canigou if the wind blows in her direction – this in spite of the glorious sunshine always gives a sharpness to the air which is rather exhilarating.'[12] Ihlee made two oil sketches in the neighbouring town of Arles-sur-Tech, which was the inspiration for *Landscape with Cat* (fig.39). One of the sketches, called *The Little Factory*, was exhibited in 1928 at the Goupil Gallery.

The road inland from Perpignan, the N116, leads to the Tet Valley (also known as the Conflent) and the town of Prades before climbing to Mont Louis, where the Mackintoshes used to visit in the summer to escape the Mediterranean heat. Ihlee painted *The Narrow House, Prades* (fig.53) in

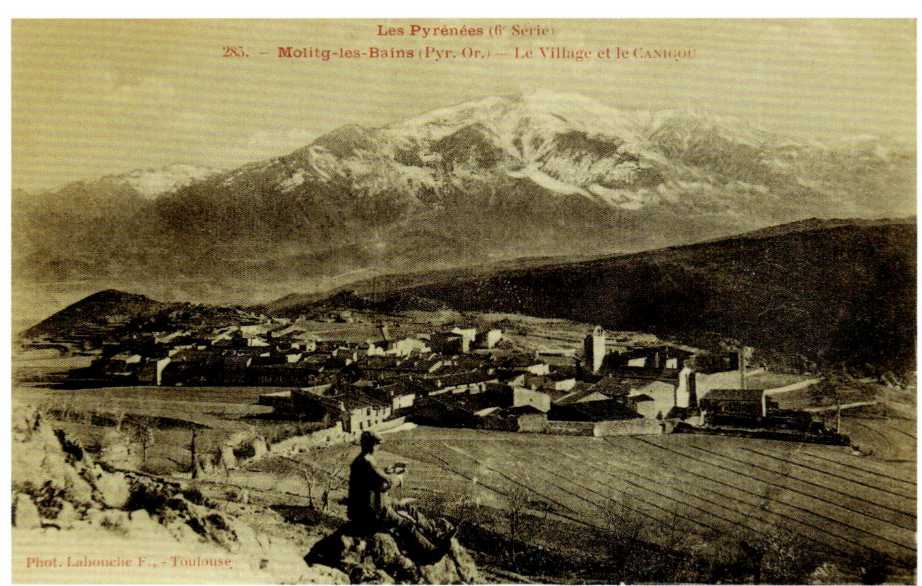

55
Molitg looking towards Prades and Mount Canigou
Postcard

1927 and two years later *Prades, Square*, but he was more attracted to a cluster of villages high above the town opposite Mount Canigou. In 1928 he produced a dozen works in and around Molitg-les-Bains, a small village with a grand hotel and spa some 2000 feet above sea level. Perhaps Ihlee, who suffered from bouts of ill health, took advantage of the various thermal treatments which are supposed to help with rheumatism and respiratory problems. The Pyrenean hot springs with their living plankton apparently do wonders for the skin.

Given that Ihlee averaged around 20 paintings a year, it would appear he spent several months in Molitg. The titles of some of his works, mostly oil sketches, such as *Rocks, Vines and Olives, The Waterfall* and *The Distant Mountain*, give a good idea of his rugged surroundings. When not enjoying the mountain air on foot, he motored along the narrow, winding roads to neighbouring villages including Campôme, Mosset and Serdinya, the subject of one of his sketches (fig.56). The following year he painted two pictures at Villefranche-de-Conflent, an ancient fortified town between Prades and Mont Louis.[13]

The P-O's third main route westward, the D117, runs from the coast just north of Perpignan towards Quillan in the Aude, passing through a region called Le Fenouillèdes which historically was neither part of Roussillon nor of Catalonia. The River Agly defines the landscape, whose rocks, olive trees and hills have a biblical feel. In 1928 Ihlee and Hereford painted in one of the largest of the villages, scattered sparsely along the route, called Saint-Paul-de-Fenouillet. Its name is the title of one of Hereford's few known works (fig.57), although, according to the local *mairie*, it does not correspond to any recognisable scene.[14]

There is no known record of Hereford's work. Beyond evidence that he exhibited occasionally with the Friday Club and ten times with the NEAC his painting career is largely a mystery. It is fair to assume, though, that he did not always accompany Ihlee. In a letter to his wife in June 1927, Mackintosh reports that 'Ihlee came along [to Port Vendres] himself last night – he wants to go to Quillan for a month or two to paint the famous gorge there but is very downhearted because Hereford does not want to move.'[15]

Nevertheless, while Hereford was working on his, possibly imaginary, composition, which features a round crenellated tower and church with iron belfry, Ihlee was painting nearby. In fact, he produced two works at Saint-Paul – *The Vineyard Gate* and *The Fallen Olive Tree*. Three years later, in 1931, he was in the neighbouring villages of Maury, Latour-de-France and Estagel and in 1934 he ventured further west, along the D117, into Aude, painting *La Garrigue* near Axat, a sawmill at Rebenty and a pair of huntsmen near Lapradelle.

The rivers running through the valleys of the Tech, the Tet and the Agly might occasionally run dry, but up until the mid 1930s Ihlee's chosen place of exile was a reliable source of inspiration. The political landscape, by contrast, was becoming increasingly unstable. Between 1936 and 1940 Ihlee's list of works peters out.

Hitler was, of course, a threat but, for Ihlee and Hereford, the more immediate menace came from Franco across the border in Spain.

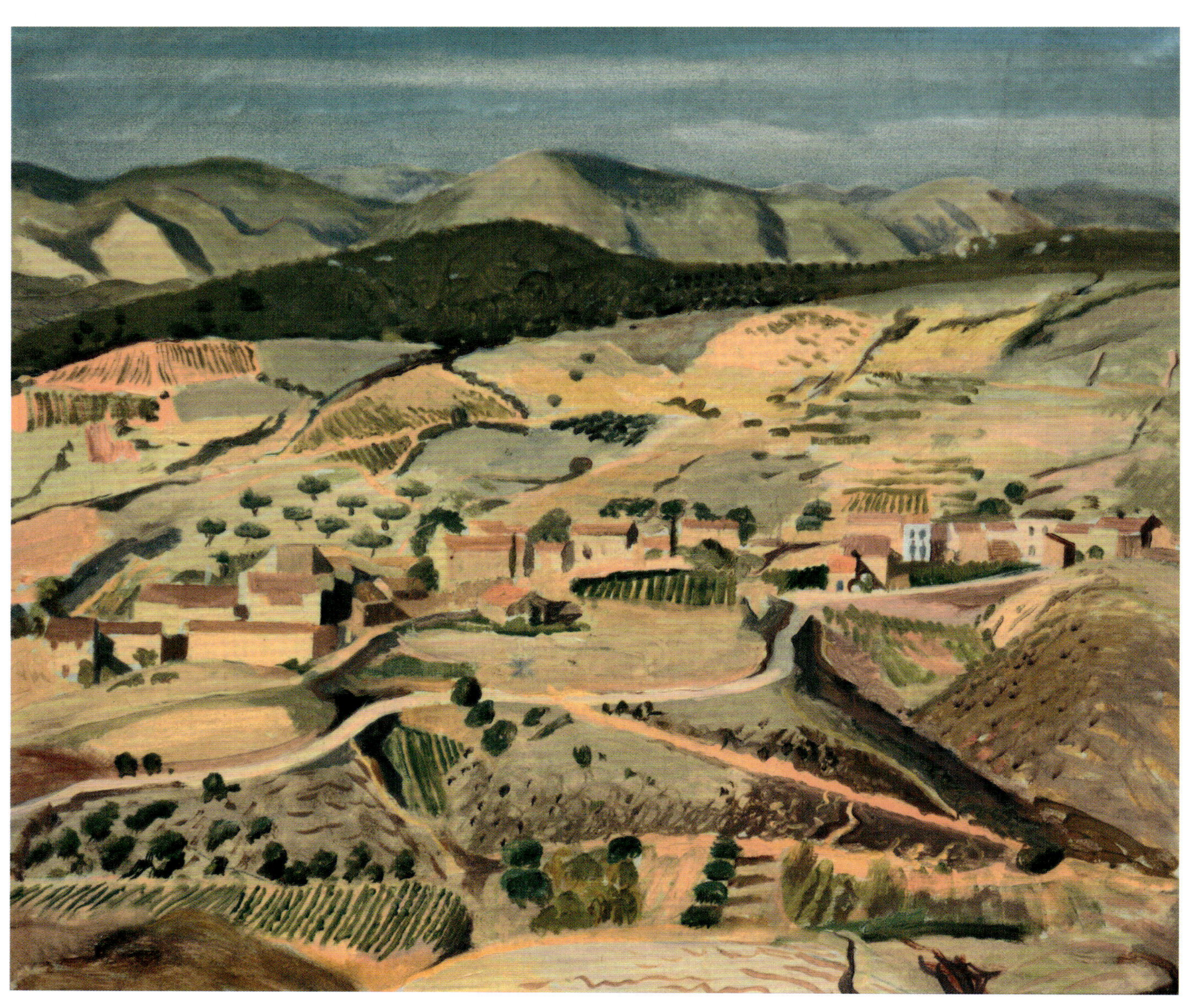

56
Serdinya, 1928
Oil on board
38.1 × 45.72 cm (15 × 18 in)
Private collection

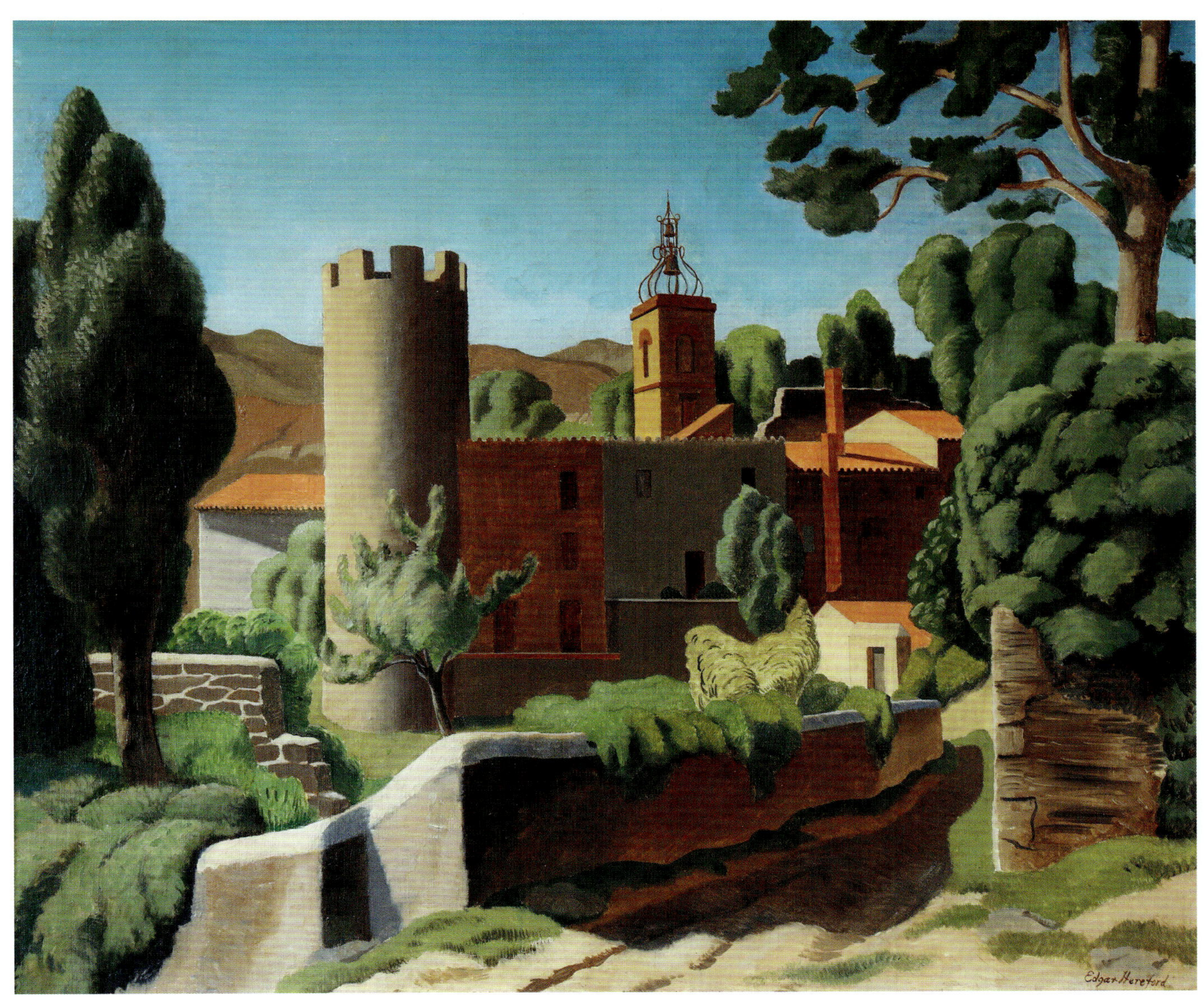

57
Edgar Hereford
Saint-Paul-de-Fenouillet, 1925
Oil on canvas
50.8 × 60.96 cm (20 × 24 in)
Private collection

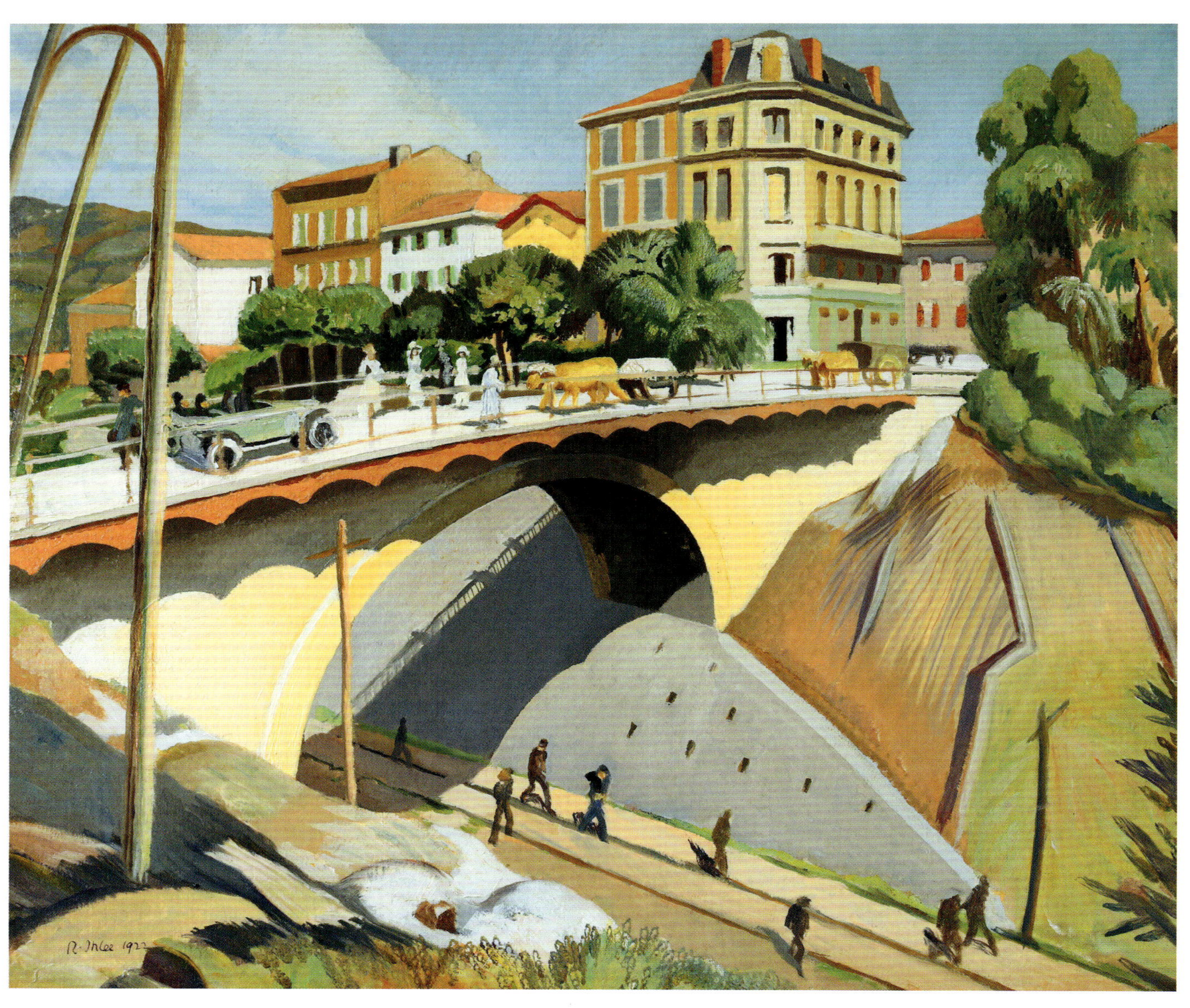

58
The Bridge at Hendaye, 1922
Oil on canvas
50.8 × 60.96 cm (20 × 24 in)
Private collection

6 Spain in Peace and War

The landscape and language of Spanish Catalonia have much in common with those of its French neighbour. Writing from Amélie-les-Bains in 1923 to her friend Jessie Newberry, Margaret Mackintosh commented: 'We are really more like Spain here than France – the people are quite a Spanish type, all wear dead black and speak Catalan amongst themselves although they understand French.'[1]

From Collioure the Spanish border town of Portbou is less than 10 miles away and the busiest crossing point at Le Perthus is in easy driving distance. And yet Ihlee seems to have painted very little in Spanish Catalonia, preferring to explore less familiar territory further south or west along the Atlantic coast.

After arriving in Collioure from Algeria in 1922, Ihlee and Hereford were soon off on their travels. They tracked the Pyrenees from the Mediterranean to the Atlantic, staying in Hendaye before heading deep into Spain. Hendaye, in the Basque country on the French side of the Spanish border, is perhaps best known as the place where Hitler met Franco in 1940 to discuss a possible alliance.[2] Ihlee produced four paintings in the coastal town, including *The Bridge at Hendaye* (fig.58), close to where the two dictators failed to reach agreement 18 years later.

The pair then made their way to Toledo in the centre of the country before heading to Málaga, the birthplace of Picasso,[3] on the south coast. Ihlee made two paintings called *Toledo*, an oil sketch (15 by 18 inches) in the winter of 1922 which he worked up into a larger painting (25 by 30 inches) the following year, a template he often followed. Ihlee's panorama of Toledo looks across the Tagus River towards the hillside town which is dominated by the towers of the Alcázar fortress. The larger version, exhibited at the NEAC in 1923 and the Chenil Gallery in 1926, was last seen in public at Bonhams, where it sold for £1150 in 1997.

Málaga's exceptionally mild winter climate would have suited Ihlee and Hereford, neither of whom prospered in the cold. The restorative warmth may explain their long stay from January to the early summer of 1923. Less welcome would have been the poverty that surrounded them. Although living conditions in Collioure were often basic, the extreme hardship faced by many Spanish peasants and fishermen would have come as a shock.

One of the poorest communities was El Palo, on the outskirts of Málaga, where many lived hand to mouth in shacks or caves.[4] Conditions were insanitary and illiteracy widespread. Ihlee's painting *El Palo* (fig.59) shows some whitewashed caves by a ramshackle, unmade road. The canvas, bought by Sir Edward Marsh, is now in York Art Gallery. From Málaga the pair travelled along the coast to Almería, where Ihlee produced a painting called *Andalusian Village*, before heading back to France.

It was not until 1935 that Ihlee returned to paint in Spain and then under very different circumstances. During the intervening decade he and Hereford had put down roots in Collioure. Ihlee had a wide circle of friends and a long-term partner in Isabelle, and probably expected to live in France for the rest of his life. In the eyes of his neighbours he was no longer a tourist but a permanent resident. While he may have gone to England for the occasional visit, he did not paint there. As his connections with English galleries diminished, his contacts with French galleries increased. Since he was trying to sell work in his adopted country the titles of his paintings were, from the early 1930s, mostly in French. On a visit to Paris in 1933, for example, he lists four pictures: *Au Square des Batignolles, St Lazare, la voie ferrée, Nu* and *Bois au Lapin*. His notebook records consistent sales throughout his exile but it is difficult to determine how much he also relied on his private income.

On the domestic front there was another change: the introduction of a child. Laure Doher was the daughter of Marguerite Doher, the married woman from Brittany with whom Hereford had a long-term relationship. As an escape from her unstable background, Laure began to spend more time in Collioure, often without her mother. She gravitated towards Rudolph and Isabelle, who became like another set of parents. When she was three she became Rudolph's ward of court. In adulthood she describes him as 'my beloved father . . . the person I loved most in the world'.[5] In 1935, when Laure was five, it is thought they took her on a holiday to Spain, unaware that the country was on the brink of civil war.

The newly constituted family spent nearly a year touring north-west Spain, first stopping at Laguardia, some 70 miles south of Bilbao in the Basque Country. The medieval fortress town is surrounded by vineyards noted for their Rioja Alavesa wines. They must have enjoyed their time there as Ihlee, who seldom finished more than two paintings a month, produced more than double that number before heading to the port of Vigo in Galicia on the Atlantic coast. Their stay in Vigo was even longer, with Ihlee completing seven paintings, including landscapes of a beach and a shipyard which he later exhibited at the Salon des Tuileries in Paris. Another painting he called *Le Chemin de la mer* (fig.60).

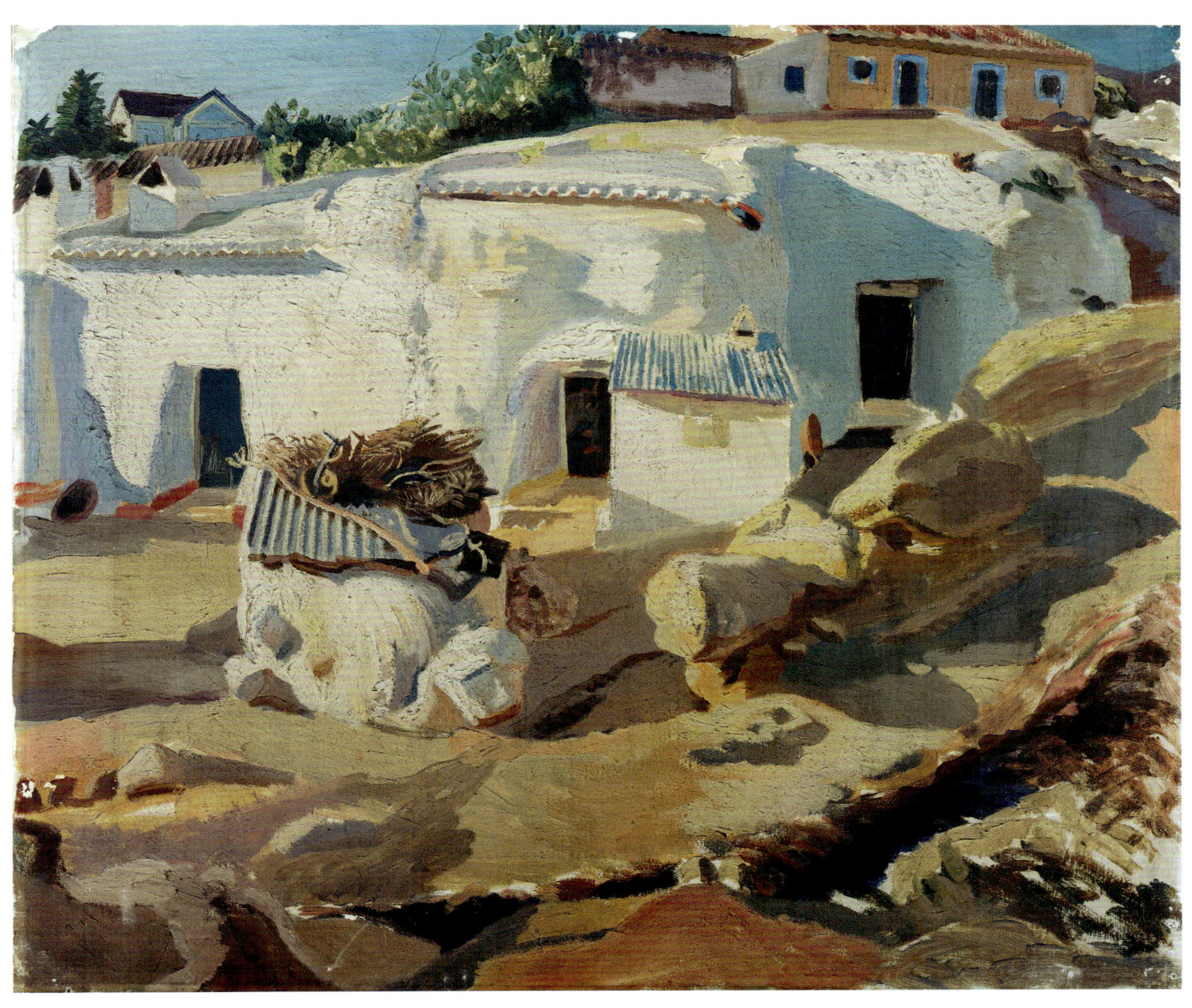

59
El Palo, 1923
Oil on canvas
50.8 × 60.96 cm (20 × 24 in)
York Art Gallery

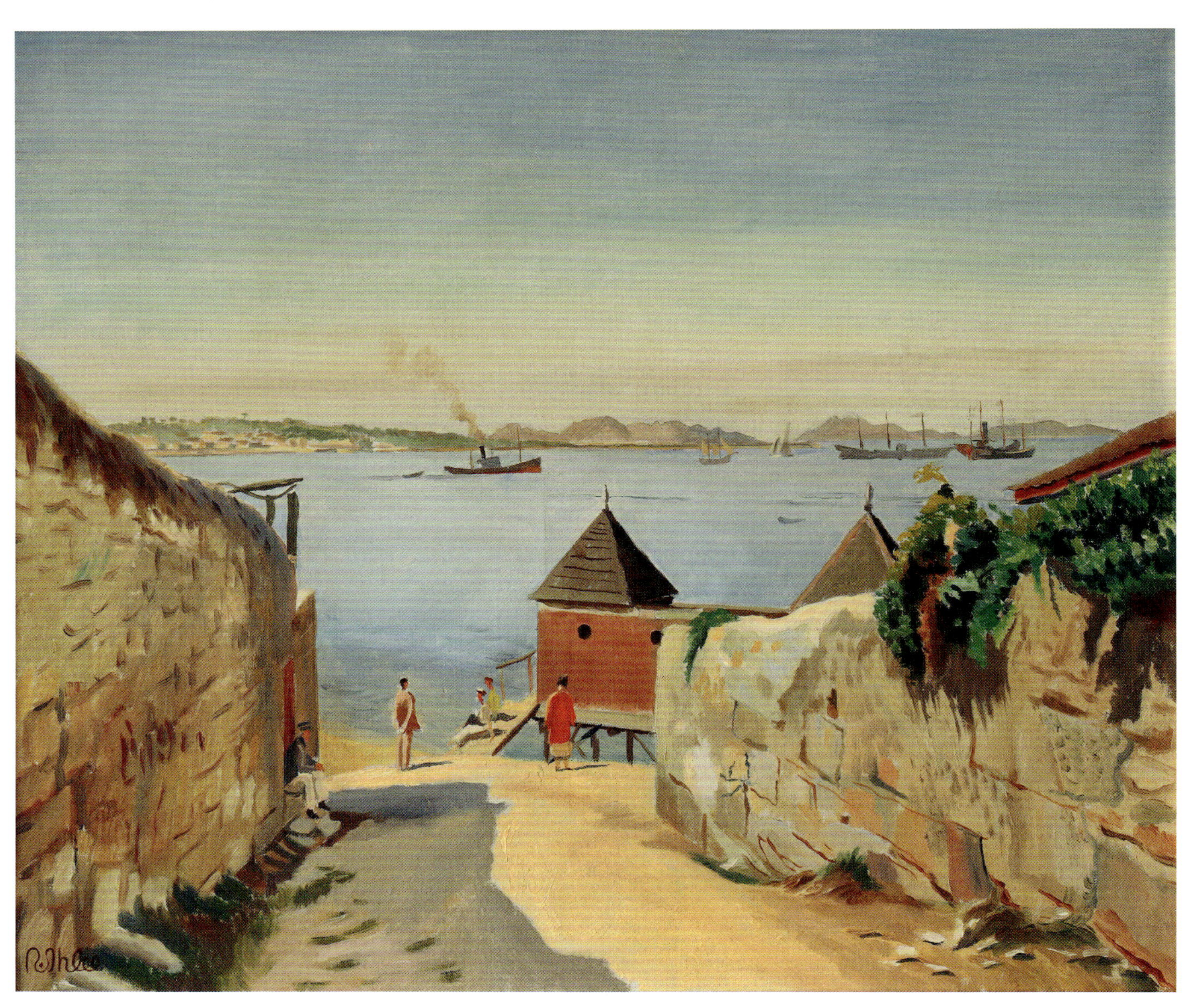

60
Le Chemin de la mer, Vigo, 1935
Oil on canvas
47 × 56 cm (18.5 × 22 in)
Private collection

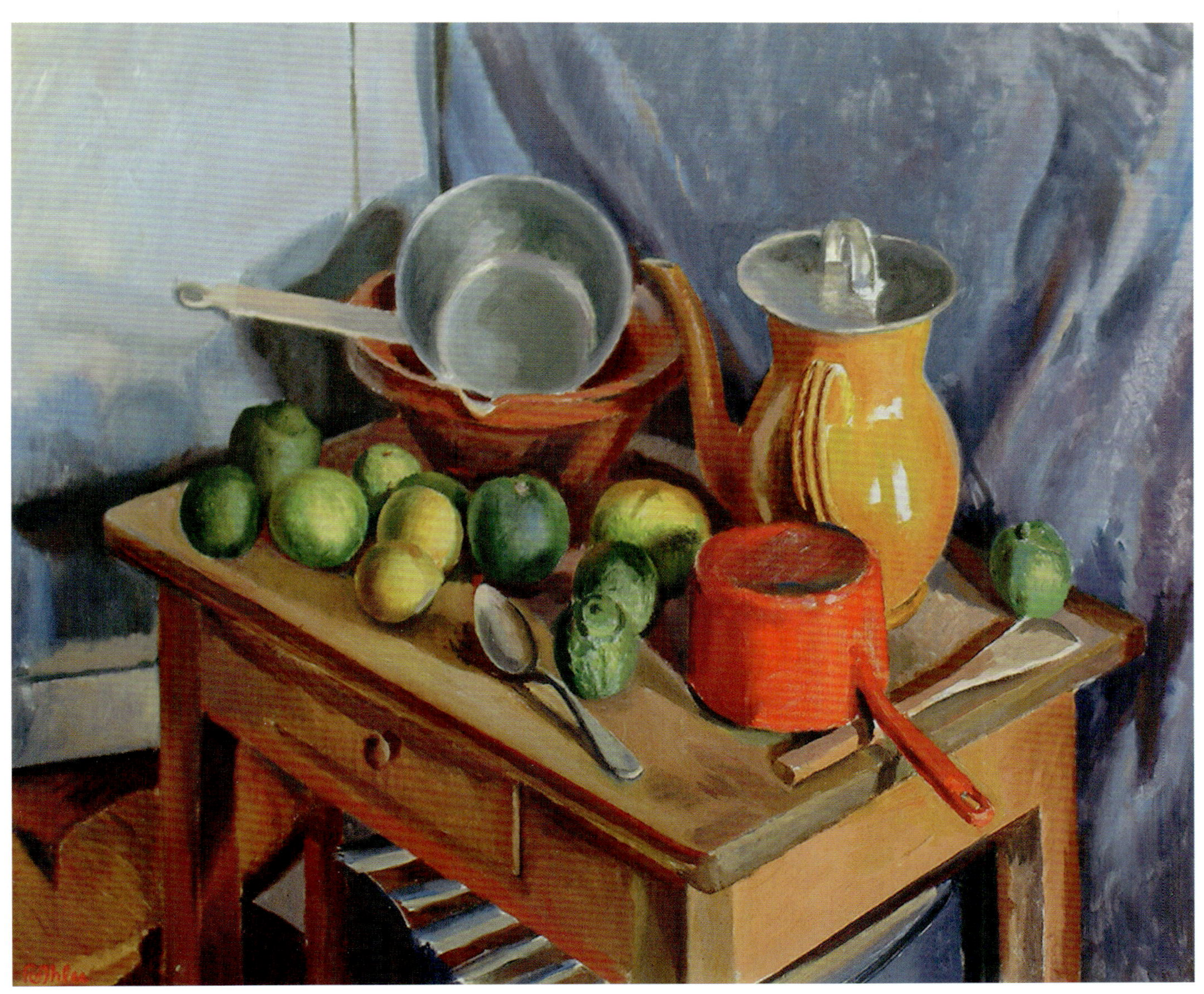

61
Casserole rouge, 1936
Oil on canvas
38.5 × 46 cm (15.3 × 18.1 in)
Private collection

In early 1936 the holidaymakers headed towards Bilbao. En route they became aware of the rising political tension. They may even have witnessed sporadic outbreaks of violence between Republican and Nationalist sympathisers – clashes which were soon to escalate into a full-blown civil war with the loss of some 200,000 lives.

With the situation becoming increasingly unstable, Ihlee was forced to abandon all of his equipment and several paintings as they hurried back to France. Blocked from travelling overland, they eventually managed to get a boat from Castro Urdiales, some 20 miles from Bilbao. In his list of works the titles of his lost paintings are written faintly in pencil. One was called *Isabelle at Window*, another *Grey Day*. A later addition in ink reads 'left at Bilbao'.

The war broke out in July, a few months after their departure. Bilbao was bombed by Nationalist forces in August. Ihlee soon stopped updating his list. He may have felt the climate was not right for painting or exhibiting. The final entries were a series of six still lives, including *Casserole rouge* (fig.61), painted in Collioure in 1936 while there was fierce fighting across the border.

In April 1937, Franco's German and Italian fascist allies bombed the Basque town of Guernica with the loss of some 250 lives. A month later Picasso produced his powerful anti-war painting of the same name. With so much suffering close at hand, it was not long before Collioure became caught up in the developing tragedy. As Republican resistance weakened, refugees began to trickle across the border into France, a trickle that became a flood with the fall of Barcelona on 26 January 1939.

The mass retreat, known as *La Retirada*, had a profound effect on the P-O. Defeated soldiers, women and children fled in huge numbers, carrying what possessions they could, in one of the harshest winters on record. Many of the wounded had to struggle across rough, mountainous terrain. Prats-de-Mollo, Arles-sur-Tech and Cerbère (see map, page 78) received tens of thousands of refugees but the greatest number came through Le Perthus (fig.62).

Entire populations of Spanish towns and villages descended on the border; in total an estimated 450,000 refugees arrived in France. Unsurprisingly, the authorities were completely overwhelmed and there were some ugly scenes as they sought to impose control. One refugee, Federica Montseny, recalled a group of wounded Republican soldiers being manhandled by French Senegalese troops in Le Perthus while women and children sought sanctuary. 'I will always remember that night at Le Perthus where women were knocking on the doors of houses begging for shelter for their children but the doors remained closed.'[6]

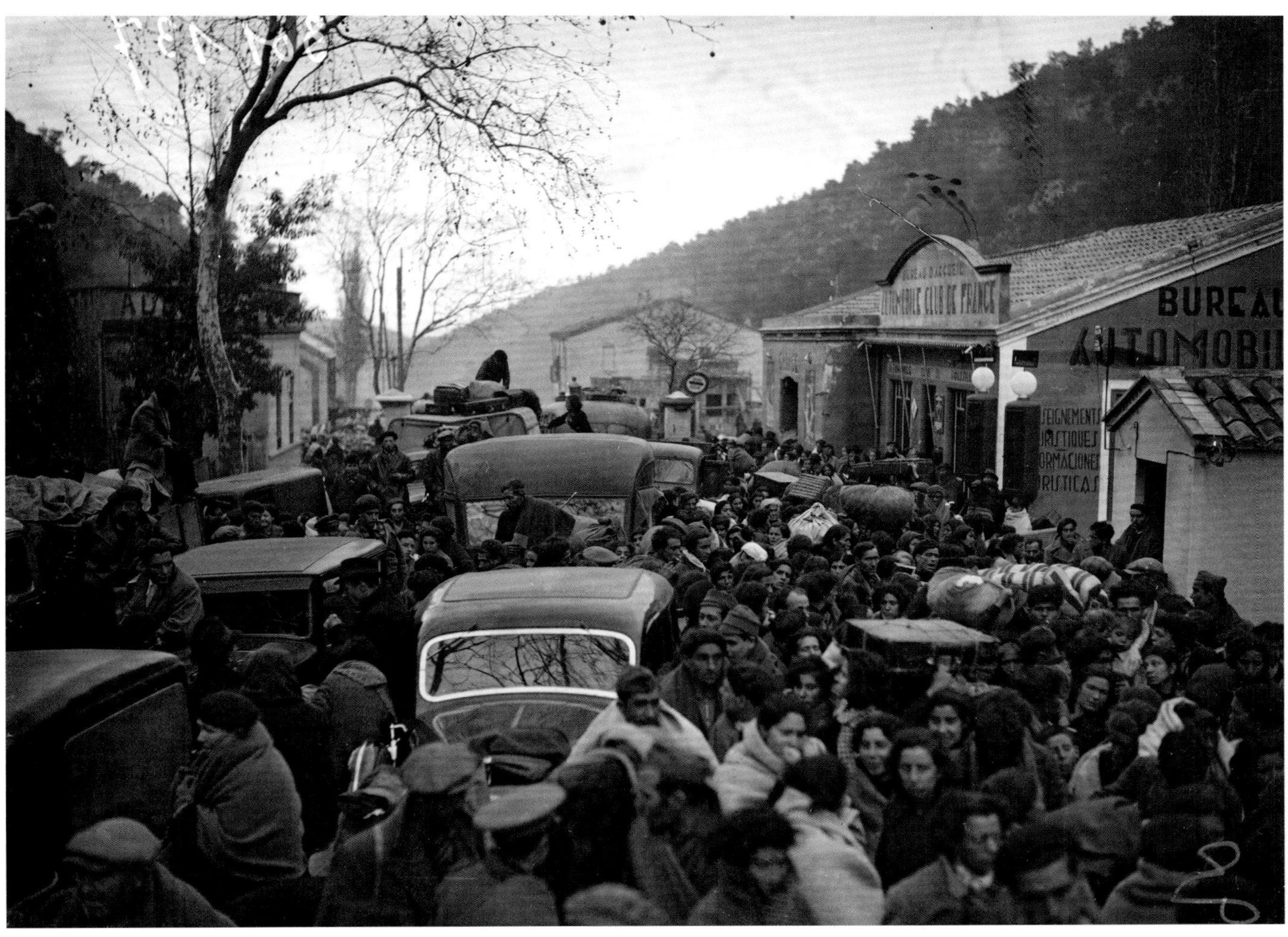

62
La Retirada, refugees at Le Perthus, February 1939

Tens of thousands were herded into makeshift camps on beaches at Argelès, St Cyprien and elsewhere. There was little or no shelter. Many had to dig holes in the sand to survive. Dysentery and TB were rife. It is thought at least 5000 died. In Collioure the Chateau Royal became a prison for refugees who were considered troublemakers. Up to 400 men were locked up in underground dungeons after being forced to break stones from six in the morning until seven at night.[7]

There were also acts of mercy. Nearby at the Hotel Bougnol-Quintana, where Ihlee and Hereford may have stayed in the 1920s, the renowned Spanish poet Antonio Machado (1875–1939) took refuge under the kindly eye of Pauline Quintana.[8] Having fled from Madrid to Barcelona, he had crossed the border from Portbou to Cerbère with his mother Ana, brother José and sister-in-law Matea. Despite the care and attention he received at the hotel, he became severely ill and died less than a month later. His grave in Collioure is still a place of pilgrimage. Another famous refugee, the cellist Pablo Casals (1876–1973), settled in Prades, vowing never to return to his native country.

The turmoil in Spain soon engulfed the whole of Europe. Little more than six months later, on 3 September 1939 France joined the war against Germany. Despite the growing Nazi threat, Ihlee and Isabelle, who had married the year before, were reluctant to leave their home and possessions. They stayed until June 1940 when the fall of Paris, the German occupation of northern France and the establishment of the Vichy puppet government in the south made them realise they could no longer afford to dither. Taking 10-year-old Laure Doher with them, they fled along the line of the Pyrenees to St Jean de Luz on the Atlantic coast, where they abandoned their car on the quayside and made a panicked getaway in a boat to Plymouth.[9]

Since Ihlee stopped recording his works in 1936, one can only guess how much he painted in the years between his flight from Spain and his flight from France. An image which probably dates from this period shows a couple near a bridge on the Route d'Argelès on the outskirts of Collioure (fig.63).[10] Is it fanciful to suggest this could be Rudolph and Isabelle stepping out into an unknown future?

What is certain is that the Collioure Ihlee left behind in 1940 was very different from the place he had fallen in love with 18 years earlier. The architecture may have been the same but the atmosphere had become polluted by war. Although some Catalans would join the resistance, many more ended up working in German factories or supporting the Vichy government either passively or actively. By 1942 Mackintosh's beloved Port Vendres was occupied by the Germans, who blew it up two years later. Ihlee's artistic life was also in ruins. Approaching 60, his prospects in war-torn England must have looked very bleak.

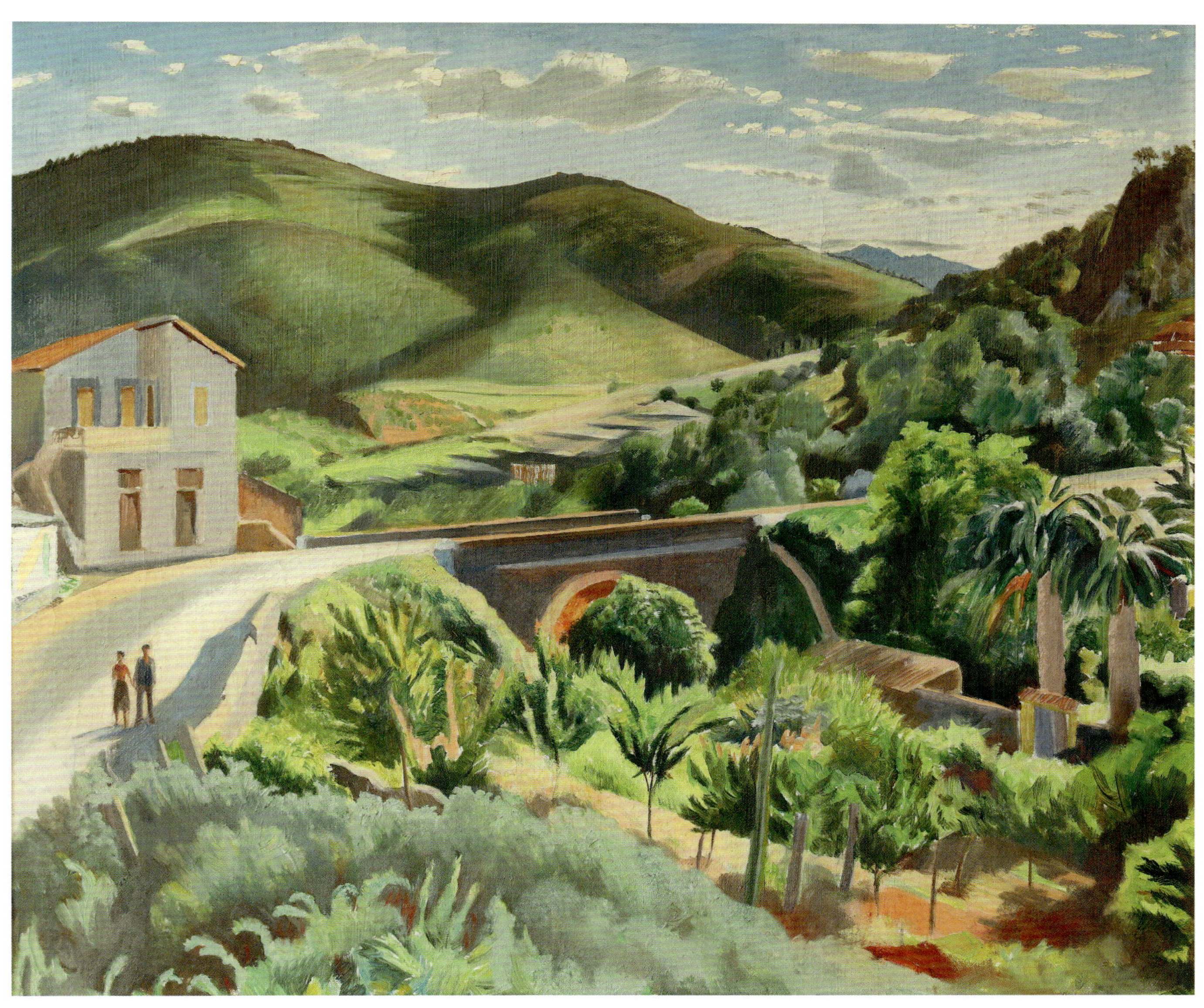

63
Road by Collioure, c.1938
Oil on canvas
50.8 × 60.96 cm (20 × 24 in)
Private collection

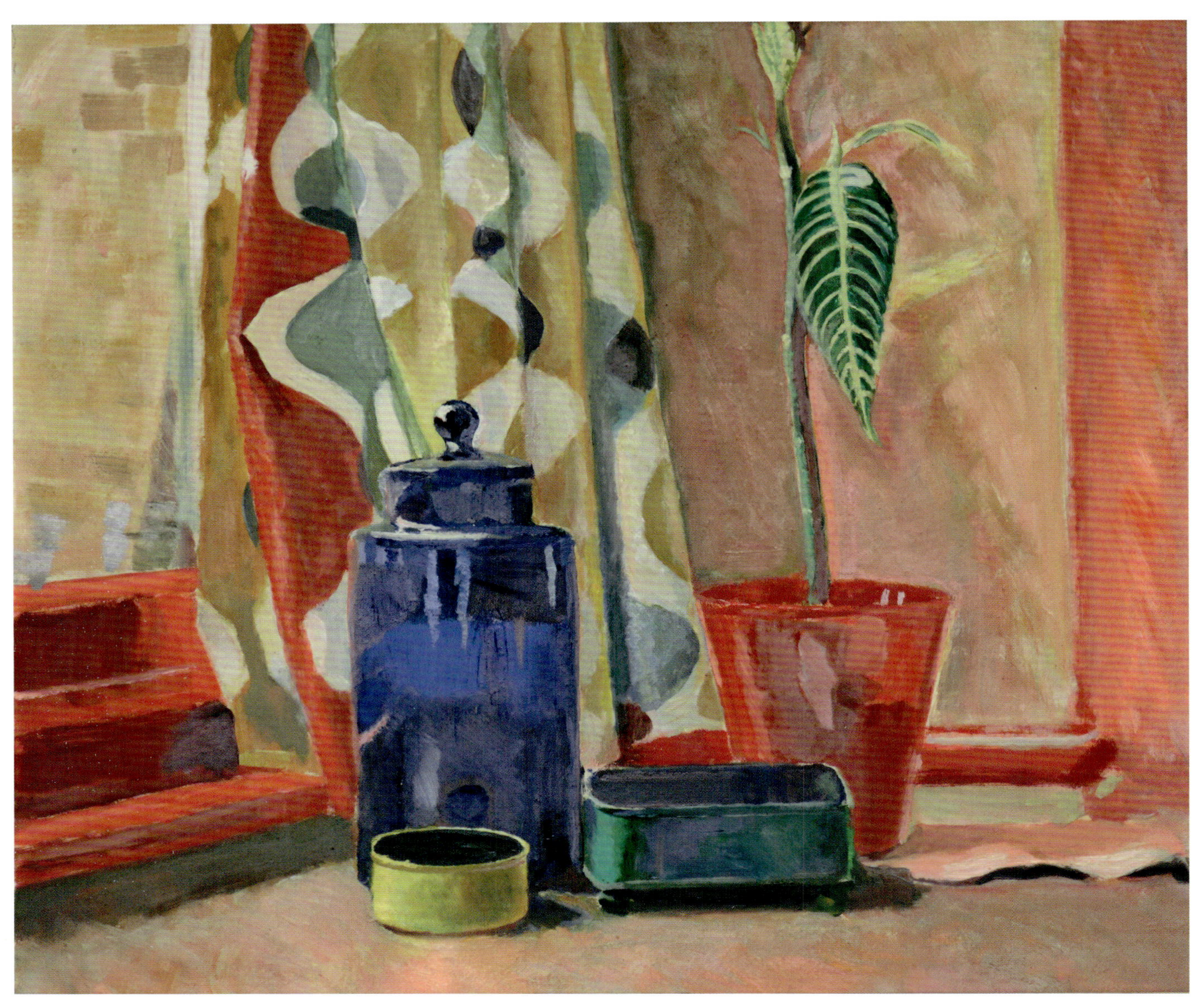

64
Still Life , West Deeping, c.1950
Oil on canvas
51 × 61 cm (20 × 24 in)
Private collection

7 Back in Britain

Rudolph and Isabelle eventually settled in a small Fenland village about 10 miles north of Peterborough. West Deeping was quite a contrast to Collioure. The countryside was flat, the climate often chilly and the threat of German air raids all too real.[1] Isabelle, who had lived all her life in France, was hampered by her lack of English, but at least she had Rudolph. The upset was greatest for Laure Doher. Separated from her mother at barely 10 years of age, she was sent to a boarding school where, at first, she could hardly understand a word that was said to her.

Anxious to help the war effort, Rudolph soon found work at a local factory as a precision tool maker. He set about it with 'such single-minded concentration that by the war's end he was almost too sick and exhausted to wish to paint'.[2] In the First World War he had had the support of his elder brother, but Fred had died in 1938 at the age of 70. A pillar of the Peterborough community, he had worked at Baker Perkins for almost half a century.

> Although in his early days he had been regarded as rather ruthless, a man who spared neither his colleagues or himself, he had mellowed as the years passed and on his death his fellow directors, in paying tribute to his devoted work for the company, had stressed the humanity of the man who had been a loyal and sympathetic friend to all, not least to the employees of the firm.[3]

Rudolph still had some surviving family, including his younger sister Gertrude, who had married John Rolt and had three grown-up children. His cousin Margaret Tomalin had married a distant relation of the artist William Orpen and was living in Ireland.[4] Margaret's elder sister Marie-Charlotte Tomalin, who had acted as Rudolph's go-between with the New English Art Club, had died in 1933. During his first decade in France all communication between Rudolph and the NEAC was 'c/o Miss Tomalin'. Although Rudolph sent pictures to the club from West Deeping in 1948 and 1949 they were painted before the war.[5] It was a chance meeting in 1950, while shopping with his wife in Peterborough, that prompted him to pick up his brushes once again.

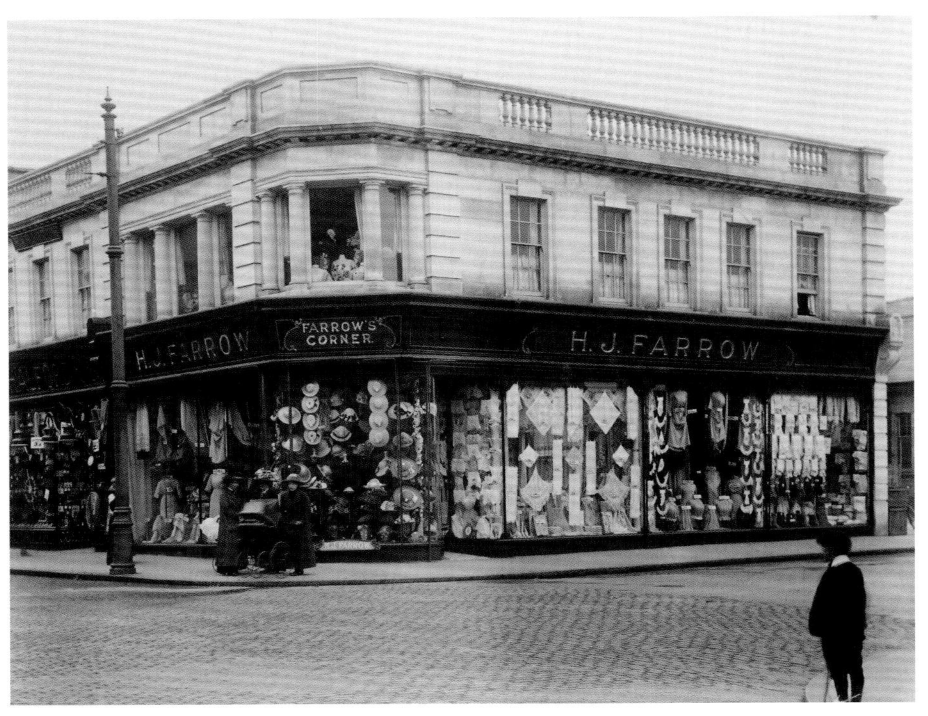

65
H.J. Farrow
Arthur Farrow's shop in Peterborough

The drapers H.J. Farrow & Son (fig.65) occupied a prime site known as Farrow's Corner. The 'son', Arthur Farrow, was then running the business. An amateur painter, he was also secretary of the Peterborough Art Society. Noticing a late middle-aged couple admiring a display of Jacqmar silk scarves,[6] he asked the man what he thought of them. 'Yes, very good, splendid colour.'

The draper warmed to the theme. 'You have an eye for colour. Perhaps you paint?'

Ihlee paused. 'Well, yes, used to – a bit.'

'You should keep it up. We have an art society here in Peterborough. Are you a member of any art club or society?'

After some hesitation Ihlee confessed to being a member of the NEAC. And so began a relationship which led to his first post-war exhibition.

The show was opened in May 1951 at St Peter's Hall in Peterborough by the Earl of Sandwich,[7] and the catalogue includes an essay by Ihlee's new friend. 'It is in France, that Ihlee truly found himself as a painter,' writes Arthur Farrow.

> His mature development, based firmly on his early classicism, benefited immensely from his later experiments and study of his great contemporaries [Maillol, Derain, Modigliani, Matisse are cited]; although he never followed them at the expense of individuality. There is a wealth of

'modern instances' to be found completely absorbed in his land and shore-scapes, enriching the perfection of his almost classical compositions with knowledge of contemporary feeling and urgent significance.

Of the 35 drawings and paintings on show most, such as *Landscape with Cat* (fig.39) and *Le Chemin de la mer* (fig.60), were painted before the war, but a few, including *Still Life: West Deeping* (fig.64), showed he had returned to the easel. Before long he was exhibiting new work at the NEAC.[8]

By this time he had renewed contact with Edgar Hereford, who had left France after the war and was living with Margot at Swinstead, about 10 miles from The Yews, the Ihlees' house in West Deeping. In 1949 the couple married, although their English life together did not last for long. Hereford died in 1953 aged 67. For Ihlee it marked the end of the most enduring friendship of his life. Having met at the Slade, the two artists had known each other for 45 years and been close companions, especially during those early days in Collioure.

In the years following the war, Ihlee, recovering from ill health, settled with Isabelle into their handsome house in West Deeping. There was little thought of returning to live in Collioure but, from the 1950s, the couple went back frequently for holidays. 'We go sponge my cousins,' Isabelle would say in her endearing franglais. In 1960 they invited Arthur Farrow and his wife Estelle to join them. 'The trip was hugely enjoyable for my parents: on each return to Collioure the Ihlees were welcomed like long-lost children,' said Nigel Farrow, who retains a particular affection for the couple.

> The first painting that I considered mine, that was not by my father, was *The Cork Wood* [fig.30], which was a fourteenth birthday present from Rudolph.[9] Visits to The Yews were much prized for Isabelle's cooking in earlier years and for the food and wine and talk in later years. The talk would as likely be of cars as of art: my father and Ihlee were enthusiastic motorists. Ihlee was in no way inhibited by the fact that his small stature meant that when he was driving he was peering at the road through rather than over the wheel.

Ihlee's great-nephew James de la Mare was another regular visitor to The Yews in the 1950s and 60s.

> As Rudolph was not interested in selling the pictures he painted, or at least did not seem to be, they accumulated in his studio, stacked vertically in

> a long line across the floor. I remember that clearly. When he was old he couldn't turn his head so when he backed his car down into the road his wife was sent there to watch out for traffic and he, staring straight ahead, put the car into reverse and put his foot on the throttle – hoping he'd keep the car in a straight line until he reached the road outside! A hazardous and alarming way of driving I used to think![10]

Laure Doher embraced the English way of life, marrying Josiah Walker, known to friends as 'JJ' and a member of a distinguished local family of medical practitioners. They had four children, who looked upon Rudolph as their grandfather. One of them, Charles, said:

> Rudolph and Isabelle played a huge part in our lives although looking back they seem an odd match. Rudolph urbane, cultured, and Isabelle quick-witted, of southern peasant stock. But as children we remember the love and care we received from them. Rudolph gave me my first train set and donated exquisite model buildings, vehicles and wagons he had scratch built himself. Isabelle showed her love through her cooking.[11]

The couple returned to Collioure most years, with Rudolph producing several more pictures of the town, including *Facades, Collioure* (fig.66), which he painted in 1959. They also travelled to Spain and, in 1962, to Ullapool in Scotland. His later work, although often pleasing, betrays signs of age and lacks the impact of his powerful images of the 1920s and 30s. But even towards the end of his life, Ihlee was thinking about how to develop his art. Writing to Arthur and Estelle Farrow in 1964, he recounts a struggle with a particular painting.

> I have done nothing beyond my first panel which I thought so pitiful but which is perhaps not quite so deplorable as I thought. I feel more and more that I would like to rid myself of the purely representational and do something with colour principally, irrespective of the things which are mere vehicles of it and only bring you back to earth if made too recognisable. But how to rid oneself of one's wretched inhibitions![12]

In 1960 Ihlee with Arthur Farrow and his son Nigel went to an exhibition at the Tate featuring one of the twentieth century's least inhibited artists. At the time it was the biggest retrospective of Picasso ever staged and was widely dubbed the exhibition of the century, with *Tatler* calling it the first 'art blockbuster'. Ihlee was, like many other artists, in awe of the Spaniard's

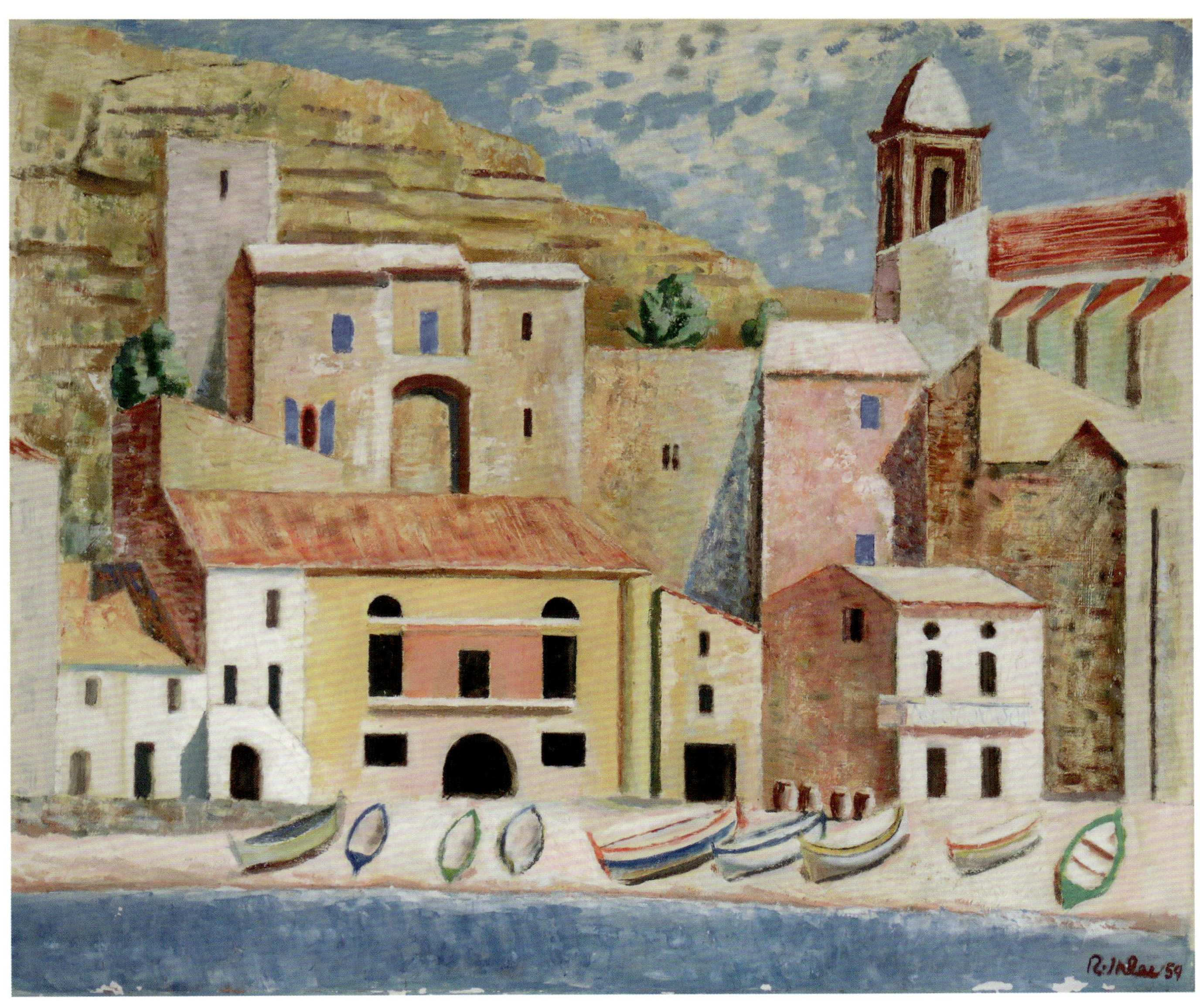

66
Facades, Collioure, 1959
Oil on canvas
51 × 61 cm (20 × 24 in)
Private collection

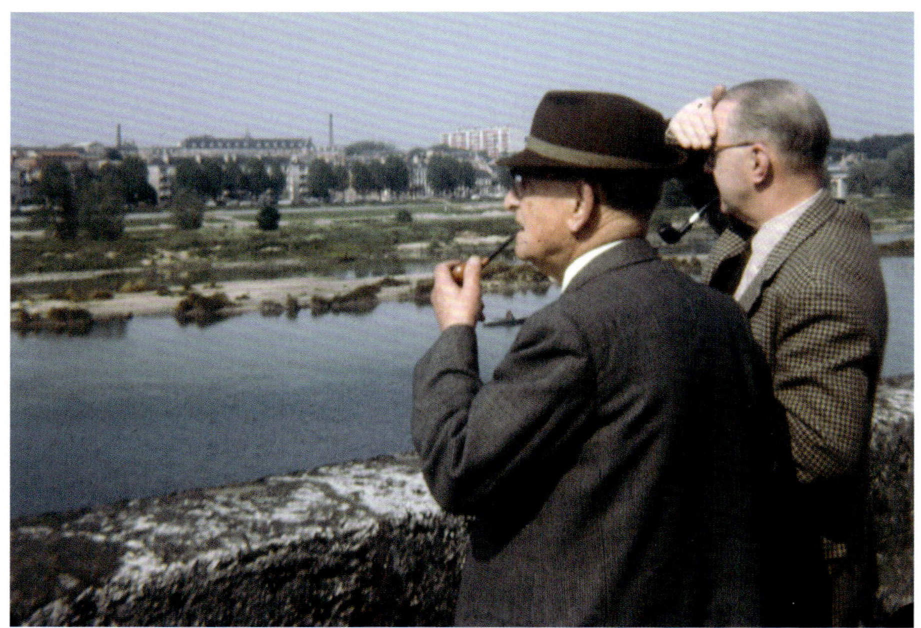

67
Rudolph Ihlee and Arthur Farrow, Orléans, 1967
Family photograph

inventive genius and had closely followed his career. 'For the joyous work of Matisse he reserves, perhaps, his greatest admiration,' noted Arthur Farrow, 'but there are individual works by Picasso, from various periods that he has found inexpressibly moving and significant.'[13]

In 1967 Rudolph and Isabelle set off once again to Collioure. For part of the journey they were accompanied by Arthur and Estelle Farrow and Nigel, his wife Sue and their first child, Miranda. The memory is still clear in Nigel's mind.

> On the way down we stopped at various points and at each stop Rudolph gazed hungrily at the views in all directions. They usually gained his approval but I remember that the stop outside Orléans elicited his trademark dismissal. 'Nothing here on which to feast the eye.' After a few days they were collected by a relation and driven to Collioure.

Rudolph was 84. One of his last paintings shows the town's market place, which he had first come across 45 years earlier in the company of Edgar Hereford. As ever, the sun is shining from a clear blue sky. From behind his easel he would have seen the Hotel Bougnol-Quintana where the pair dined with Charles Rennie Mackintosh. He was surrounded by memories – the chateau, the lighthouse, the mountain backdrop, the Mediterranean – but he would never take the road to Collioure again. Like Mackintosh, decades before, he was suffering from cancer; of the prostate, in his case. It killed him the following year.

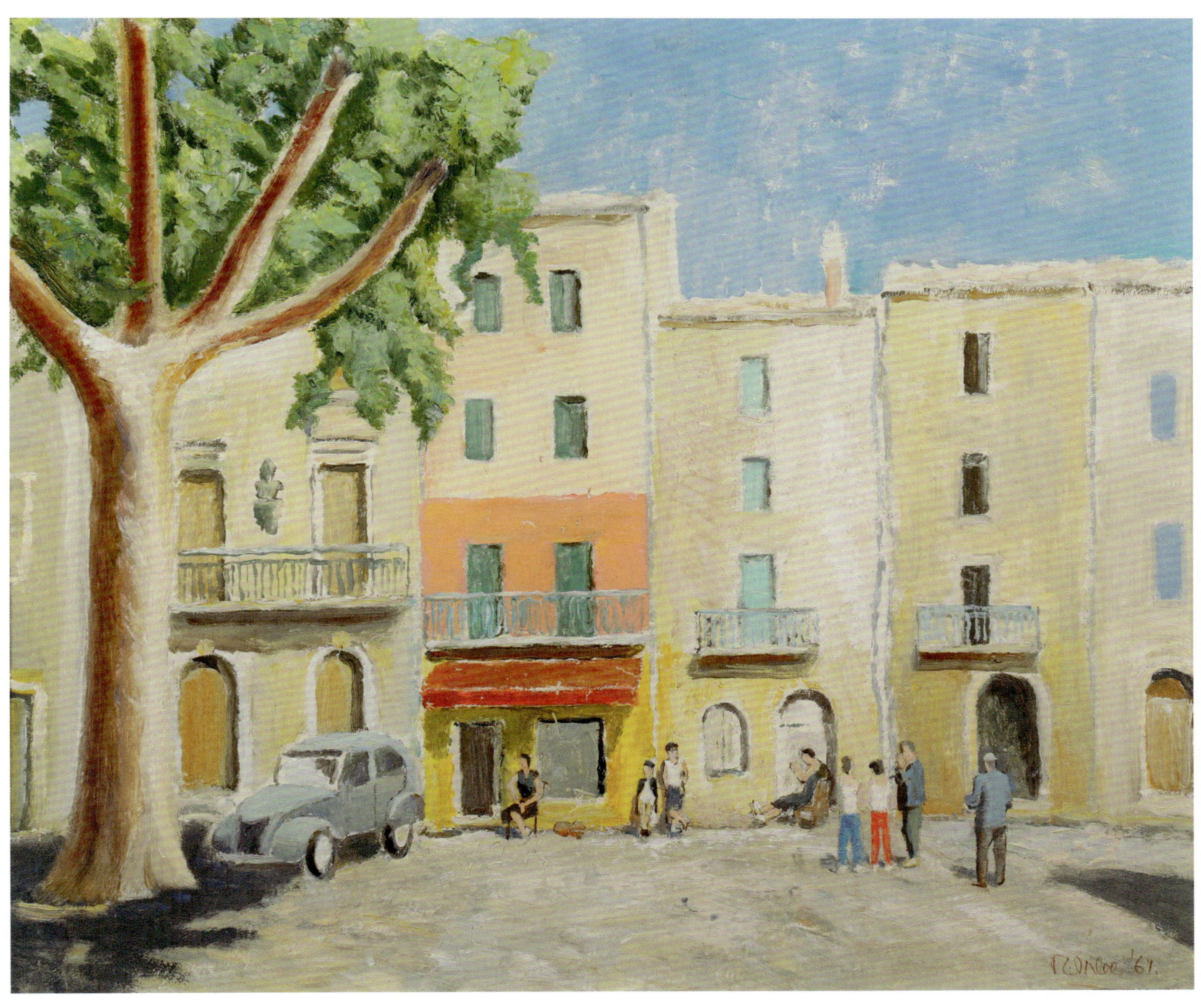

68
Market Place, 1967
Oil on canvas
51 × 61 cm (20 × 24 in)
Private collection

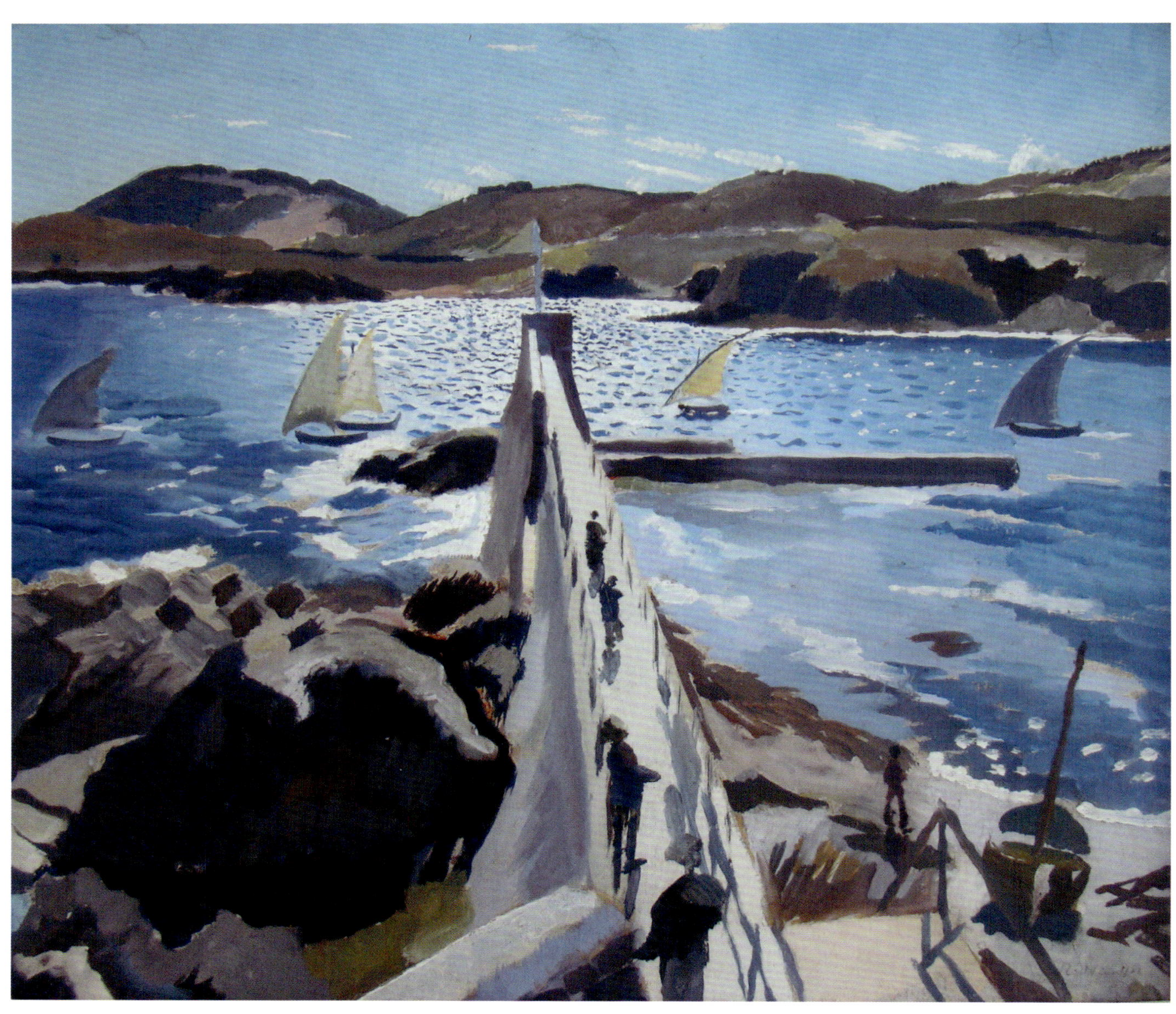

69
The Jetty, Collioure, 1922
Oil on board
38 × 46 cm (15 × 18 in)
Private collection

Although Ihlee spent his final years in England, it was in Collioure that he felt most alive. And it was in that corner of Catalonia that he developed his personality as a painter. By the time of his death, in 1968, the character of the port was changing. The local economy was starting to rely on tourism rather than a dwindling supply of anchovies and sardines. And yet, especially out of season, the magic of the place survives. A century ago, not long after his arrival, Ihlee sketched some fishing boats setting out beyond the jetty across a sparkling sea (fig.69): they would have needed a fine catch to match his exceptional haul.

Afterword

Having retraced the artist's steps I now look upon my Ihlee landscape with a different eye. While *Petites Maisons, Faubourg, Collioure* (fig.1) still recalls the warmth, light and colours of the P-O, it also makes me think of the events and choices which shaped its creator's life. You could say he was unlucky. With a brilliant student career behind him, he seemed to have the art world at his feet, especially after his second one-man show. But that same year, when he was 27 and newly married, the First World War intervened. By the time it was over he was depressed and soon to be divorced.

After the war the London art scene began to lose its appeal and he decided on a life abroad. His exile, liberating though it was, harmed his career and explains why many less talented artists of that generation are now better known than him.

Ihlee found both pleasure and satisfaction following his own path and would not have liked to have been pigeonholed as a particular type of painter. With his German heritage, English education and exile in France he resists easy categorisation. His early Brittany paintings certainly recall the likes of Augustus John and Henry Lamb, while other works such as *Interior, 28 Drayton Gardens* (fig.25) show some affinity with the Camden Town Group. It could also be said that some of his later landscapes display elements of Post-Impressionism and the occasional hint of Surrealism. Reviewers of a retrospective in 1978 puzzled how to place him.

Frances Spalding reckoned that after arriving in Collioure 'he exchanged the Pre-Raphaelite timelessness of his early work for a French breeziness'.[1] The correspondent of *The Times* detected in *My Window, Collioure* (fig.28) 'a Camden Town sort of dryness and precision married with an almost Fauvist intensity'.[2] The critic in the *Daily Telegraph* wrote that he 'shows himself to have been a child of his times but also to have had in his work a pronounced personal character'.[3]

Ihlee himself never admitted to any overriding influence or belonged to any movement or group. Unless, perhaps, you count that talented band of contemporaries at the Slade. And what became of them? Lightfoot, Currie and Gertler committed suicide, Dickson Innes died of TB, Derwent Lees lost his mind and, of the 'Coster Gang', none lived beyond 70. Maybe he was not so unlucky after all!

Although Ihlee did not like the business of art and, in particular, the self-promotion that it often involves (there's no known self-portrait), I am sure he would have liked to have sold those paintings that James de la Mare noticed in stacks on his visits to The Yews. And it is probable he felt unappreciated in later life, when he is often described as shy and reserved, albeit with a dry sense of humour. But that is not how Mackintosh saw him in his prime, when he 'showed his feelings like a young child' and lived life to the full.

From his arrival in Collioure at the age of 39 to his departure aged 57, he escaped the pressures of a metropolitan existence. It was the Mediterranean landscape and lifestyle, rather than other artists, that had the greatest influence on this prolific period of his career. Many of the Catalan pictures, recorded more fully in this book than ever before, show the delight he took in those beautiful, relaxed surroundings. The slower rhythm of life, the mountain and sea air, the support of a great friend, the love of a new wife – all these are reflected in a body of work which deserves to be appreciated more widely.[4]

Notes

Introduction

1 James Dickson Innes visited Collioure three times between 1908 and 1912, on the last occasion with Derwent Lees. Both artists started at the Slade in 1905, the same year as Edgar Hereford and the year before Ihlee. Innes died aged 27 from TB. Derwent Lees was an Australian by birth who moved from being a student at the Slade to an assistant on the teaching staff. He suffered from schizophrenia for much of his adult life and died in a mental institution.

2 Ihlee told his Peterborough friend Arthur Farrow that he was never able to recover several paintings which he had left with a Paris dealer before the outbreak of the Second World War. Ihlee's notes indicate the dealer could have been based in Rue de l'Armorique in the fifteenth arrondissement.

3 Frank Rutter (1876–1937) was an influential art critic, most notably for the *Sunday Times*. Paul George Konody (1872–1933) was a Hungarian-born art critic for, among others, the *Observer* and the *Daily Mail* and the author of several books.

4 Sir Edward Marsh (1872–1953) was a high-ranking civil servant who became an important collector and patron of the arts, encouraging Ihlee and many of his contemporaries including Mark Gertler and Stanley Spencer. He bought at least six works by Ihlee.

5 From the introduction to the catalogue of Ihlee's one-man show at the Chenil Gallery, 1926.

6 Letter to Ihlee from Marsh quoted in the catalogue of a retrospective exhibition of Ihlee's works at the Belgrave Gallery, London in 1978.

7 *An Exhibition of Practical Art*, organised by the Arts League of Service at the Twenty-One Gallery in the autumn of 1919.

8 Sir Edward Marsh writing in 1951 to Arthur Farrow, who had organised an exhibition of Ihlee's work in Peterborough. Personal correspondence.

9 Arthur Farrow, a draper from Peterborough, became a close friend of Ihlee after the artist moved to nearby West Deeping after the Second World War.

1 A Brilliant Beginning

1 James de la Mare (1939–2014) was Rudolph Ihlee's great-nephew, the grandson of Klara Ryan (née Ihlee), one of Rudolph's elder sisters.

2 The Museumslandschaft Hessen Kassel has 31 works by Johann Eduard Ihlée, 16 paintings and 15 drawings.

3 Baker Perkins is an engineering firm still operating in Peterborough which as a result of mergers and takeovers has had a number of different names. See *The History of Baker Perkins* by Augustus Muir, W. Heffer & Sons, 1968.

4 Fred Ihlee left around 30 ship models to the Science Museum, more than anyone else except the Admiralty. https://collection.sciencemuseumgroup.org.uk/people/cp39504/frederick-charles-ihlee

5 According to an article by James de la Mare published online for the Baker Perkins Historical Society. www.bphs.net/groupfacilities/w/wernerpfleidererperkins.

6 Ihlee was apprenticed to Ferranti in Trafford Park, Manchester. Having paid his younger brother's indentures, Fred was annoyed when he gave it up to go to the Slade. Letter from Anne Houben (Ihlee's niece) to Irving Grose.

7 According to Anne Houben, at some time in the family's possession there were several early watercolours dating from 1901.

8 Henry Tonks (1862–1937) qualified as a surgeon before starting to teach at the Slade at the age of 30.

9 Paul Nash, *Outline*, Lund Humphries, 2016, p.71.

10 C.R.W. Nevinson, *Paint and Prejudice*, Harcourt, Brace and Co., 1938, p.34.

11 *ibid.*, p.37. Now perhaps the least well known, 'Claus[e]' was William Lionel Clause (1887–1946) who later became honorary secretary of the NEAC.

12 From Adrian Allinson's unpublished memoirs, McFarlin Library, University of Tulsa, quoted in John Woodeson, *Mark Gertler*, Sidgwick and Jackson, 1972, p.55. Allinson also gave up medicine to go to the Slade.

13 *ibid.*, p.65.

14 Frances Spalding, *Vanessa Bell*, Weidenfeld and Nicolson, 1983, p.56.

15 Nash, *Outline*, p.75.

16 Walter Sickert formed the Fitzroy Street Group before the Camden Town Group. On Saturdays members exhibited and were expected to contribute towards the rent of the studio in Fitzroy Street. Wendy Baron, *Perfect Moderns*, Ashgate, 2000, gives a detailed account of the various groups.

17 Private letter to Ihlee, from family archive.

18 Gerard Chowne, a former Slade student, taught at Liverpool University before founding the Sandon Studios in the city.

19 Their Slade index cards both give the address 211 Hampstead Rd.

20 Woodeson, *Mark Gertler*, p.67.

21 Nevinson, *Paint and Prejudice*, p.57.

22 Woodeson, *Mark Gertler*, p.68.

23 Catalogue of 1972 exhibition of works by Maxwell Gordon Lightfoot at the Walker Art Gallery, Liverpool, p.31.

24 Nash, *Outline*, pp 103–4.

25 *Daily Telegraph*, 3 March 1912.

26 *Morning Post*, 4 March 1912.

27 *Rhythm* ran from the summer of 1911 to March 1913. Ihlee's *The Quarrel* (The Higgins, Bedford) was among the images featured in the last edition. Murry's letter to Marsh is in Edinburgh University Library.

28 Edward Hereford (1837–1921) exhibited 62 pictures at the Dudley Gallery (later the New Dudley Gallery), and also showed at the Walker Art Gallery, Liverpool (2), the Royal Institute of Painters in Watercolour (2), the Royal Scottish Academy (1) and Manchester City Art Gallery (1).

29 William Rothenstein's parents, like Ihlee's, emigrated from Germany. Along with Roger Fry he was one of the most influential

figures in the London art world.

30 Albert Rutherston, the youngest of the six Rothenstein siblings, anglicised his name during the First World War. He had a one-man show at the Carfax two years before Ihlee's first solo exhibition there.
31 Private letter, from Ihlee family archive.
32 Christian Millet suggests that the bait may have been a mixture of cod's eggs and flour which was commonly used for catching sardines.
33 Rupert Brooke, Siegfried Sassoon, Robert Graves and D.H. Lawrence were among the better known 'Georgian Poets'. Marsh envisaged a volume of 50 'Georgian Drawings' by around 20 artists but it never materialised.
34 Article by Sickert in *The New Age*, 14 May 1914.
35 Letter to Ihlee from Arthur Clifton, 3 March 1914.

2 War and Divorce

1 According to the Baker Perkins Historical Society's website, the company was subjected to 'venomous attacks suggesting that it was trading with the enemy'. www.bphs.net/groupfacilities/w/wernerpfleidererperkins.
2 A set of Ihlee's lithographs is held by the Imperial War Museum.
3 The mural was in the Holdings Building of Baker Perkins' old Westwood plant, the remains of which are now occupied by Virgin Media.
4 Ihlee quoted in Baker Perkins' in-house journal, *Group News*, October 1966.
5 In 1916 Farnsworth Smith was living in St James Square, Holland Park, London. It is believed he later married Sophia in France.
6 In 1906 Sir Thomas Horridge (1857–1938) was elected Liberal MP for Manchester, defeating the Prime Minister Arthur Balfour, before resuming his legal career in 1910.
7 In his memorial tribute to Oliver Brown (1885–1966), Sir Kenneth Clark said: 'He loved art, he loved artists and he was even tolerant of collectors.'
8 *The Memoirs of Oliver Brown*, Evelyn, Adams & MacKay, 1968, p.62.
9 *ibid.*, pp 51–2.
10 The name Arts League of Service alluded to the League of Nations and was chosen to reflect a mood of post-war optimism. Duncan Grant and Cedric Morris were also among Ihlee's co-exhibitors.
11 *Bal* was painted in Guilvinec in Brittany.
12 *Mélanie* was also painted in Guilvinec and later exhibited in Australia.
13 The oils were priced between £12, *La Femme des Roches*, and £80, *Breton Peasants*.
14 Picasso's exhibition at the Leicester Galleries was in January 1921. Other artists showing at the gallery that year included Wyndham Lewis, C.R.W. Nevinson and Albert Rutherston.
15 *Sunday Times*, 20 March 1921.
16 *Daily Telegraph*, 16 March 1921.

3 Algeria, Collioure and Charles Rennie Mackintosh

1 The Senegalese Tirailleurs (riflemen) were an infantry corps employed throughout the French colonies and also in mainland France where many trained in and around Collioure.
2 In a letter to Henri Manguin (1874–1949) Matisse described the light in Biskra as 'blinding'. Quoted in Hilary Spurling, *The Unknown Matisse*, Penguin, 2000, p.358.
3 Philippe Zilcken, *Impressions d'Algerie*, H. Floury, 1910, p.32, quoted in Spurling, *The Unknown Matisse*, p.359.
4 Carolina McCabe, 'The Disappearing Tradition of Amazigh Facial and Body Tattoos', *Morocco World News*, 7 April 2019.
5 Exh. spring 1924, Scottish Academy, sold to Mrs Peploe, India Street, Edinburgh, £25. Ihlee's list.
6 Dr Sériziat and P. Soulier, *Collioure et ses environs*, 1902, reprinted 2005 by Le Livre d'Histoire-Lorisse, p.31. Paul Soulier (1850–1930) was a friend of Matisse, who painted scenes of Collioure from one of his properties. Ihlee gave one of his paintings, *By the Railway*, 1922, to his son Honoré and through his connection with the Soulier family may have met Matisse.
7 Letter to Otto Theis, 9 July 1923, in *A Life in Letters*, a biographical blog by Scott's granddaughter Denise Scott Fears, alifeinletters2017.wordpress.com/2017/10/26/collioure/.
8 *My Window* was exhibited at the Chenil Gallery in 1926, price £60. Ihlee's list.
9 From north to south: Plage Nord, Plage St Vincent, Plage Boramar, Plage de Port d'Avall, Plage du Boutigue, Plage de la Balette.
10 Ihlee's *Le Grand Café* now bears little resemblance to the Hotel Frégate after extensive remodelling.
11 Patrick O'Brian lived in Collioure between 1949 and 1998. First published in 1953, *The Catalans* was republished by HarperCollins in 2005; pp 132–3.
12 Sériziat and Soulier, *Collioure et ses environs*, p.179.
13 Gérard Bonet, *Les Pyrénées-Orientales dans la guerre*, Horvath, 1992, p.20.
14 Sériziat and Soulier, *Collioure et ses environs*, p.153.
15 *The Red Arch*, exh. Goupil Gallery, 1926, price £60. Ihlee's list.
16 Sériziat and Soulier, *Collioure et ses environs*, p.155.
17 *ibid.*, p.161.
18 Evelyn Scott, letter to Lola Ridge, September 1923, in *A Life in Letters*.
19 *ibid.*
20 *Festival at Laroque* was exhibited at the Chenil Gallery in 1926, price £25. Ihlee's list.
21 The hotel passed from René Pous to his son Joseph Pous and is now run by Joseph's daughter, Manée Pous.
22 Alistair Moffat, *Remembering Charles Rennie Mackintosh*, Colin Baxter, 1989, p.131.
23 Pamela Robertson and Philip Long, *Charles Rennie Mackintosh in France*, National Galleries of Scotland, 2005, p.9.
24 Richard Emerson, 'Mackintosh and Textiles', *Charles Rennie Mackintosh Society Journal* 100, Spring 2016.
25 James Herbert MacNair was married to Margaret Mackintosh's sister Frances. He taught at the Sandon Studios alongside Gordon Maxwell Lightfoot's mentor Gerard Chowne.
26 Letter dated 13 May 1927, *The Chronycle: The Letters of Charles*

Rennie Mackintosh to Margaret Macdonald Mackintosh, 1927, Hunterian Art Gallery, University of Glasgow, 2001, p.50.

27 Letter dated 19 June 1927, *ibid.*, pp 96–7.
28 Letter dated 22 May 1927, *ibid.*, pp 61–2.
29 Letter dated 28 May 1927, *ibid.*, pp 70–1.
30 Letter dated 3 June 1927, *ibid.*, p.78.
31 Letter dated 25 May 1927, *ibid.*, p.66.
32 On 17 May 1927 Mackintosh went to Collioure to visit Ihlee and Hereford and found 'when I got there they had gone to Perpignan with Madame and Fernando' (ibid., p.58). In his list, Ihlee notes he gave 'Pauline' *Senegalese at Collioure*, painted in 1922. That year he also gave *By the Railway* to Honoré Soulier.
33 Letter dated 7 June 1927, *The Chronycle*, p.84.
34 Letter dated 11 June 1927, *ibid.*, p.89.
35 Letter dated 13 May 1927, *ibid.*, p.52.
36 Moffat, *Remembering Charles Rennie Mackintosh*, p.149. The book is partly a transcript of a 1987 STV documentary in which, despite having lived in England for 46 years, Isabelle spoke in French and was subtitled.
37 According to Ihlee's adopted grandson, Charles Walker.

4 Artists about Town

1 Jack Knewstub (1872–1959) was a brother-in-law of both William Rothenstein and William Orpen.
2 *Sunday Times*, 4 April 1926.
3 For example Nash's *The Edge of the Wood*, c.1919, Reading Museum and Town Hall.
4 This unusual building was designed by the Danish architect Viggo Dorph-Petersen (1851–1937) around 1900.
5 William Marchant (1868–1925) worked as an art dealer in Paris before managing the Goupil Gallery in London, which was destroyed by German bombs in 1941.
6 *Observer*, 13 March 1927.
7 *L'Heure de la soupe* was painted in 1924 and exhibited at the NEAC the following year. Ihlee's list.
8 *Terrace Consolation* was painted in 1932 and exhibited at the Galerie Campistro in Perpignan before being acquired by the museum at Collioure. Ihlee's list.
9 Jean Peské emigrated to France at the age of 21 after receiving a large inheritance. Like Ihlee, he painted in Brittany, Collioure and elsewhere in France.
10 Gaston Pams (1918–81) was born in Port Vendres. He was imprisoned by the Gestapo in 1944 and later became a prominent left-wing politician.
11 Port Vendres had been occupied by the Germans since 1942. Before leaving the German commander, Walter Denys, oversaw the destruction of much of the port on 19 August 1944.
12 Vergé-Sarrat painted in Biskra in 1928.
13 Maillol lived on and off at La Métairie, Banyuls, from 1910 until his death in 1944.
14 A poster promoting the rail link from Paris to Collioure via Toulouse and Perpignan appeared in 1934. See *Le Pays Catalan à l'affiche*, Mare Nostrum, 2014.
15 A reference to Alphonse Daudet's 1872 novel *Tartarin de Tarascon*, about a hunting-obsessed French town.
16 Evelyn Scott, letter to Lola Ridge, September 1923, in *A Life in Letters*.
17 The Salon des Indépendents has been holding annual exhibitions in Paris since 1884. The Salon des Tuileries was founded in 1923.
18 A small gallery in Perpignan where Ihlee exhibited around 15 paintings in both 1931 and 1932.

5 Romance in Languedoc-Roussillon and Brittany

1 Payra-sur-l'Hers is a small village about eight miles south-west of Castelnaudary which claims to be the birthplace of the white bean and meat stew called cassoulet.
2 Jules Joly and Etienne Frenay, *Dans les Pyrénées Orientales: Notre ecole au bon vieux temps*, Horvath, 1990, p.xxiv.
3 *ibid.*, p.xxvii.
4 According to Arthur Farrow's wife Estelle.
5 Information from Charles Walker, grandson of Margot Doher.
6 *Bathers*, exhibited Leicester Galleries, March 1921, price £25. Ihlee's list.
7 Information from Christian Millet, Président de l'Association Patrimoine de Plougasnou.
8 La Fête des Filets Bleus was started in 1905 to raise money for local fishermen who, in the preceding years, had suffered during a severe sardine shortage.
9 For example *Four Breton Women* by Paul Gauguin, 1886, Neue Pinakothek Art Museum, Munich.
10 Picasso, who was in Ceret in 1911, 1912, 1913 and 1953, donated 57 artworks to the museum, many of which are ceramics of bullfighting scenes.
11 According to family legend Ihlee, at various times, met Picasso and Matisse. Ihlee's ward Laure Walker (née Doher) spoke of sitting on Matisse's knee.
12 Letter from Margaret Mackintosh to Jessie Newberry, December 1923, *Charles Rennie Mackintosh in France*, p.116.
13 Campôme is a mountain village of around 100 people some four miles from Prades. Mosset is a slightly larger village (population around 300) whose highest point is 8000 feet above sea level. Villefranche-de-Conflent is among the best preserved fortified towns in France, dating from 1098 with later defences by Vauban in the eighteenth century.
14 The iron belfry is characteristic of many churches in the region but, despite the title, locals say it bears no relation to present-day Saint-Paul-de-Fenouillet.
15 Letter dated 22 June 1927, *The Chronycle*, p.102.

6 Spain in Peace and War

1 The appendix of *Charles Rennie Mackintosh in France* includes three letters from Margaret Mackintosh sent from the P-O to Jessie Newberry, including this one from Amélie-les-Bains in December 1923.
2 The largely inconclusive meeting took place on 23 October 1940 at the railway station at Hendaye.

3 Picasso was born in Malaga in 1881 and spent the first ten years of his life there.
4 Photos of the caves and shacks in El Palo at around the time of Ihlee's visit can be found at elpalo.org/imagenes-para-el-recuerdo-de-la-barriada-de-el-palo/.
5 Letter from Laure Walker to Jeremy Hill (Maggie Tomalin's grandson), 14 July 1995. Monksgrange Archive.
6 Quoted in Bonet, *Les Pyrénées-Orientales dans la guerre*, p.32.
7 *ibid.*, p.38.
8 Machado's last days are recounted in Jacques Issorel, *Collioure 1939: Les derniers jours d'Antonio Machado,* Mare Nostrum, 2002.
9 Their escape route from France is mentioned by Ihlee's great friend Arthur Farrow in his introduction to the catalogue of an exhibition of Ihlee's drawings and paintings in Peterborough in 1951.
10 The house in the picture was one of the first in Collioure to have a telephone. Built by Augustin and Marguerite Vivès in 1927, it was requisitioned by the Germans during the war.

7 Back in Britain

1 There were at least six air raids on Peterborough, where warning sirens sounded 650 times during the war.
2 From Arthur Farrow's introductory essay to the catalogue of Ihlee's 1951 exhibition in Peterborough.
3 Muir, *The History of Baker Perkins*, p.113.
4 Margaret Tomalin married Edward Richards-Orpen (1884–1967), an Irish politician and furniture maker. According to Ihlee's list Maggie Orpen owned several of her cousin's paintings, including *L'Heure de la soupe* and *The Red Arch.*
5 At the NEAC in 1948 Ihlee exhibited *Le Chemin de la mer*, painted in Vigo in 1935, and in 1949 he exhibited *Road by Collioure*, also painted before the war.
6 Jacqmar was based in Mayfair and owned by Joseph (Jack) Lyons and his wife Mary, whose names were combined for the label.
7 George Montague, ninth Earl of Sandwich (1874–1962) was a notable art collector and pre-war trustee of the Tate. He became president of the Peterborough Art Society at the request of Arthur Farrow.
8 NEAC records show that Ihlee exhibited new paintings from 1956 most years until 1966. His last entry was *Hot Afternoon.*
9 Ihlee did much to encourage Nigel Farrow's interest in art. He now runs the art publishing company which produced this book.
10 James de la Mare's anecdote is from a website associated with the history of Baker Perkins, www.westwoodworks.net.
11 The 'grandchildren' referred to Rudolph as Tont and Isabelle as Tat; the Farrow family called them Tonton and Tati.
12 The extract from the 1964 letter is one of several helpful fragments provided by Irving Grose, who organised an exhibition of Ihlee's paintings and drawings in 1978.
13 Arthur Farrow, introductory essay to the catalogue of Ihlee's 1951 exhibition in Peterborough.

Afterword

1 *Art Review*, vol.XXX, No.20, October 1978.
2 John Russell Taylor in *The Times*, 25 October 1978.
3 *Daily Telegraph*, 23 October 1978.
4 Many of Ihlee's paintings were sold after his death. There were two local selling exhibitions in 1968 (Sleaford) and 1975 (Oakham), and the Belgrave Gallery staged two shows in London and Sheffield in 1978 with a catalogue essay by Irving Grose, whose research has helped greatly with this book. Since 1984 more than 130 of his paintings have appeared at auction in England while others have found a home in France.

Bibliography

Baile de Laperriere, Charles, *The New English Art Club Exhibitors 1886–2001*, Vol.2, Hilmarton Manor Press, Calne, 2002

Baron, Wendy, *Perfect Moderns: A History of the Camden Town Group*, Ashgate Publishing, Aldershot, 2000

Billcliffe, Roger, *Mackintosh Watercolours*, John Murray, London, 1979

Bonet, Gérard, *Les Pyrénées Orientales dans la guerre, 1939–1944*, Horvath, Saint Étienne, 1992

Boyd Hancock, David, *A Crisis of Brilliance*, Old Street Publishing Ltd, London, 2009

Brown, Oliver, *Exhibition*, Evelyn Adams and Mackay, London, 1968

Causey, Andrew, *Paul Nash: Landscape and the Life of Objects*, Lund Humphries, London, 2013

Clifton, Arthur, *Drawings by R. Ihlee*, exh. cat., Carfax Gallery, March 1912

Clifton, Arthur, *Paintings and Drawings by R. Ihlee*, exh. cat., Carfax Gallery, March 1914

Crawford, Alan, *C.R. Mackintosh: The Chelsea Years, 1915–23*, exh. cat., Hunterian Art Gallery, Glasgow, 1994

Crichton, Robin, *Monsieur Mackintosh*, Luath Press Ltd, Edinburgh, 2006

Emerson, Richard, 'Mackintosh and Textiles', *Charles Rennie Mackintosh Society Journal* 100, 2016

Engert, Gail, *Maxwell Gordon Lightfoot*, Walker Art Gallery, Liverpool, 1972

Farrow, A.H., *Paintings and Drawings by Rudolph Ihlee*, exh. cat., Peterborough Arts Council, Peterborough, 1951

Forcada, Eric, *De La Chute de Barcelone à La Retirada*, Mare Nostrum, Perpignan, 2014

Forcada, Eric, *Le Pays Catalan à l'affiche*, Mare Nostrum, Perpignan, 2014

Forcada, Eric, *Port Vendres 1944*, Semilibres, Perpignan, 2019

Fothergill, John, *James Dickson Innes*, Faber and Faber, London, 1946

Grose, Irving, *Rudolph Ihlee, 1883–1968*, exh. cat., Belgrave Gallery, London, 1978

Gruetzner Robins, Anna, *Walter Sickert: The Complete Writings on Art*, Oxford University Press, Oxford, 2000

Hamnett, Nina, *Laughing Torso*, Ray Long and Richard R. Smith, New York, 1932

Hassall, Christopher, *Edward Marsh, Patron of the Arts: A Biography*, Longmans, London, 1959

Holroyd, Michael, *Augustus John*, Vintage, London, 1997

Issorel, Jacques, *Collioure 1939: Les derniers jours d'Antonio Machado*, Mare Nostrum, Perpignan, 2002

Johnson, Lesley, *An Honest Patron: A Tribute to Sir Edward Marsh*, Bluecoat Gallery, Liverpool, 1976

Joll, Evelyn, *Watercolours and Drawings*, Cecil Higgins Gallery, Bedford, 2002

Joly, Jules, and Etienne Frenay, *Dans les Pyrénées Orientales: Notre école au bon vieux temps*, Horvath, Saint Étienne, 1990

Knewstub, Jack, *Rudolph Ihlee*, exh. cat., Chenil Gallery, London, 1926

McCabe, Carolina, 'The Disappearing Tradition of Amazigh Facial and Body Tattoos', *Morocco World News*, 7 April 2019

Matamoros, Joséphine, and Dominique Szymusiak, *Matisse, Derain: 1905, un été à Collioure*, Découvertes Gallimard, Paris, 2005

Moffat, Alistair, *Remembering Charles Rennie Mackintosh*, Colin Baxter Photography, Lanark, 1989

Muir, Augustus, *The History of Baker Perkins*, W. Heffer and Sons, Cambridge, 1968

Nash, Paul, *Outline: An Autobiography*, new edn, ed. David Boyd Haycock, Lund Humphries, London, 2016 (first published 1949)

Nevinson, C.R.W., *Paint and Prejudice*, Harcourt, Brace and Co., New York, 1938

O'Brian, Patrick, *The Catalans*, HarperCollins, London, 2005 (first published by Harcourt, Brace and Company, New York, 1953)

Pous, Joseph and Michel Descossy, *Couleurs de Collioure*, Editions Equinoxe, Saint-Rémy-de-Provence, 2009

Raguenaud, Virginie, *The Colors of Catalonia*, Gemma, Boston, 2012

Robertson, Pamela (ed.), *The Chronycle: The Letters of Charles Rennie Mackintosh to Margaret Macdonald Mackintosh, 1927*, Hunterian Art Gallery, University of Glasgow, 2001

Robertson, Pamela, and Philip Long, *Charles Rennie Mackintosh in France*, National Galleries of Scotland, Edinburgh, 2005

Robins, Anna, and Francis Farmar, *The New English Art Club Centenary Exhibition*, Christie's, London, 1986

Rothenstein, William, *Men and Memoirs, 1900–1922*, Vol.2, Faber and Faber, London, 1932

Scott Fears, Denise, *A Life in Letters: A Biography of Evelyn Scott*, alifeinletters2017.wordpress.com

Sériziat, Dr, and P. Soulier, *Collioure et ses environs*, Le Livre d'Histoire, Paris, 2005 (first published 1905)

Spalding, Frances, *Vanessa Bell*, Weidenfeld and Nicolson, London, 1983

Spurling, Hilary, *The Unknown Matisse*, Vol.1, Penguin, London, 1998

Sturgis, Matthew, *Walter Sickert*, Harper Perennial, London, 2005

Vinen, Richard, *The Unfree French: Life Under the Occupation*, Penguin, London, 2007

Woodeson, John, *Mark Gertler*, Sidgwick & Jackson, London, 1972

Zilcken, Philippe, *Impressions d'Algérie*, H. Floury, Paris, 1910

List of Works

The most complete record of Ihlee's work dates from his arrival in Collioure in 1922 until the outbreak of the Spanish Civil War in 1936. During that period he made a meticulous list under the following headings: title, medium, size, where painted, frame, price and history (exhibitions, sales, gifts, etc). Titles are either in French or English depending on where he intended to exhibit the painting. He would number paintings with four digits, two for the year and two for the order in which they were painted. *L'Heure de la soupe*, for example, is numbered 2408, being the eighth painting completed in 1924. He also made a more selective list before he settled in Collioure, including some paintings pre-dating the First World War but excluding many, such as those from his two Carfax Gallery exhibitions. The catalogues of those exhibitions omit the dimensions of his drawings and paintings so I have listed their titles at the end of the first section.

Ihlee exhibited most frequently at the New English Art Club. Between 1910, the year of his first recorded NEAC exhibit, and 1966, his last, he showed a total of 105 pictures. Besides his one-man shows at the Carfax, Leicester and Chenil galleries, Ihlee exhibited elsewhere in London including the Alpine Club Gallery, the French Gallery, the Goupil Gallery, the Grafton Galleries, the Redfern Gallery and the Whitechapel Gallery. He was also busy outside the capital, exhibiting in Belfast, Birmingham, Bradford, Derby, Edinburgh, Hull, Liverpool and Oldham. In the 1930s he exhibited in Paris and Perpignan.

Although Ihlee painted until his death in 1968, he did not record his works in the same way in the last 30 years of his life. What follows, therefore, is not exhaustive but is, nevertheless, the most complete published record of his work to date; 485 titles in total. Since he painted principally in England (E1–E52), Algeria (A1–A25), Spain (S1–S29), Brittany (B1–B58), Languedoc-Roussillon (LR1–LR64) and the rest of France (RF1–RF10), his work is grouped under those geographical headings, with the addition of a special category for Collioure (C1–C140) where he did the bulk of his work. The last section is an incomplete list of paintings dating from his post-war years at West Deeping (WD1–WD33).

England

Ihlee's addresses in England included 13 Burstock Rd, Putney (c.1906), 211 Hampstead Rd (c.1909), 12 Castletown Road, London (1913–c.1915, with first wife Sophia), 84 Aldermans Drive, Peterborough (c.1915–18), 28 Drayton Gardens, London (1918–c.1921 with Edgar Hereford) (Fig 26), and The Yews, West Deeping, Near Peterborough (c.1940–68, with second wife Isabelle).

- E1 *Aldwych*, 1908, pencil/watercolour, London, 24.7 × 37.5 cm (10 × 11 in), sold Christie's 1991, £286
- E2 *The Blind Girl*, 1912, drawing, London, 19.5 × 14.8 cm (7.6 × 5.8 in), exh. Carfax Gallery, bought by Charles Rutherston, gifted by him to Manchester City Art Gallery in 1925
- E3 *Woman Ironing*, 1912, drawing, illustrated in *Rhythm*, December 1912, bought by Sir Edward Marsh, donated to Contemporary Art Society
- E4 *The Quarrel*, 1912, pencil, ink, chalk, 20 × 24.7 cm (8 × 10 in), illustrated in *Rhythm*, March 1913, The Higgins Museum and Art Gallery, Bedford
- E5 *The Magic Wand*, 1912, oil, 83 × 111 cm (32.5 × 43.5 in) exh. NEAC
- E6 *Pounding the Bait*, 1913, sepia pen and ink on paper, London, 32.1 × 26.9 cm (12.6 × 10.6 in), exh. Carfax Gallery 1914, 15 gns, Aberdeen Art Gallery
- E7 *Young Jewess*, 1913, oil, Castletown Rd (CR), 50.8 × 60.96 cm (20 × 24 in), exh. Leicester Galleries (LG) March 1921 and Derby 1922, given to Arthur Farrow
- E8 *Portrait of a Woman*, 1913, oil, CR, 33.5 × 26 cm (14 × 10 in), exh. Chenil Gallery, bought by Charles Rutherston, sold Christie's 1995, £862
- E9 *New Boots*, 1913, oil, CR, 50.8 × 61 cm (20 × 24 in), exh. Carfax Gallery 1914, 60 gns
- E10 *The Children's Matinée*, oil, CR, 1913, 40 × 57.5 cm (16 × 22.5 in), exh. Carfax Gallery 1914, 60 gns
- E11 *Nene Bridge*, c.1918, oil, Peterborough, 50.8 × 60.96 cm (20 × 24 in), exh. LG March 1921, £40 (sold)
- E12 *War Work at Westwood Works*, a suite of 12 lithographs from line drawings, 1918, Peterborough, 38.7 × 27.3 cm (15 × 10 in), edition of 50, Imperial War Museum
- E13 *Still Life*, c.1918, oil, painted at Drayton Gardens (DG), 50.8 × 60.96 cm (20 × 24 in), exh. NEAC winter 1919–20
- E14 *Girl's Head*, 1919, oil, DG, 50.8 × 60.96 cm (20 × 24 in), exh. NEAC winter 1919–20
- E15 *The Quarrel*, 1919, watercolour, 26.3 × 30.4 cm (10.3 × 12 in), bought by Sir Edward Marsh, donated to the Contemporary Art Society, presented to Glasgow Museums 1927
- E16 *Workman Resting*, c.1919, charcoal, bought by Sir Edward Marsh, donated to Contemporary Art Society, presented to Cyfarthfa Castle Museum and Art Gallery, Merthyr Tydfil 1956
- E17 *Words*, 1919, coloured drawing (CD), DG, 48.26 × 60.96 cm (19x 24 in), exh. NEAC winter 1919–20, sold to Sir Edward Marsh
- E18 *The Model*, 1919, CD, DG, 48.26 × 60.96 cm (19 × 24 in), exh. NEAC winter 1919–20. Victoria and Albert Museum
- E19 *Berkeley Square*, 1921, oil, DG, 38.1 × 45.72 cm (15 × 18 in), exh. NEAC summer 1921
- E20 *Calvary*, 1921, oil, DG, 63.5 × 76.2 cm (25 × 30 in), exh. NEAC summer 1921
- E21 *Study Blue Chalk*, c.1921, drawing, DG, 48.26 × 60.96 cm (19 × 24 in), exh. LG March 1921, 6 gns
- E22 *Portrait Study 1*, c.1921, drawing, DG, 48.26 × 60.96 cm (19 × 24 in), exh. LG March 1921, 6 gns; exh. Derby 1922
- E23 *Concert*, c.1921, CD, DG, 48.26 × 60.96 cm (19 × 24 in), exh. LG March 1921, 12 gns (sold)
- E24 *Nude Sitting*, c.1921, chalk, DG, 48.26 × 60.96 cm (19 × 24 in), exh. LG March 1921, 6 gns (sold)
- E25 *Toilet*, c.1921, drawing, chalk, DG, 48.26 × 60.96 cm (19 × 24 in), exh. LG March 1921, 6 gns (sold)
- E26 *Farm Labourer*, c.1921, brush, DG, 48.26 × 60.96 cm (19 × 24 in), exh. LG March 1921, 6 gns
- E27 *The Burden*, c.1921, CD, DG, 48.26 × 60.96 cm (19 × 24 in), exh. LG March 1921, 10 gns (sold)
- E28 *Mr Pedotti*, c.1921, drawing, DG, 48.26 × 60.96 cm (19 × 24 in), exh. LG March 1921, 6 gns (given to Pedotti)
- E29 *Nude Sitting*, c.1921, lithograph, DG, 48.26 × 60.96 cm (19 × 24 in), exh. LG March 1921, 3 gns (sold)
- E30 *Pigs*, c.1921, brush, DG, 48.26 × 60.96 cm (19 × 24 in), exh. LG March 1921, 8 gns
- E31 *Nude Reclining*, c.1921, lithograph, DG, 48.26 × 60.96 cm (19 × 24 in), exh. LG March 1921, 3 gns (sold)
- E32 *Nude Back View*, c.1921, chalk, DG, 48.26 × 60.96 cm (19 × 24 in), exh. LG March 1921, 6 gns
- E33 *The Shelter*, c.1921, CD, DG, 48.26 × 60.96 cm (19 × 24 in), exh. LG March 1921, 10 gns
- E34 *Nude*, c.1921, oil, DG, 45.72 × 53.34 cm (18 × 21 in), exh. Derby 1921, £25
- E35 *The Tube*, c.1921, Watercolour, DG, 48.26 × 60.96 cm (19 × 24 in) exh Derby 1921, £10

E10 *The Children's Matinée*, 1913, Private collection

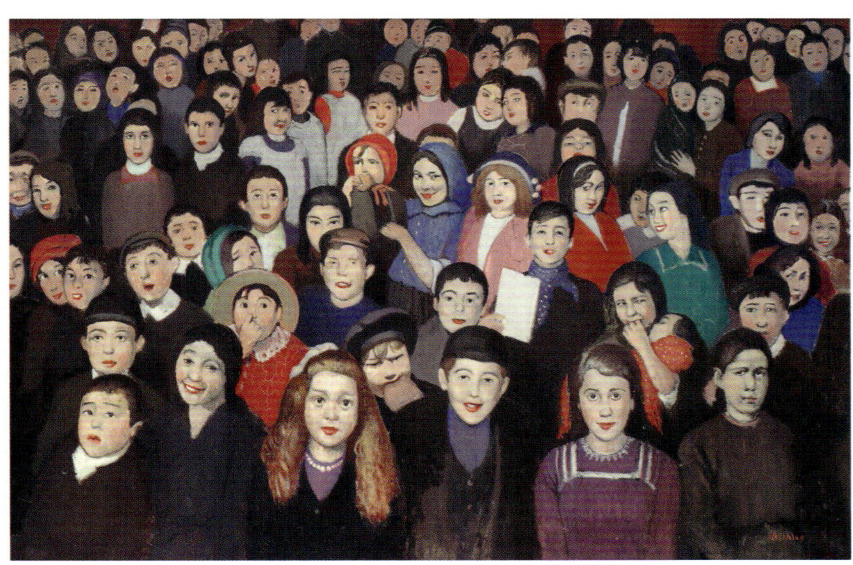

E36 *Sleep*, c.1913, drawing, CR, 48.26 × 60.96 cm (19 × 24 in), exh. Derby 1921, £6

E37 *Portrait Study 2*, c.1921, chalk, DG, 48.26 × 60.96 cm (19 × 24 in), exh. Derby 1921, £8 (sold)

E38 *Bust*, c.1921, charcoal, DG, 48.26 × 60.96 cm (19 × 24 in), exh. Derby 1921, £6

E39 *Nude Standing*, c.1921, chalk, DG, 48.26 × 60.96 cm (19 × 24 in), exh. Derby 1921, £6

E40 *King George and the Green Candle*, c.1921, oil, DG, 50.8 × 60.96 cm (20 × 24 in), sold to Gertrude Ihlee (sister)

E41 *The Deserted House*, c.1921, oil, Nether Stowey, 33.02 × 40.64 cm (13 × 16 in), exh. LG March 1921, £15 (sold)

E42 *Odalisque*, 1920, oil, DG, 50.8 × 60.96 cm (20 × 24 in), exh. LG March 1921, £35

E43 *The Idol at the Window*, c.1921, oil, DG, 50.8 × 60.96 cm (20 × 24 in), exh. LG March 1921, £25

E44 *Mr Pedotti*, c.1921, oil, DG, 38.1 × 45.72 cm (15 × 18 in), exh. LG March 1921, £25

E45 *Three Graces*, c.1921, oil, DG, 63.5 × 76.2 cm (25 × 30 in), exh. LG March 1921, £40

E46 *A Portrait Sketch*, c.1921, oil, DG, 25.4 × 35.56 cm (10 × 14 in), exh. LG March 1921, £25 (sold)

E47 *Drayton Gardens*, c.1921, oil, DG, 33.02 × 40.64 cm (13 × 16 in), exh. Goupil Gallery 1921

E48 *Jenefer*, c.1921, oil, DG, 33.02 × 40.64 cm (13 × 16 in), exh. NEAC winter 1921–2, sold

E49 *Study of a Bottle 1*, c.1921, oil, DG, 33.02 × 40.64 cm (13 × 16 in), exh. Friday Club

E50 *Study of a Bottle 2*, c.1921, oil, DG, 33.02 × 40.64 cm (13 × 16 in)

E51 *In the King's Road*, c.1921, oil, DG, 45.2 × 53.34 cm (18 × 21 in), exh. NEAC 1922

E52 *Creswell Place*, c.1921, oil, DG, 33.02 × 40.64 cm (13 × 16 in)

E53 *Billie*, c.1921, oil, DG, 33.02 × 40.64 cm (13 × 16 in)

E54 *Man with Spotted Tie*, 1921, oil, DG, 41 × 33 cm (16 × 13 in)

In March 1912 Ihlee showed 38 drawings at the Carfax Gallery with the following titles:
1 *Le Célibitaire*, 2 *Samson and Delilah*, 3 *In the Shadows*, 4 *It Rains*, 5 *The Dinner Hour*, 6 *Miner's Crouch*, 7 *Women Deriding a Dwarf*, 8 *Promenade*, 9 *Rêverie*, 10 *Woman Asleep*, 11 *The Window*, 12 *Conversation*, 13 *Revenge of Satan*, 14 *The Sisters*, 15 *The Repast*, 16 *Sonia*, 17 *Study of a Head*, 18 *The Necklace*, 19 *The Loose Blouse*, 20 *Sabbath*, 21 *Illustration: Little Claus at the Farmer's*, 22 *Girl Reading*, 23 *Portrait Drawing*, 24 *Interval*, 25 *The Collar Finisher*, 26 *'Give Me to Drink'*, 27 *Aria*, 28 *The Reader*, 29 *The Girls' Heads*, 30 *Mother and Child*, 31 *Ketch in a Music Hall*, 32 *The Downgoing*, 33 *Evening*, 34 *The Young Mother*, 35 *The Firstborn*, 36 *Houses on Hill*, 37 *The Auditorium*, 38 *Workgirls*

In March 1914 Ihlee showed 19 paintings and 16 drawings at the Carfax Gallery with the following titles and prices:

Paintings: 1 *Head of Woman No.1* (24 gns), 2 *A Pool* (25 gns), 3 *Head of Woman No.2* (24 gns), 4 *Le Bon Dieu sort de l'église* (50 gns), 5 *New Boots aka The Bootshop* (60 gns), 6 *The Godless One* (160 gns), 7 *The Children's Matinée* (60 gns), 8 *The Red Sun* (20 gns), 9 *Behind the Garage* (40 gns), 10 *In the Country* (130 gns), 11 *Breton Woman Washing* (40 gns), 12 *Across the Table* (25 gns), 13 *Portrait*, 14 *On the Road* (120 gns) 15 *The Well* (100 gns), 16 *In the Fields* (60 gns), 17 *Temporary Neighbours* (50 gns), 18 *The Knitter* (24 gns), 19 *The Idler* (25 gns)
Drawings: 20 *Pounding the Bait* (15 gns), 21 *Study for 'The Magic Wand'* (8 gns), 22 *On the Balcony* (6 gns), 23 *Nude* (6 gns), 24 *Alf Weller* (6 gns), 25 *The Pet* (15 gns), 26 *Study of Heads* (7 gns), 27 *Maria Hervé No.1* (7 gns), 28 *Young Girl* (6 gns), 29 *Maria Hervé No.2* (8 gns), 30 *Shepherd Boy* (7 gns), 31 *Study for 'The Magic Wand'* (8 gns), 32 *Study for 'The Magic Wand'* (8 gns), 33 *Study for 'Le Bon Dieu sort de l'église'* (7 gns), 34 *Quéron François* (12 gns), 35 *Geese* (7 gns)

Brittany

Ihlee made several trips to Brittany before and after the First World War, mostly in the company of Edgar Hereford, whose future wife Marguerite Doher lived near Morlaix in Finistère. Their favourite painting spots included Trégastel on the Côte d'Armor, Le Diben near Plougasnou in northern Finistère and Audierne, Concarneau and Guilvinec in southern Finistère. They visited the region in 1913, 1914, 1919, 1920, 1921, 1923 and 1931.

B1 *The Well*, 1913, oil, 50.9 × 61 cm (20 × 24 in), exh. Carfax Gallery 1914, sold to Charles Rutherston, gifted to Manchester City Art Gallery

B2 *Breton Folk*, 1913, oil, 91.44 × 121.92 cm (36 × 48 in), exh. Belgrave Gallery, London 1978

B3 *Group of Breton Folk*, 1913, oil, 66.04 × 91.44 cm (26 × 36 in), exh. Belgrave Gallery 1978

B4 *The Two Maids*, 1914, oil, 45.72 × 38.1 cm (18 × 15 in)

B5 *Peapicker Resting*, 1914, oil, 45.72 × 38.1 cm (18 × 15 in), exh. Friday Club 1919

B6 *Berry Pickers*, 1919, oil, 50.8 × 60.96 cm (20 × 24 in), exh. Belgrave Gallery 1978

B7 *The Small Estate, Brittany*, 1920, oil, 45.72 × 38.1 cm (15 × 18 in), exh. LG 1921, £15

B8 *Village Street, Brittany*, 1920, oil, 66 × 53.34 cm (26 × 21 in), exh. LG 1921, £40

B9 *Black Cattle*, c.1920, oil, 63.5 × 76.2 cm (25 × 30 in), exh. LG 1921, £50, Derby 1921, Whitechapel 1924

B10 *Breton Woman*, c.1921, oil, 40.64 × 33.02 cm (16 × 13 in), exh. Belgrave Gallery 1978

B11 *Gosses*, 1921, oil, 71.12 × 91.44 cm (28 × 36 in), exh. LG 1921, £60

B12 *Augustine*, 1921, oil, 60.96 × 50.8 cm (24 × 20 in), exh. Goupil Gallery 1921

B13 *The Red Gate Posts*, c.1921, oil, 40.64 × 33 cm (16 × 13 in), exh. LG 1921, £16, Government Art Collection

B14 *Breton Girl*, 1921, drawing, 38 × 30 cm (15 × 11 in), exh. Belgrave Gallery 1978

B15 *Three Boys by a Wall (study for Gosses)*, 1921, drawing, 38 × 30 cm (15 × 11 in), exh. Belgrave Gallery 1978

B16 *Three Breton Girls*, 1921, drawing, 38 × 30 cm (15 × 11 in), exh. Belgrave Gallery 1978

B17 Peasant Girl Standing, c.1920, drawing, Le Diben, 48.26 × 60.96 cm (19 × 24 in), exh. LG 1921, £6

B18 *Rocks Trégastel*, c.1920, oil, Le Diben, 25.4 × 35.56 cm (10 × 14 in), exh. LG 1921, £15

B19 *Bathers*, c.1920, oil, Le Diben, 38.1 × 45.72 cm (15 × 18 in), exh. LG 1921, £25

B20 *Room 17*, c.1920, oil, Trégastel, 40.64 × 55.88 cm (16 × 22 in), exh. Derby 1921, £20

B21 *Peasant Girl Seated*, c.1920, drawing, Le Diben, 48.26 × 60.96 cm (19 × 24 in), exh. Derby 1921, £6

B22 *Peasant Girl with Basket*, c.1920, drawing, Le Diben, 48.26 × 60.96 cm (19 × 24 in), exh. Derby 1921, £6

B23 *La Femme des rochers*, c.1920, oil, Le Diben, 25.4 × 35.56 cm (10 × 14 in), exh. Derby 1921, £12

B24 *Primel Station*, c.1920, oil, Le Diben, 33.02 × 40.64 cm (13 × 16 in), exh. LG 1921, £25

B25 *The Three Fishermen*, c.1920, oil, Le Diben, 50.8 × 60.96 cm (20 × 24 in), exh. LG 1921, £30

B26 *Les deux brodeuses*, 1921, oil, Guilvinec, 50.8 × 60.96 cm (20 × 24 in), exh. Goupil Gallery 1921

B27 *Shipyard 1*, 1921, oil, Guilvinec, 38.1 × 45.72 cm (15 × 18 in), exh. Goupil Gallery 1921

B28 *Mélanie*, c.1921, drawing, Guilvinec, 48.26 × 60.96 cm (19 × 24 in)

B29 *Breton Boy*, c.1921, drawing, Guilvinec, 48.26 × 60.96 cm (19 × 24 in)

B30 *Les deux brodeuses*, c.1921, drawing, Guilvinec, 48.26 × 60.96 cm (19 × 24 in)

B31 *Bigoudène Back View*, c.1921, drawing, Guilvinec, 48.26 × 60.96 cm (19 × 24 in)

B32 *Mélanie with Flower*, c.1921, drawing, Guilvinec, 48.26 × 60.96 cm (19 × 24 in)

B33 *La Boiteuse*, c.1921, drawing, Guilvinec, 48.26 × 60.96 cm (19 × 24 in)

B34 *Mélanie*, c.1921, ink, Guilvinec, 48.26 × 60.96 cm (19 × 24 in)

B35 *3 Bigoudènes Front*, c.1921, drawing, Guilvinec, 48.26 × 60.96 cm (19 × 24 in)

B36 *3 Bigoudènes Back*, c.1921, drawing, Guilvinec, 48.26 × 60.96 cm (19 × 24 in)

B37 *La Boiteuse*, c.1921, oil, Guilvinec, 33.02 × 40.64 cm (13 × 16 in)

B38 *Mélanie*, c.1921, oil, Guilvinec, 50.8 × 60.96 cm (20 × 24 in), exh. NEAC winter 1921/2, 25 gns (sold)

B39 *Bal*, c.1921, oil, Guilvinec, 63.5 × 76.2 cm (25 × 30 in), exh. NEAC winter 1921/2

B40 *The High Road*, c.1921, oil, Guilvinec, 38.1 × 45.72 cm (15 × 18 in), exh. Whitechapel 1923, Derby 1923

B41 *Madame Baltés*, c.1921, oil, Guilvinec, 25.4 × 35.56 cm (10 × 14 in), exh. Friday Club

B42 *Shipyard 2*, c.1921, oil, Guilvinec, 38.1 × 45.72 cm (15 × 18 in)

B43 *Augustine en Bigoudène*, c.1921, oil, Guilvinec, 38.1 × 45.72 cm (15 × 18 in)

B44 *Léchiagat Evening*, c.1921, oil, Guilvinec, 38.1 × 45.72 cm (15 × 18 in)

B45 *Sea View, Guilvinec*, c.1921, oil, Guilvinec, 25.4 × 35.56 cm (10 × 14 in)

B46 *View from Window*, c.1921, oil, Guilvinec, 25.4 × 35.56 cm (10 × 14 in)

B47 *Smiling Bigoudène*, c.1921, oil, Guilvinec, 25.4 × 35.56 cm (10 × 14 in), exh. Derby 1922

B48 *Mélanie Head*, c.1921, oil, Guilvinec, 25.4 × 35.56 cm (10 × 14 in), exh. Goupil Gallery 1923

B49 *Monsieur Tirilly*, c.1921, oil, Guilvinec, 25.4 × 35.56 cm (10 × 14 in)

B50 *Church Guilvinec*, c.1921, oil, Guilvinec, 25.4 × 35.56 cm (10 × 14 in)

B51 *Guilvinec across the Water*, c.1921, oil, Guilvinec, 38.1 × 45.7 cm (15 × 18 in)

B52 *Audierne Fisherman*, c.1921, oil, Guilvinec, 38.1 × 45.72 cm (15 × 18 in)

B53 *Little Bay – Audierne*, c.1923, oil, Audierne, 38.1 × 45.72 cm (15 × 18 in), exh. NEAC 1925, £15 (sold), collection, Cyfarthfa Castle Museum and Art Gallery, Merthyr Tydfil

B54 *The Quay at Audierne*, c.1923, oil, Audienne, 38.1 × 45.72 cm (15 × 18 in), exh. Chenil Gallery 1926, £20 (sold)

B55 *Reflections*, c.1923, oil, Concarneau, 50.8 × 60.96 cm (20 × 24 in), exh. Chenil Gallery 1926, £25 (sold)

B56 *The Bad Actress*, c.1923, oil, Concarneau, 38.1 × 45.72 cm (15 × 18 in), exh. Redfern Gallery 1924, £15

B57 *Breton Farm*, 1931, oil, Brittany, 38.1 × 45.72 cm (15 × 18 in), exh. Galerie Campistro, Perpignan 1931

B58 *Winter Brittany*, 1931, oil, 38.1 × 45.72 cm (15 × 18 in), given to Albert Doher

Algeria

A1 *Ouled Nayl*, 1922, oil, Biskra, 50.8 × 60.96 cm (20 × 24 in), exh. Goupil Gallery 1922, Derby 1923

A2 *Nocturne Biskra*, 1922, oil, Biskra, 50.8 × 60.96 cm (20 × 24 in), exh. NEAC 1922, Scottish Academy 1923, bought by Mrs Peploe of India St, Edinburgh (wife of painter Samuel Peploe)

A3 *Ante-chamber Moorish Baths*, 1922, oil, Biskra, 50.8 × 60.96 cm (20 × 24 in)

A4 *The Quay, Algiers*, 1922, oil, Algiers, 38.1 × 45.72 cm (15 × 18 in), exh. Chenil Gallery 1926

A5 *Palms against Sunlight*, 1922, oil, Biskra, 38.1 × 45.72 cm (15 × 18 in), exh. Chenil Gallery 1926

A6 *Ouled Silver & Blue*, 1922, oil, Biskra, 38.1 × 45.72 cm (15 × 18 in), exh. Chenil Gallery 1926

A7 *Ouled on Balcony*, 1922, oil, Biskra, 38.1 × 45.72 cm (15 × 18 in), exh. Chenil Gallery 1926

A8 *Hotel du Zibans*, 1922, oil, Biskra, 38.1 × 45.72 cm (15 × 18 in), exh. Chenil Gallery 1926

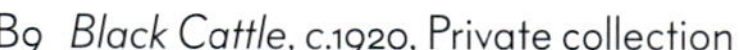

B9 *Black Cattle*, c.1920, Private collection

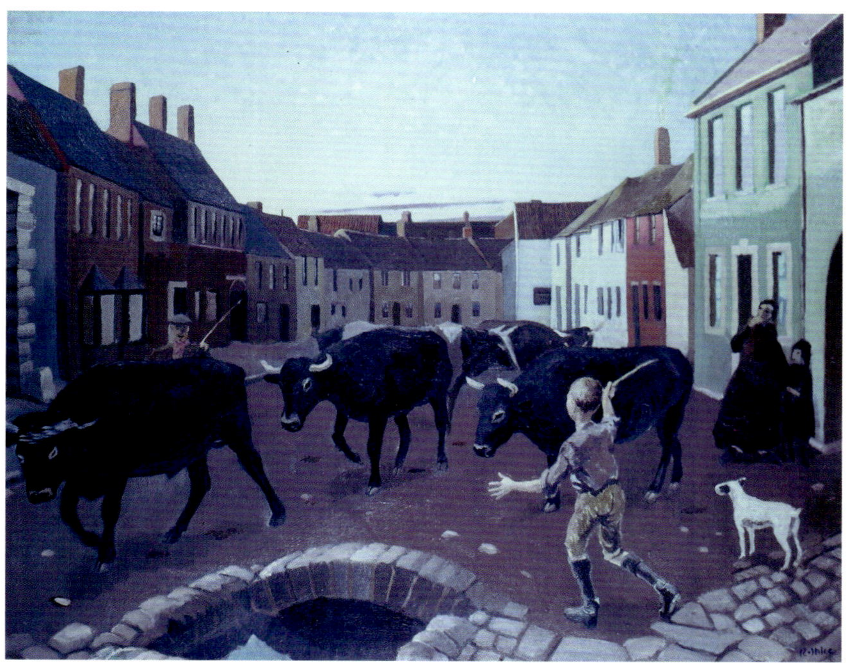

A9 *Rifle Range, Biskra*, 1922, oil, Biskra, 38.1 × 45.72 cm (15 × 18 in)

A10 *Senegalese Soldiers*, 1922, oil, Biskra, 38.1 × 45.72 cm (15 × 18 in), exh. NEAC 1923

A11 *Corn Merchant's Yard*, 1922, oil, Biskra, 38.1 × 45.72 cm (15 × 18 in), exh. NEAC 1923

A12 *Senegalese Gardening*, 1922, oil, Biskra, 38.1 × 45.72 cm (15 × 18 in), exh. Redfern Gallery 1924

A13 *Near the Station Biskra*, 1922, oil, Biskra, 38.1 × 45.72 cm (15 × 18 in)

A14 *Palms & Cracked Earth*, 1922, oil, Biskra, 38.1 × 45.72 cm (15 × 18 in)

A15 *Girl with Red Shawl*, 1922, oil, Biskra, 38.1 × 45.72 cm (15 × 18 in)

A16 *Jardin militaire*, 1922, oil, Biskra, 38.1 × 45.72 cm (15 × 18 in), exh. Chenil Gallery 1926

A17 *The Milkman*, 1922, oil, Biskra, 38.1 × 45.72 cm (15 × 18 in)

A18 *Young Arab Girl*, 1922, oil, Biskra, 38.1 × 45.72 cm (15 × 18 in)

A19 *Arab Boy*, 1922, oil, Biskra, 38.1 × 45.72 cm (15 × 18 in)

A20 *Palm Grove Interior*, 1922, oil, Biskra, 38.1 × 45.72 cm (15 × 18 in), exh. Chenil Gallery 1926

A21 *Mother Ouled Nayl*, 1922, oil, Biskra, 38.1 × 45.72 cm (15 × 18 in), exh. NEAC 1922

A22 *The Beggar*, 1922, oil, Biskra, 38.1 × 45.72 cm (15 × 18 in)

A23 *Palms against Sunlight 2*, 1922, oil, Biskra, 38.1 × 45.72 cm (15 × 18 in)

A24 *Little Arab Girl (Tattoo)*, 1922, oil, Biskra, 38.1 × 45.72 cm (15 × 18 in), exh. Goupil Gallery 1922, Bradford 1923

A25 *The Fritter Merchant*, 1922, oil, Biskra, 38.1 × 45.72 cm (15 × 18 in)

Collioure

C1 *By the Railway*, 1922, oil, 63.5 × 76.2 cm (25 × 30 in), exh. French Gallery 1922, 40 gns, Australia 1923

C2 *Sunset at Collioure*, 1922, oil, 63.5 × 76.2 cm (25 × 30 in), exh. Derby 1923

C3 *Simone qui lave*, 1922, oil, 63.5 × 76.2 cm (25 × 30 in), exh. NEAC 1922, £40, Whitechapel 1923, Derby 1923, Bradford 1924

C4 *The Handsome Fisher*, 1922, oil, 50.8 × 60.96 cm (20 × 24 in)

C5 *Collioure from the Railway*, 1922, oil, 50.8 × 60.96 cm (20 × 24 in), exh. NEAC 1923, £20

C6 *Fernande*, 1922, oil, 38.1 × 45.72 cm (15 × 18 in), exh. Chenil Gallery 1926, £16

C7 *By the Railway*, 1922, oil sketch, 38.1 × 45.72 cm (15 × 18 in), given to Honoré Soulier

C8 *Senegalese at Collioure*, 1922, oil, 38.1 × 45.72 cm (15 × 18 in), given to Pauline (Quintana?)

C9 *The Jetty*, 1922, oil, 38.1 × 45.72 cm (15 × 18 in), exh. Chenil Gallery 1926, £16

C10 *Interior*, 1924, oil, 76.2 × 76.2 cm (30 × 25 in)

C11 *Cafetière*, 1924, oil, 50.8 × 60.96 cm (20 × 24 in)

C12 *Sugar Fishes*, 1924, oil, 38.1 × 45.72 cm (15 × 18 in)

C13 *The Palm in the Garden*, 1924, oil, 63.5 × 76.2 cm (25 × 30 in), exh. Chenil Gallery 1926, £60

C14 *Palm and Viaduct*, 1924, oil, 38.1 × 45.72 cm (15 × 18 in)

C15 *Still Life*, 1924, oil, 38.1 × 45.72 cm (15 × 18 in)

C16 *The Grey Castle*, 1924, oil, 38.1 × 45.72 cm (15 × 18 in), exh. Chenil Gallery 1926, £20

C17 *L'Heure de la soupe*, 1924, oil, 63.5 × 76.2 cm (25 × 30 in), exh. NEAC 1924

C18 *Gardens at Collioure*, 1924, oil, 60.96 × 50.8 cm (24 × 20 in)

C19 *The Grand Café*, 1924, oil, 63.5 × 76.2 cm (25 × 30 in), exh. Belgrave Gallery 1978

C20 *The Dry River*, 1924, oil, 50.8 × 60.96 cm (20 × 24 in), exh. NEAC 1925

C21 *The Paper Girl*, 1924, oil, 76.2 × 63.5 cm (30 × 25 in), exh. NEAC 1925

C22 *My Window Collioure*, 1925, oil, 63.5 × 76.2 cm (25 × 30 in), exh. Chenil Gallery 1926, £60

C23 *The House by the Pines*, 1925, oil, 60.96 × 50.8 cm (24 × 20 in), exh. Chenil Gallery 1926, £40

C24 *The Faubourg*, 1925, oil, 38.1 × 45.72 cm (15 × 18 in), exh. Chenil Gallery 1926, £20

C25 *The Temple*, 1925, oil, 76.2 × 63.5 cm (30 × 25 in), exh. Chenil Gallery 1926, £60

C26 *The Tree Stumps*, 1925, oil, 50.8 × 60.96 cm (20 × 24 in), exh. Chenil Gallery 1926, £40

C27 *Behind the House*, 1925, oil, 60.96 × 50.8 cm (24 × 20 in), exh. Chenil Gallery 1926, £40

C28 *The Arch*, 1925, oil, 96.52 × 81.28 cm (38 × 32 in)

C29 *The Car by the Trees*, 1925, oil, 76.2 × 63.5 cm (30 × 25 in), exh. Chenil Gallery 1926, £60

A11 *Corn Merchant's Yard, Biskra*, 1922, Private collection

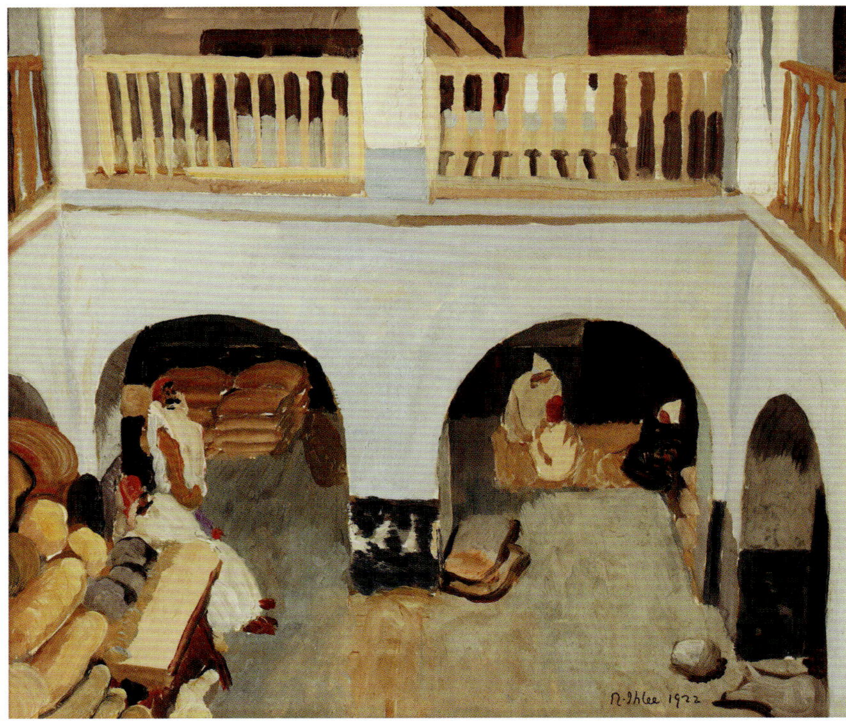

C30 *The Cork Wood*, 1925, oil, 63.5 × 76.2 cm (25 × 30 in), exh. Venice 1926, Goupil Gallery 1927

C31 *The Heath*, 1925, oil, 63.5 × 76.2 cm (25 × 30 in), exh. Chenil Gallery 1926, £60

C32 *The Festival at Laroque*, 1925, oil, 40.64 × 33 cm (16 × 13 in), exh. Chenil Gallery 1926, £25

C33 *Beside the Bridge*, 1925, oil, 63.5 × 76.2 cm (25 × 30 in), exh. Walker Art Gallery 1926

C34 *Corkwood Interior*, 1925, oil, 38.1 × 45.72 cm (15 × 18 in), exh. Chenil Gallery 1926, £20

C35 *Avenue*, 1925, oil, 76.2 × 63.5 cm (30 × 25 in), exh. Chenil Gallery 1926, £60

C36 *The Red Wood*, 1925, oil, 60.96 × 50.8 cm (24 × 20 in), exh. Chenil Gallery 1926, £40

C37 *By the Milestone*, 1925, oil, 63.5 × 76.2 cm (25 × 30 in), exh. Chenil Gallery 1926, £60

C38 *The Clear Road*, 1925, oil, 50.8 × 60.96 cm (20 × 24 in), exh. Chenil Gallery 1926, £40

C39 *St Luke's*, Summer, 1925, oil, 50.8 × 60.96 cm (20 × 24 in), exh. Chenil Gallery 1926, £40

C40 *The Turn by the Railway*, 1925, oil, 50.8 × 60.96 cm (20 × 24 in), exh. Chenil Gallery 1926, £40

C41 Le Boulou, 1926, oil, 50.8 × 60.96 cm (20 × 24 in), exh. Goupil Gallery 1927

C42 *Les Trois Arbres*, 1926, oil, 60.96 × 50.8 cm (24 × 20 in), exh. Salon d'Automne 1926, 1200 francs

C43 *Les Alentours du village*, 1926, oil, 50.8 × 60.96 cm (20 × 24 in), exh. Salon d'Automne 1926, 1200 francs

C44 *The Red Arch*, 1926, oil, 63.5 × 76.2 cm (25 × 30 in), exh. NEAC 1926, £60

C45 *The Cellars of Port Vendres*, 1926, oil, 50.8 × 60.96 cm (20 × 24 in), exh. NEAC 1927

C46 *The Facade*, 1926, oil, 63.5 × 76.2 cm (25 × 30 in), exh. Goupil Gallery 1927

C47 *Out of My Window*, 1926, oil, 38.1 × 45.72 cm (15 × 18 in)

C48 Under the Trees, 1926, oil, 76.2 × 65.5 cm (30 × 25 in)

C49 *The Gutter*, 1926, oil, 63.5 × 76.2 cm (25 × 30 in), exh. NEAC 1927

C50 *Landscape with Jug*, 1926, oil, 63.5 × 76.2 cm (25 × 30 in), exh. NEAC 1927

C51 *The Cutting*, 1926, oil, 38.1 × 45.72 cm (15 × 18 in), exh. NEAC 1927

C52 *The Terrace*, 1926, oil, 38.1 × 45.72 cm (15 × 18 in), exh. Goupil 1927

C53 *La Place*, 1926, oil, 50.8 × 60.96 cm (20 × 24 in), exh. Goupil Gallery 1927

C54 *Military Architecture*, 1926, oil, 63.5 × 76.2 cm (25 × 30 in), exh. Goupil Gallery 1927

C55 *The Square Fort*, 1926, oil, 38.1 × 45.72 cm (15 × 18 in)

C56 *Landscape with Cat*, 1926, oil, 81.28 × 96.52 cm (32 × 38 in), exh. NEAC 1927

C57 *The Rocky Valley*, 1926, oil, 38.1 × 45.72 cm (15 × 18 in)

C58 *Houses and Tombs*, 1927, oil, 50.8 × 60.96 cm (20 × 24 in)

C59 *Rain among the Hills*, 1927, oil, 38.1 × 45.72 cm (15 × 18 in)

C60 *Coconut Palms*, 1927, oil, 38.1 × 45.72 cm (15 × 18 in)

C61 *The Castle, Vignette*, 1927, oil, 38.1 × 45.72 cm (15 × 18 in)

C62 *Landscape with Mule*, 1927, oil, 38.1 × 45.72 cm (15 × 18 in), exh. NEAC 1929

C63 *The Cooper's Yard*, 1927, oil, 38.1 × 45.72 cm (15 × 18 in), exh. NEAC 1929

C64 *The Soapy Stream*, 1927, oil,, 63.5 × 76.2 cm (25 × 30 in), exh. Imperial Art Gallery 1930, Sleaford 1968, 40 gns (sold)

C65 *The Aloe*, 1927, oil, 38.1 × 45.72 cm (15 × 18 in)

C66 *Paysage jaune*, 1927, oil, 38.1 × 45.72 cm (15 × 18 in), exh. Salon des Indépendants, 1200 francs

C67 *The Castle by the Sea*, 1927, oil, 88.9 × 53.34 cm (35 × 21 in)

C68 *The Disused Church*, 1927, oil, 63.5 × 76.2 cm (25 × 30 in)

C69 *Fort Miradou Precincts*, 1927, oil, 38.1 × 45.72 cm (15 × 18 in), Hunterian Art Gallery, Glasgow

C70 *Autumn Landscape*, 1927, oil, 50.8 × 60.96 cm (20 × 24 in)

C71 *The Old Town*, 1927, oil, 38.1 × 45.72 cm (15 × 18 in)

C72 *Design, Grey and Yellow*, 1927, oil, 50.8 × 60.96 cm (20 × 24 in)

C73 *Rain among the Hills*, study, 1927, oil, 38.1 × 45.72 cm (15 × 18 in)

C74 *Towards the Mountain*, 1927, oil, 100 × 81 cm (39 by 32 in)

C75 *Le Château*, 1927, oil, Coll, 81 × 100 cm (32 × 39 in), exh. Salon des Indépendants, 5000 francs

C76 *Red Landscape*, 1927, oil, 83.82 × 129.54 cm (38 × 51 in), exh. NEAC 1929

C77 *Le Port*, 1928, oil, 50.8 × 60.96 cm (20 × 24 in), exh. Salon des Indépendants 1929

C78 *The Waterfall*, 1928, oil, 63.5 × 76.2 cm (25 × 30 in), exh. NEAC 1929, Ferens Gallery, Hull 1930, £40

C79 *Albas*, 1928, oil, 1928, 83.82 × 129.54 cm (38 × 51 in)

C80 *The Distant Mountain*, 1929, oil, 100 × 81cm (39 × 32 in), exh. NEAC 1929

C81 *Nocturnal Conversation (The Plot)*, 1929, oil, 100 × 81 cm (39 × 32 in), exh. NEAC 1929

C82 *Group*, 1929, oil, 38.1 × 45.72 cm (15 × 18 in)

C83 *Village Pump, Night*, 1930, oil, 50.8 × 60.96 cm (20 × 24 in), exh. Galerie Campistro, Perpignan 1931

C84 *Still Life, Lemons*, 1930, oil, 38.1 × 45.72 cm (15 × 18 in), exh. Galerie Campistro 1931

C85 *Sea Shore*, 1930, oil, 63.5 × 76.2 cm (25 × 30 in)

C86 *Bay, Faubourg*, 1930, oil, 63.5 × 76.2 cm (25 × 30 in), exh. Galerie Campistro 1931

C87 *Glacis, Collioure*, 1930, oil, 38.1 × 45.72 cm (15 × 18 in), exh. Galerie Campistro 1931

C88 *Seated Figure*, 1930, oil, 38.1 × 40.64 cm (16 × 18 in)

C89 *Winter in the South*, 1931, oil, 50.8 × 60.96 cm (20 × 24 in)

C90 *Profile*, 1931, oil, 38.1 × 45.72 cm (15 × 18 in), exh. Galerie Campistro 1931

C91 *The Red Blouse*, 1931, oil, 50.8 × 60.96 cm (20 × 24 in), exh. Galerie Campistro 1931

C92 *Ecole maternelle*, 1931, oil, 38.1 × 45.72 cm (15 × 18 in)

C93 *Terrace Consolation*, 1932, oil, 50.8 × 60.96 cm (20 × 24 in), exh. Galerie Campistro, 1932, Musée d'Art Moderne, Collioure

C94 *Sous les arbres*, 1932, oil, 60 × 73 cm (24 × 28 in), exh. Galerie Campistro 1932

C95 *Le Mas*, 1932, oil, 60 × 73 cm (24 × 28 in), exh. Galerie Campistro 1932

C96 *Petites Maisons, Collioure (Faubourg)*, 1932, oil, 38.1 × 45.72 cm (15 × 18 in), exh. Galerie Campistro 1932

C97 *Les Arbres nus*, 1932, oil, 60 × 73 cm (24 × 28 in), exh. Salon des Tuileries 1933, Goupil Gallery 1937

C98 *Les Filets, Collioure*, 1932, oil, 50.8 × 60.96 cm (20 × 24 in), exh. Galerie Campistro 1932

C99 *Château Villerouge*, 1933, oil, 50.8 × 60.96 cm (20 × 24 in), exh. Salle Arago 1934

C100 *La Placette, étude*, 1933, oil, 38.1 × 45.72 cm (15 × 18 in)

C101 *La Placette*, 1933, oil, 63.5 × 76.2 cm (25 × 30 in), exh. Salon des Tuileries 1933, Salle Arago 1934, NEAC 1935, £60

C102 *La Cabane*, 1933, oil, 50.8 × 60.96 cm (20 × 24 in), exh. Salle Arago 1934

C103 *La Descente du Miradou*, 1933, oil, 60 × 73 cm (24 × 28 in), exh. Salon des Indépendants 1933

C104 *L'Ane sous l'arbre*, 1933, oil, 47 × 56 cm (18.5 × 22 in), exh. Salle Arago 1934
C105 *Portrait au fond gris*, 1933, oil, 38.1 × 45.72 cm (15 × 18 in), exh. Salle Arago 1934
C106 *Portrait (Marcelle)*, 1933, oil, 47 × 56 cm (18.5 × 22 in), exh. Salle Arago 1934
C107 *Jeune Fille au corsage bleu*, 1933, oil, 38.1 × 45.72 cm (15 × 18 in), exh. Salle Arago 1934
C108 *Portrait de peintre Moros*, 1933, oil, 50.8 × 60.96 cm (20 × 24 in), exh. Salon des Tuileries 1934
C109 *Le Fort St Elme*, 1933, oil, 50.8 × 60.96 cm (20 × 24 in), exh. Salle Arago 1934
C110 *Temps sombre à Collioure*, 1933, oil, 50.8 × 60.96 cm (20 × 24 in), exh. Salle Arago 1934
C111 *Les Remparts du Miradou*, 1933, oil, 50.8 × 60.96 cm (20 × 24 in), exh. Salle Arago 1934
C112 *Maisons du Faubourg*, 1933, oil, 50.8 × 60.96 cm (20 × 24 in), exh. Salle Arago 1934
C113 *Montagnes et orangiers*, 1933, oil, 60 × 73 cm (24 × 28 in), exh. Salle Arago 1934, NEAC 1935, Birmingham 1936, Collection Hull University
C114 *Le Canigou*, 1934, oil, 50.8 × 60.96 cm (20 × 24 in), exh. Salon des Tuileries 1934, NEAC 1936
C115 *Au Racou*, 1934, oil, 50.8 × 60.96 cm (20 × 24 in)
C116 *Nu blonde*, 1934, oil, 50.8 × 60.96 cm (20 × 24 in)
C117 *Paysage du printemps*, 1934, oil, 47 × 56 cm (18.5 × 22 in), exh. Salon des Tuileries 1935, NEAC 1935, Leicester Galleries 1936, £25
C118 *Clos St Pierre*, 1934, oil, 47 × 56 cm (18.5 × 22 in)
C119 *Coin ombragé*, 1934, oil, 60 × 73 cm (24 × 28 in)
C120 *Palmiers*, 1934, oil, 47 × 56 cm (18.5 × 22 in)
C121 *La Route, le soir*, 1934, oil, 50.8 × 60.96 cm (20 × 24 in)
C122 *Après-midi gris*, 1934, oil, 50.8 × 60.96 cm (20 × 24 in)
C123 *La Baie du Faubourg*, 1934, oil, 50.8 × 60.96 cm (20 × 24 in), exh. Goupil Gallery 1937
C124 *La Placette ombragée*, 1934, oil, 50.8 × 60.96 cm (20 × 24 in), exh. Salon des Tuileries 1936
C125 *Poivrons*, 1934, oil, 47 × 56 cm (18.5 × 22 in)
C126 *La Plage du Racou*, 1934, oil, 50.8 × 60.96 cm (20 × 24 in)
C127 *Collioure de chez Monsieur Le Brun*, 1934, oil, 60 × 73 cm (24 × 28 in), exh. Salon des Tuileries 1935, NEAC 1935, Leicester Galleries 1936, £50
C128 *La Poule en verre*, 1935, oil, 38.1 × 45.72 cm (15 × 18 in), exh. Salon des Tuileries 1935, NEAC 1935, £15
C129 *Nature morte*, 1935, oil, 38.1 × 45.72 cm (15 × 18 in)
C130 *L'Espagnole, Rosaleo*, 1935, oil, 50.8 × 60.96 cm (20 × 24 in)
C131 *L'Interieur*, 1934, oil, 47 × 56 cm (18.5 × 22 in)
C132 *Still Life with Green Jug*, 1936, oil, 50.8 × 60.96 cm (20 × 24 in)
C133 *Still Life with Bread and Bottle*, 1936, oil, 50.8 × 60.96 cm (20 × 24 in)
C134 *Still Life with Leeks*, 1936, oil, 60 × 73 cm (24 × 28 in)
C135 *Still Life with Red Pot*, 1936, oil, 60 × 73 cm (24 × 28 in)
C136 *Still Life with Casserole Rouge*, 1936, oil, 60 × 73 cm (24 × 28 in)
C137 *Still Life, Villa Franca*, 1936, oil, 60 × 73 cm (24 × 28 in)
C138 *Petite Nature Morte aux fruits*, 1936, oil, 38.1 × 45.72 cm (15 × 18 in)
C139 *Outskirts of Collioure*, c.1938, oil, 51 × 61cm (20 × 24 in)
C140 *Tour de Madeloc*, c.1938, oil, 46 × 56 cm (18 × 22 in)

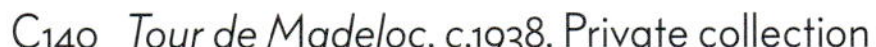

C140 *Tour de Madeloc*, c.1938, Private collection

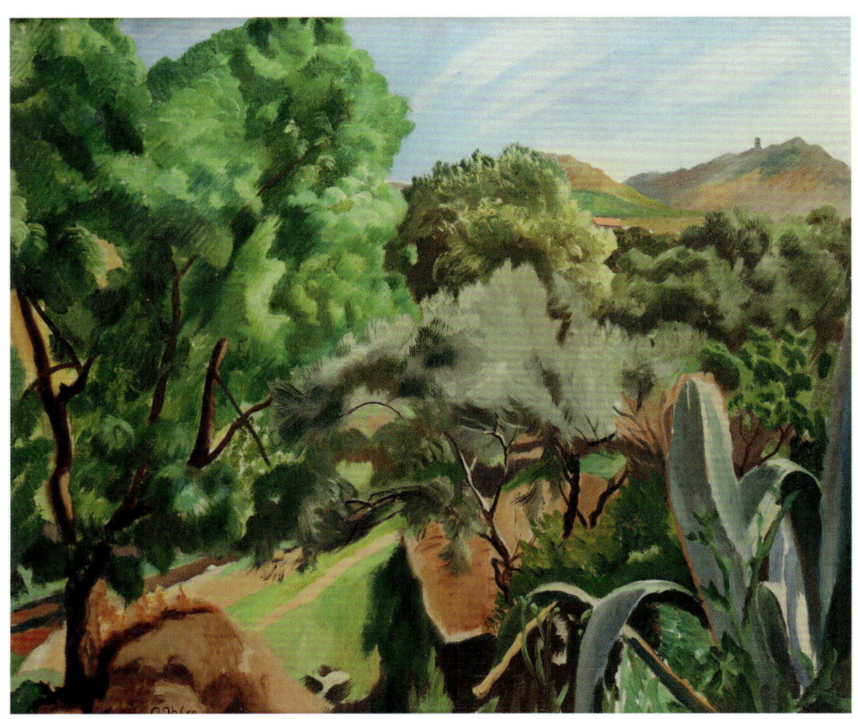

Languedoc-Roussillon

Ihlee and Hereford visited several places in easy driving distance of Collioure in the Languedoc-Roussillon region, which consisted of five departments; the Pyrénées-Orientales (P-O), the Aude (AU), Hérault (HE), the Gard (G) and Lozère (L). The region has since been expanded to 13 departments and renamed Occitanie.

LR1 *Port Vendres*, 1924, oil, PV (P-O), 76.2 × 63.5 cm (30 × 25 in), exh. Goupil Gallery 1924
LR2 *The Little Factory*, 1926, oil, Arles-sur-Tech (P-O), 38.1 × 45.72 cm (15 × 18 in), exh. Goupil Gallery 1928
LR3 *Arles Sketch*, 1926, oil, Arles-sur-Tech (P-O), 38.1 × 45.72 cm (15 × 18 in)
LR4 *A Stream*, 1927, oil, Elne (P-O), 38.1 × 45.72 cm (15 × 18 in)
LR5 *The Valley*, 1927, oil, Mosset (P-O), 38.1 × 45.72 cm (15 × 18 in)
LR6 *Off the Road*, 1927, oil, Molitg (P-O), 38.1 × 45.72 cm (15 × 18 in)
LR7 *The Narrow House*, 1927, oil, Prades (P-O), 38.1 × 45.72 cm (15 × 18 in)

LR8 *The Stone Wall*, 1927, oil, Molitg (P-O), 38.1 × 45.72 cm (15 × 18 in)

LR9 *Towards the Mountain*, 1927, oil, Clara (P-O), 38.1 × 45.72 cm (15 × 18 in)

LR10 *Les Arbres, la nuit*, 1928, oil, Perpignan (P-O), 81 × 100 cm (32 × 39 in), exh. Salon des Indépendants 1929, 5000 francs, Goupil Gallery 1929, £80

LR11 *The Distant Mountain*, 1928, oil, Molitg (P-O), 38.1 × 45.72 cm (15 × 18 in), given to fellow artist Henri Vergé-Sarrat

LR12 *The Terrace*, 1928, oil, Molitg (P-O), 38.1 × 45.72 cm (15 × 18 in)

LR13 *Behind the Chapel*, 1928, oil, Molitg (P-O), 38.1 × 45.72 cm (15 × 18 in)

LR14 *The Road by the Rocks*, 1928, oil, Molitg (P-O), 50.8 × 60.96 cm (20 × 24 in)

LR15 *Study Campôme*, 1928, oil, Campôme (P-O), 38.1 × 45.72 cm (15 × 18 in)

LR16 *Rock, Vines and Olives*, 1928, oil, Molitg (P-O), 38.1 × 45.72 cm (15 × 18 in)

LR17 *Barrage*, 1928, oil, Molitg (P-O), 38.1 × 45.72 cm (15 × 18 in)

LR18 *Waterfall*, 1928, oil, Molitg (P-O), 38.1 × 45.72 cm (15 × 18 in)

LR19 *Waterfall 2*, 1928, oil, Molitg (P-O), 38.1 × 45.72 cm (15 × 18 in)

LR20 *Approaching the Bridge*, 1928, oil, Molitg (P-O), 38.1 × 45.72 cm (15 × 18 in)

LR21 *In the Pine Wood*, 1928, oil, Molitg (P-O), 38.1 × 45.72 cm (15 × 18 in)

LR22 *On the Edge of the Wood*, 1928, oil, Molitg (P-O), 38.1 × 45.72 cm (15 × 18 in)

LR23 *Serdinya*, 1928, oil, Joncet (P-O), 38.1 × 45.72 cm (15 × 18 in)

LR24 *The Vineyard Gate*, 1928, oil, St-Paul-de-Fenouillet (P-O), 38.1 × 45.72 cm (15 × 18 in)

LR25 *The Fallen Olive Tree*, 1928, oil, St-Paul-de-Fenouillet (P-O), 38.1 × 45.72 cm (15 × 18 in)

LR26 *Maury, the Golden Village*, 1928, oil, Maury (P-O), 38.1 × 45.72 cm (15 × 18 in)

LR27 *Olive Trees*, 1928, oil, Maury (P-O), 38.1 × 45.72 cm (15 × 18 in)

LR28 *The Marble Bridge*, 1928, oil, Albas (AU), 38.1 × 45.72 cm (15 × 18 in)

LR29 *Albas from Cemetery*, 1928, oil, Albas (AU), 38.1 × 45.72 cm (15 × 18 in)

LR30 *The Gorge*, 1928, oil, Félines-Minervois (HE), 38.1 × 45.72 cm (15 × 18 in)

LR31 *Campôme*, 1929, oil, Campôme (P-O), 120 × 100 cm (47.2 × 39.3 in)

LR32 *Fort Villefranche*, 1929, oil, Villefranche-de-Conflent (P-O), 38.1×45.72 cm (15×18 in)

LR33 *Square, Prades*, 1929, oil, Prades (P-O), 38.1 × 45.72 cm (15 × 18 in)

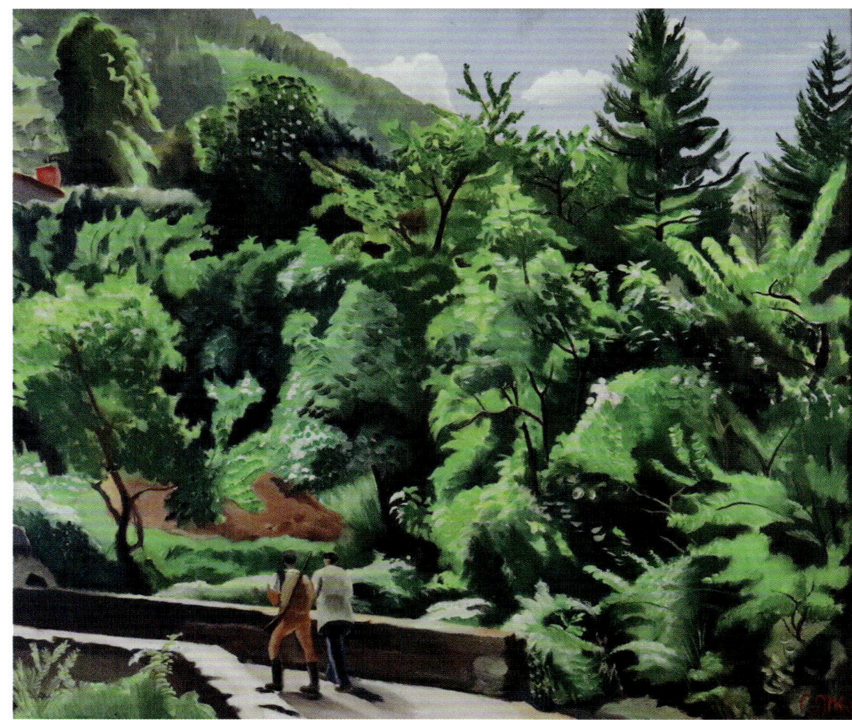

LR61 *Paysage boisé, Lapradelle*, 1934, Louise Kosman Fine Art

LR34 *Bridge*, 1929, oil, Villefranche-de-Conflent (P-O), 38.1 × 45.72 cm (15 × 18 in)

LR35 *Wine Country*, 1929, oil, Prades (P-O), 38.1 × 45.72 cm (15 × 18 in)

LR36 *River*, 1929, oil, St Chinian (HE), 38.1 × 45.72 cm (15 × 18 in)

LR37 *Roquebrun*, 1929, oil, Roquebrun (HE), 38.1 × 45.72 cm (15 × 18 in)

LR38 *Pierre Rue*, 1929, oil, St Chinian (HE), 38.1 × 45.72 cm (15 × 18 in)

LR39 *The Reservoir*, 1929, oil, St Chinian (HE), 38.1 × 45.72 cm (15 × 18 in)

LR40 *Roquebrun*, 1930, oil, St Chinian (HE), 100 × 120 cm (39.3 × 47.2 in), exh. NEAC 1932

LR41 *Nocturnes Félines*, 1930, oil, Félines (HE), 38.1 × 45.72 cm (15 × 18 in)

LR42 *Spanish Castle*, 1930, oil, St-Paul-de-Fenouillet (P-O), 63.5 × 76.2 cm (25 × 30 in), exh. Galerie Campistro 1931

LR43 *Winter in the South*, 1931, oil, Estagel (P-O), 50.8 × 60.96 cm (20 × 24 in), exh. Galerie Campistro 1931

LR44 *Agly Valley*, 1931, oil, Estagel (P-O), 38.1 × 45.72 cm (15 × 18 in), exh. Galerie Campistro 1931

LR45 *Grey Landscape*, 1931, oil, Estagel (P-O), 38.1 × 45.72 cm (15 × 18 in), exh. Galerie Campistro 1931

LR46 *Paysage Estagel*, 1931, oil, Estagel (P-O), 38.1 × 45.72 cm (15 × 18 in), exh. Galerie Campistro 1931

LR47 *Latour-de-France from Bend*, 1931, oil, Latour-de-France (P-O), 38.1 × 45.72 cm (15 × 18 in), exh. Galerie Campistro 1931

LR48 *Latour-de-France*, 1931, oil, Latour-de-France (P-O), 50.8 × 60.96 cm (20 × 24 in), exh. Galerie Campistro 1931

LR49 *Les Macons Félines*, 1931, oil, Félines (HE), 38.1 × 45.72 cm (15 × 18 in), exh. Galerie Campistro 1932

LR50 *Bend Félines*, 1932, oil, Félines (HE), 38.1 × 45.72 cm (15 × 18 in), exh. Galerie Campistro 1932

LR51 *Aux Tamarins, Port Vendres*, 1933, oil, PV (P-O), 47 × 56 cm (18.5 × 22 in), exh. Salle Arago 1934

LR52 *Vue de Port Vendres*, 1933, oil, PV (P-O), 38.1 × 45.72 cm (15 × 18 in), exh. Salle Arago 1934

LR53 *Portrait de Madame Martin*, 1933, oil, Félines (HE), 56 × 47 cm (22 × 18.5 in), exh. Salon des Indépendants 1933

LR54 *Port Vendres, le phare*, 1933, oil, PV (P-O), 47 × 56 cm (18.5 × 22 in), exh. Salle Arago 1934

LR55 *Les Pins, Port Vendres*, 1934, oil, PV (P-O), 60 × 73 cm (24 × 28 in)

LR56 *Au dessus de Port Vendres*, 1934, oil, PV (P-O), 50.8 × 60.96 cm (20 × 24 in)

LR57 *Trawlers, Port Vendres*, 1934, oil, PV (P-O), 38.1 × 45.72 cm (15 × 18 in)

LR58 *La Garrigue*, 1934, oil, Axat (AU), 60 × 73 cm (24 × 28 in), exh. NEAC 1937, £25

LR59 *Axat*, 1934, oil, Axat (AU), 60 × 73 cm (24 × 28 in), exh. NEAC 1936

LR60 *Sawmill at Rebenty*, 1934, oil, Rebenty (AU), 50.8 × 60.96 cm (20 × 24 in), exh. NEAC 1938

LR61 *Paysage boisé*, 1934, oil, Lapradelle (AU), 50.8 × 60.96 cm (20 × 24 in)

LR62 *Paysage de montagne*, 1934, oil, Rebenty (AU), 38.1 × 45.72 cm (15 × 18 in)

LR63 *Paysage au chasseur*, 1934, oil, Lapradelle (AU), 47 × 56 cm (18.5 × 22 in)

LR64 *L'Aude à Axat*, 1934, oil, Axat (AU), 60 × 73 cm (24 × 28 in), exh. NEAC 1936

Spain

Although Collioure is less than 10 miles from the Spanish border Ihlee appears to have painted very little, if at all, in Spanish Catalonia with its principal cities of Barcelona and Girona and rugged coastline – the Costa Brava. Instead, towards the end of 1922 and for much of 1923, he travelled via Toledo to Málaga and Almería in the far south of the country. More than a decade later he explored Galicia with Isabelle, staying at Laguardia and Vigo before the Spanish Civil War intervened in 1936, forcing him to leave four paintings in Bilbao.

S1 *Toledo Sketch*, 1922, oil, Toledo, 38.1 × 45.72 cm (15 × 18 in)

S2 *Villa*, 1922, oil, Málaga, 38.1 × 45.72 cm (15 × 18 in)

S3 *Over a Garden Wall*, 1923, oil, Málaga, 50.8 × 60.96 cm (20 × 24 in), exh. NEAC June 1924, £26, Walker Art Gallery 1924

S4 *Conejo*, 1923, oil, Málaga, 50.8 × 60.96 cm (20 × 24 in), exh. Chenil Gallery 1926

S5 *The Hillside Nursery*, 1923, oil, Málaga, 63.5 × 76.2 cm (25 × 30 in), exh. NEAC June 1923, £40 (sold)

S6 *Maria*, 1923, oil, Málaga, 38.1 × 45.72 cm (15 × 18 in)

S7 *The Garden of Innocence*, 1923, oil, Malaga, 63.5 × 76.2 cm (25 × 30 in), exh. Wembley 1924, Walker Art Gallery 1925

S8 *Toledo*, 1923, oil, Toledo, 63.5 × 76.2 cm (25 × 30 in), exh. NEAC 1923, Chenil Gallery 1926, £60

S9 *The Harbour, Malaga*, 1923, oil, Málaga, 63.5 × 76.2 cm (25 × 30 in), exh. Goupil Gallery 1923, Whitechapel 1924, £40

S10 *The Road by the Sea*, 1923, oil, Málaga, 50.8 × 60.96 cm (20 × 24 in), exh. NEAC 1925, Chenil Gallery 1926, £20

S11 *El Palo*, 1923, oil, Málaga, 50.8 × 60.96 cm (20 × 24 in), £25, sold to Sir Edward Marsh, now in York Art Gallery

S12 *Andalusian Village*, 1923, oil, Almería, 50.8 × 60.96 cm (20 × 24 in), exh. NEAC June 1924, £26

S13 *Soir à Laguardia*, 1935, oil, Laguardia, 47 × 56 cm (18.5 × 22 in)

S14 *Paysage de Galice*, 1935, oil, Laguardia, 47 × 56 cm (18.5 × 22 in)

S15 *Fontaine, Laguardia*, 1935, oil, Laguardia, 50.8 × 60.96 cm (20 × 24 in)

S16 *Porteuse d'eau*, 1935, oil, Laguardia, 50.8 × 60.96 cm (20 × 24 in)

S17 *Le Chantier*, 1935, oil, Laguardia, 50.8 × 60.96 cm (20 × 24 in)

S18 *Le Bassin des Chalutiers*, 1935, oil, Vigo, 47 × 56 cm (18.5 × 22 in)

S19 *Le Bâteau de Canjas*, 1935, oil, Vigo, 50.8 × 60.96 cm (20 × 24 in)

S20 *Le Port de Vigo*, 1935, oil, Vigo, 60 × 73 cm (24 × 28 in)

S21 *Shipyard Vigo*, 1935, oil, Vigo, 50.8 × 60.96 cm (20 × 24 in), exh. Salon des Tuileries, NEAC 1937, Bradford 1938

S22 *L'Usine blanche*, 1935, oil, Vigo, 47 × 56 cm (18.5 × 22 in)

S23 *Le Chemin de la mer*, 1935, oil, Vigo, 47 × 56 cm (18.5 × 22 in)

S24 *Vigo plage*, 1935, oil, Vigo, 60 × 73 cm (24 × 28 in)

S25 *Isabelle at Window*, 1936, oil, Vigo, 47 × 56 cm (18.5 × 22 in), left at Bilbao

S26 *Castro de Vigo, the Harbour*, 1936, oil, Vigo 47 × 56 cm (18.5 × 22 in), left at Bilbao

S27 *Castro de Vigo, Sunny Day*, 1936, oil, Vigo, 50.8 × 60.96 cm (20 × 24 in)

S28 *A Grey Day*, 1936, oil, Vigo, 50.8 × 60.96 cm (20 × 24 in), left at Bilbao

S29 *Boats at Estepona*, 1961, oil, 50.8 × 60.96 cm (20 × 24 in) exh. NEAC 1961, £37

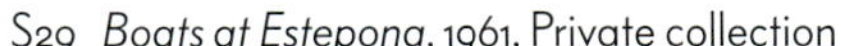
S29 *Boats at Estepona*, 1961, Private collection

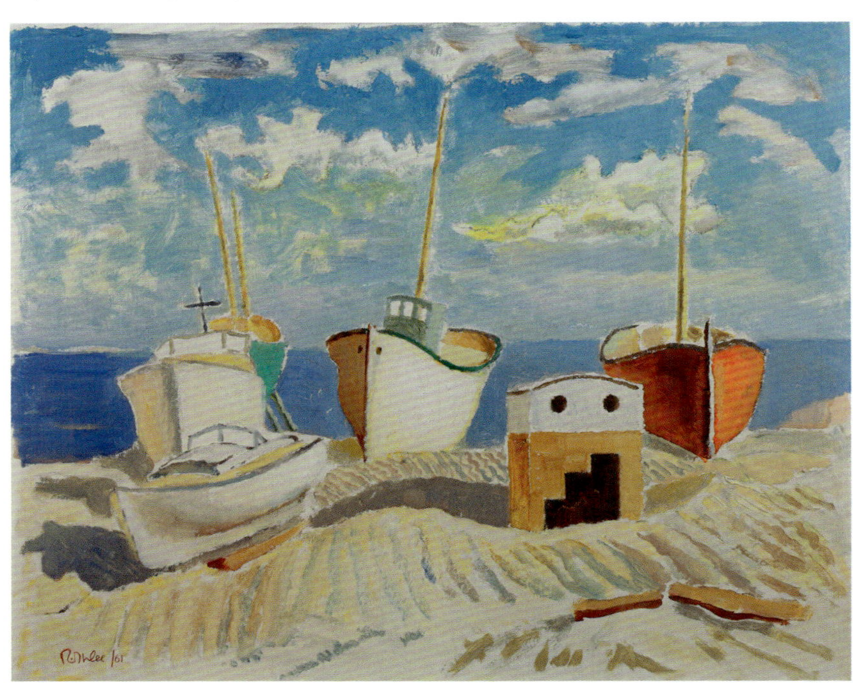

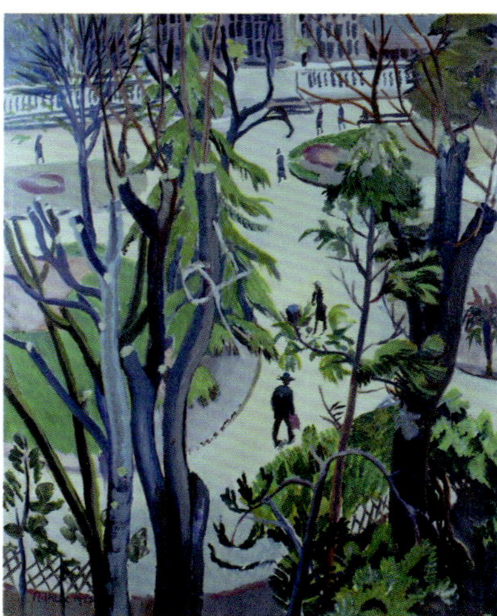

RF1 *Public Gardens, Avignon*, 1922, Private collection

Rest of France

RF1 *Public Gardens, Avignon*, 1922, oil, 38.1 × 45.72 cm (15 × 18 in), exh. Chenil Gallery 1926, £20

RF2 *Marseilles*, 1922, oil, Marseilles, 50.8 × 60.96 cm (20 × 24 in)

RF3 *Still Life, Hendaye*, 1922, oil, Hendaye, 50.8 × 60.96 cm (20 × 24 in), exh. NEAC 1923, £20

RF4 *The Bridge at Hendaye*, 1922, oil, Hendaye, 50.8 × 60.96 cm (20 × 24 in), £20

RF5 *View of Hendaye*, 1922, oil, 38.1 × 45.72 cm (15 × 18 in), exh. Redfern Gallery 1924, £12

RF6 *Behind Hendaye*, 1922, oil, 38.1 × 45.72 cm (15 × 18 in), £12

RF7 *Bois au Lapin*, Paris, 1933, oil, Paris, 60 × 73 cm (24 × 28 in), exh. Salle Arago 1934

RF8 *Nu*, 1933, oil, Paris, 60 × 73 cm (24 × 28 in), exh. Salle Arago 1934

RF9 *Au Square des Batignolles*, 1933, oil, Paris, 38.1 × 45.72 cm (15 × 18 in), exh. Salle Arago 1934

RF10 *St Lazare, la voie ferrée*, 1933, oil, Paris, 47 × 56 cm (18.5 × 22 in), exh. Salon d'Automne 1933

Post Second World War

Ihlee took a break from painting after his escape from France in 1940 and did not resume until around 1950, by which time he and Isabelle were settled at The Yews in West Deeping. From 1956 to his death in 1968 he exhibited 28 paintings at the NEAC. Not all their measurements and media are recorded.

WD1 *Still Life 1, West Deeping*, c.1950, oil on board, 50 × 60 cm (19.6 × 23.6 in), exh. Peterborough 1951

WD2 *Still Life, Cockerel*, c.1950, oil on canvas, 38 × 46 cm (15 × 18 in), exh. Peterborough 1951

WD3 *Mediterranean Shore*, c.1954, exh. NEAC 1956, £42

WD4 *Tape and Pins*, c.1955, exh. NEAC 1956, £86

WD5 *Jug and Candlestick*, c.1956, exh. NEAC 1957, £47

WD6 *Architectural Shapes*, c.1956, exh. NEAC 1957, £42

WD7 *Red Landscape*, c.1957, exh. NEAC 1958, £63

WD8 *Denia*, 1958, oil on board, 46 × 54.5 cm (18 × 21.5 in), exh. NEAC 1958, £63, sold Bellmans 2018, £350

WD9 *The Sea Was Green*, 1959, exh. NEAC 1959, £26

WD10 *Shacks*, 1959, exh. NEAC 1959, £53

WD11 *Facades*, 1959, oil on board, 50 × 60 cm (19.6 × 23.6 in), exh. NEAC 1959, £74

WD12 *Estepona*, 1959, exh. NEAC 1959, £73

WD13 *Canigou*, 1961, exh. NEAC 1961, £21

WD14 *Collioure Again*, 1961, exh. NEAC 1961, £26

WD15 *Old Stones*, 1961, exh. NEAC 1961, £47

WD16 *Rachel*, 1962, oil on board, 64 × 53 cm (25 × 21 in), exh. NEAC 1962, £95, sold Gorringes 2017, £1400

WD17 *Old Collioure*, 1962, exh. NEAC 1962, £42

WD18 *Ullapool*, 1962, oil on board, 46 × 55 cm (18 × 21.5 in), exh. NEAC 1962, £53, sold Sotheby's 2004, £1700

WD19 *The Harbour at Ullapool*, 1962, oil on board, 38 × 46 cm (15 × 18 in)

WD20 *Blue Shadows*, 1962, exh. NEAC 1962, £47

WD21 *Girl's Head*, 1963, exh. NEAC 1963, £37

WD22 *Reflections*, 1963, exh. NEAC 1963, £47

WD23 *Fort*, 1963, exh. NEAC 1963, £84

WD24 *Beach*, 1963, exh. NEAC 1963, £84

WD25 *Blue Bay*, 1964, exh. NEAC 1964, £42

WD26 *Avenue*, 1964, oil on board, 38 × 46 cm (15 × 18 in), exh. NEAC 1964, £32, sold Bonhams 2011, £600

WD27 *By Artificial Light*, 1966, exh. NEAC 1966, £42

WD28 *The Red Turret*, 1966, oil on canvas, 76 × 91.5 cm (30 × 36 in)

WD29 *Hotel Terrace, Collioure*, 46 × 38 cm (18 × 15 in)

WD30 *Fishing Boats in Dry Dock*, 1966, oil on board, 91.5 × 61 cm (36 × 24 in), exh. NEAC 1966, £84

WD31 *Portrait of a Frying Pan*, 1966, exh. NEAC 1966, £47

WD32 *Hot Afternoon*, 1966, exh. NEAC 1966, £26

WD33 *Market Place, Collioure*, 1967

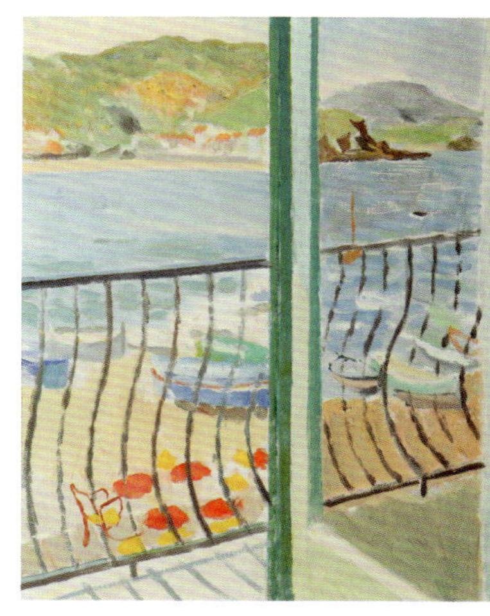

WD29 *Hotel Terrace, Collioure*
Private collection

Timeline

1883
Born to parents Heinrich and Victoria. Spends early years at a large Victorian house in Arterberry Rd, Wimbledon called 'Cronberg'
1891
Father dies and mother returns to Germany, leaving Rudolph in the care of his aunt and uncle and elder brother Frederick
1902–6
Apprenticed to Ferranti
1906–10
Studies at the Slade
1909
Shares Melville Nettleship Prize for figure composition with Maxwell Gordon Lightfoot
1911
Exhibits at Vanessa Bell's Friday Club. Suicide of Maxwell Gordon Lightfoot
1912
First London solo show at the Carfax Gallery. Starts contributing illustrations to *Rhythm* magazine
1913
Visits Brittany with Edgar Hereford. Marries Sophia Roith at Fulham Register Office
1914
Second one-man show at Carfax Gallery
1914–18
Works as a draughtsman at a factory in Peterborough, now called Baker Perkins, run by his brother Fred
1918
Produces a suite of 12 drawings for lithographs of war work at the factory, which made field ovens and guns for the allied forces. Files for divorce against Sophia
1919
Exhibits at Friday Club and Arts League of Service. Meets Charles Rennie Mackintosh and his wife Margaret
1920
Elected member of New English Art Club
1921
One-man show at the Leicester Galleries
1922
Painting expedition to Algeria with Edgar Hereford before the pair settle in Collioure
1923–7
With Ihlee's encouragement, Charles Rennie Mackintosh and his wife base themselves at Port Vendres within walking distance of Collioure
1926
One-man show at Chenil Gallery. Exhibits for the first of many times at the Salon d'Automne, Paris
1927
Meets Isabelle Mons who later becomes his second wife. Mackintosh becomes ill and Ihlee accompanies him back to England
1928
Death of Mackintosh from cancer. Ihlee exhibits at the Salon des Indépendants in Paris and spends several weeks in the mountain village of Molitg near Prades
1931
Solo exhibition at the Galerie Campistro in Perpignan
1932
Second exhibition at the Galerie Campistro
1934
Solo exhibition at the Salle Arago in Perpignan
1935
Second exhibition at the Salle Arago
1935–6
Ihlee is painting in Spain on the eve of the outbreak of the Spanish Civil War. He flees, leaving behind several paintings in Bilbao
1938
Marries Isabelle in Collioure. Death of brother Fred
1940
After France's surrender to Germany Ihlee returns to England with Isabelle and Laure Doher, the 10-year-old daughter of Hereford's partner Marguerite Doher. Several paintings left in Paris
1942–5
Works in a machine tool factory to help the war effort. Settles in West Deeping near Peterborough
1949
Hereford marries Marguerite Doher and settles in Swinstead, not far from Ihlee
1951
One-man show at St Peter's Hall, Peterborough supported by the Arts Council
1953
Death of Edgar Hereford
1968
Exhibition of paintings (1920–30) at Sleaford. Death of Ihlee
1975
Exhibition at Rutland Sixth Form College, Oakham
1978
Exhibition at Graves Gallery, Sheffield and Belgrave Gallery in London
1999
Death of Isabelle Ihlee

Other Artists in Collioure

Although in 1905 the famous Fauves, Matisse and Derain, did more than anyone else to put the Catalan fishing port on the artistic map, many other artists have had a brush with Collioure.

Paul Signac (1863–1935) produced notable pointillist studies some 20 years earlier and his contemporary Henri Martin (1860–1943) painted Collioure in similar style at roughly the same time as Ihlee and Hereford in the 1920s and 30s. A less flamboyant Fauve, Albert Marquet (1875–1947), spent several months in Collioure in 1912 before returning to the Catalan coast in later life. Other notable visitors included Tsuguharu Foujita (1886–1968), who, in 1920, was in Collioure with Nina Hamnett (1890–1956), and, 20 years later, Raoul Dufy (1877–1953), who coined the rhyme 'Collioure sans voiles c'est un soir sans étoiles' ('Collioure without sails is like a night without stars').

Of the British contingent, James Dickson Innes, as previously mentioned, was a repeat visitor to the Vermilion Coast (fig.70), as were some other artists of Ihlee's generation including Derwent Lees. Roger Fry, who lectured Ihlee and Hereford on History of Art at the Slade, stayed in Port Vendres in the 1920s, as did Ethelbert White (1891–1972) who, like Ihlee, was a member of the NEAC. Jessica Dismorr was in the region in 1925 with her friend Catherine Giles (1878–1955). Among their surviving works are a modernist study of Collioure by Dismorr (fig.71) and a watercolour

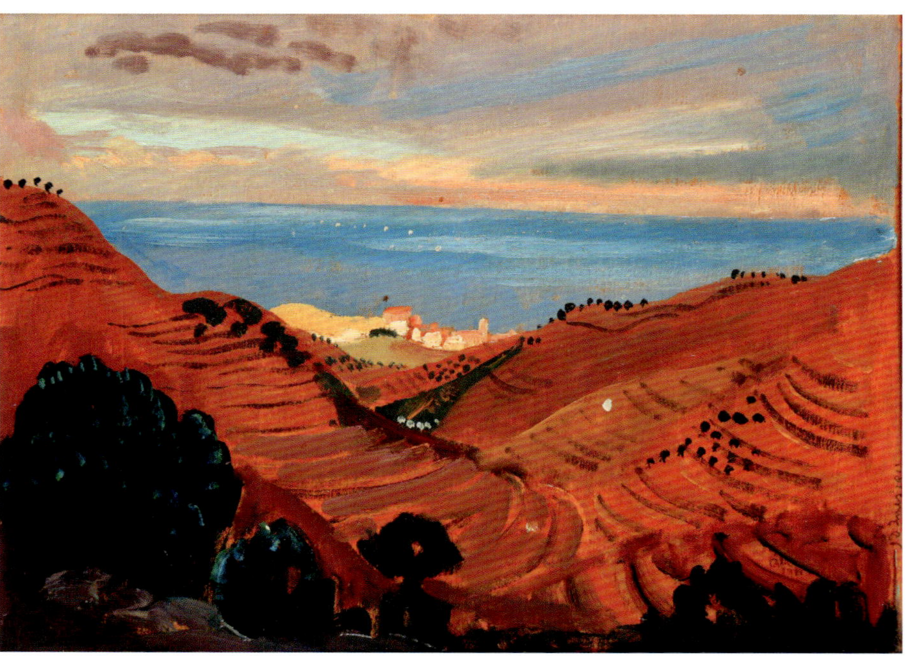

70
James Dickson Innes
Collioure from the Hills, c.1911
Oil on board
23.4 × 33 cm (9.25 × 13 in)
Private collection

of Amélie-les-Bains by Giles. The German expressionist painter Max Pechstein (1881–1955) was in Collioure in 1931 shortly before being hounded by the Nazis for his 'degenerate' art.

After the war, as Collioure gradually changed from working fishing port to congested tourist destination, the number of visiting artists increased although, perhaps, the quality of work did not. In the 1950s when Ihlee began revisiting the region he could have hardly avoided bumping into some fellow painters. Among the best of the British artists were Norman Janes (1892–1980), Philip Naviasky (1894–1983) and William Wilson (1905–72).

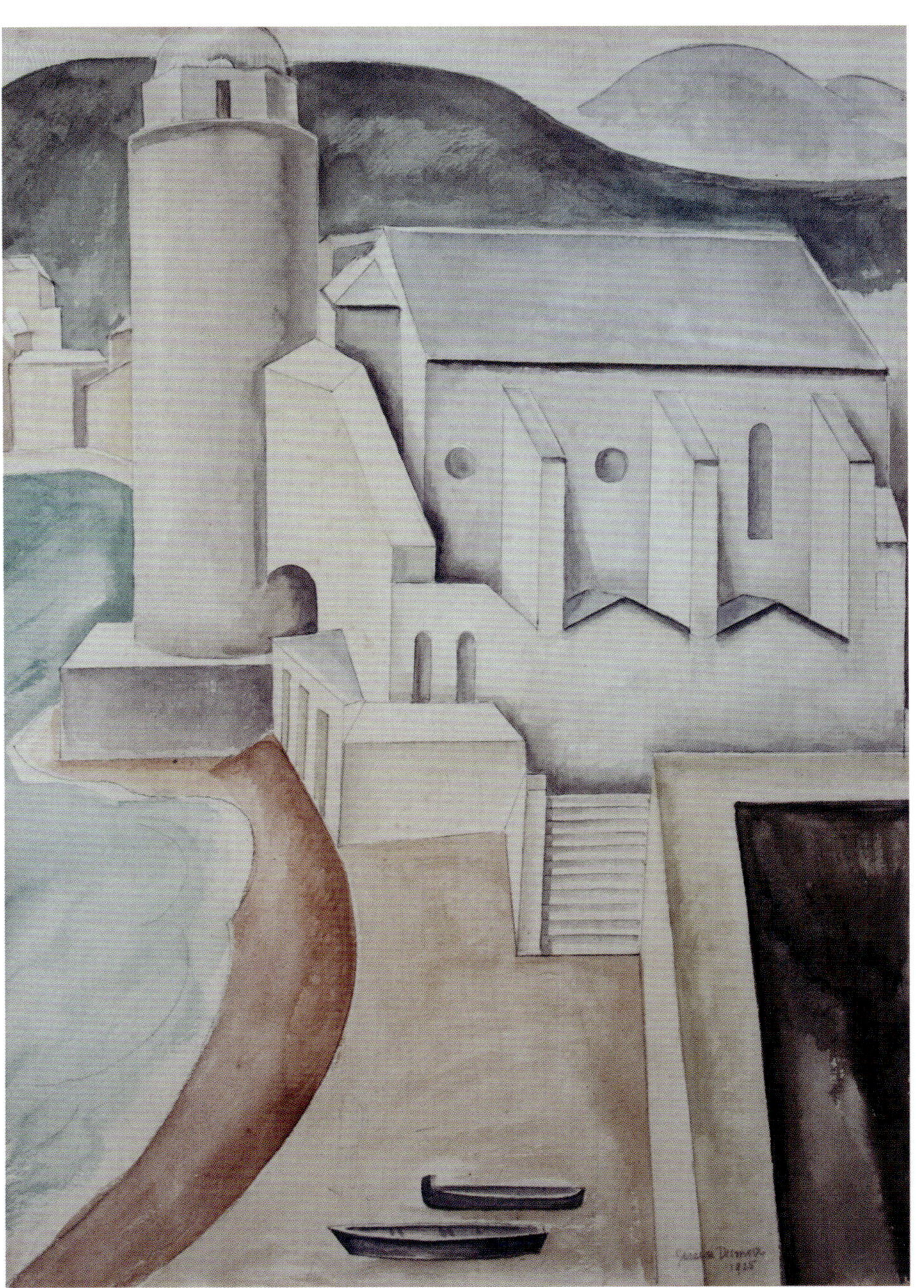

71
Jessica Dismorr
Collioure, 1925
Watercolour and pencil on paper
37.5 × 27 cm (15 × 10.6 in)
Private collection

Image Credits

We would like to thank the following for allowing us to reproduce images. Other works are in private collections. Copyright of works by Ihlee and Hereford is held by the family estate.

Figs 5 and 35 Hunterian Art Gallery, University of Glasgow
Fig.7 Museumslandschaft Hessen Kassel
Figs 8, 9, 25 and 69 Monksgrange Archives
Fig.10 University College London (Bridgeman Images)
Figs 11 and 21 Tate Archive and Gallery
Fig.12 Charles Miller Ltd, Specialist Marine and Scientific Auctioneers
Fig.13 Trustees of the Cecil Higgins Art Gallery (The Higgins, Bedford)
Fig.15 Manchester Art Gallery (Bridgeman Images)
Fig.16 Aberdeen Art Gallery
Fig.20 Liss Fine Art (Bridgeman Images)
Figs 22, 23, 29, B11 and RF1 Irving Grose
Figs 24, 61 and E10 Bonhams
Fig.26 Andrew Bunce Fine Art
Fig.28 Liss Fine Art (Bridgeman Images)
Fig.31 University of Hull Art Collection
Figs 41, 42 Musée d'Art Moderne, Collioure
Fig.51 Christie's Images (Bridgeman Images)
Fig.59 York Museums Trust (York Art Gallery)
Fig.62 Copyright Excelsior, L'Equipe/Roger Viollet
Fig.71 Woolley and Wallis Saleroom, Salisbury
Fig.LR61 Louise Kosman Fine Art

Works in Public Collections

Pounding the Bait (drawing), Aberdeen Art Gallery
The Quarrel (drawing), The Higgins, Bedford
Little Bay – Audierne (oil) and *Workmen Resting* (charcoal), Cyfarthfa Castle Museum & Art Gallery, Merthyr Tydfil
Fort Precincts (oil) and Ihlee's notebook with lists of works, Hunterian Art Gallery, University of Glasgow
The Quarrel (watercolour), Kelvingrove Art Gallery and Museum, Glasgow
The Red Gate Posts (oil), Government Art Collection
Montagnes et orangiers (oil), Hull University
The Well (oil), Manchester Art Gallery
Terrace Consolation (oil), Musée d'Art Moderne, Collioure
Biskra Scene (Oil), New College, Oxford
El Palo (oil), York Art Gallery

Acknowledgements

There are four people without whom it would have been difficult if not impossible to produce this book. In his youth Nigel Farrow knew Rudolph Ihlee and, as chairman of Lund Humphries, asked me to write about him. Irving Grose organised exhibitions of Ihlee's work in 1978 when he produced a catalogue based on extensive research, which he generously shared. Grant Waters gave me a copy of Ihlee's list of paintings between 1922 and 1936 which became the backbone of the Collioure narrative. Charles Walker (son of Laure Walker, née Doher), who looked upon Ihlee as a grandfather, granted permission to reproduce his work.

In Collioure, Claire Muchir and Nadine Skilbeck at the Musée d'Art Moderne were very supportive, as were Jacques Issorel, Monique Alonso, Christine Corbel and Valia Boulay, the niece of Henri Vergé-Sarrat. Denise Scott-Fears, whose grandmother, Evelyn Scott, was in Collioure at the same time as Ihlee and Hereford, was kind enough to let me reproduce extracts from her letters. I am also very grateful to Joseph Sharples from the Hunterian in Glasgow who allowed us to quote at length from the letters of Charles Rennie Mackintosh, whose friendship with Ihlee and Hereford provided an invaluable insight into their lives in the south of France. I would also like to thank Robin Crichton and Pamela Robertson for additional help with Charles Rennie Mackintosh, and HarperCollins Publishers Ltd (Olivia Bignold-Jordan) for allowing me to reproduce an extract from *The Catalans* by Patrick O'Brian.

Christian Millet, a historian from Brittany, was able to identify some of the works Ihlee painted there and Jeremy Hill, grandson of Maggie Tomalin, provided useful family background and the youthful photos of Ihlee from the Monksgrange Archive. The staff at the Tate Archive and Library were unfailingly helpful, as was Robert Winckworth from the Slade archive. Thanks also for the co-operation of various public galleries which hold Ihlee's work, including Hull University (John Bernasconi), Aberdeen Art Gallery (Griffin Coe), Manchester City Art Gallery (John Peel), York Art Gallery (Melanie Baldwin), Cecil Higgins Art Gallery (Victoria Partridge), Contemporary Arts Society (Tania Adams). Several dealers, owners and auction houses have also been helpful, including Bonhams (Andrew Currie), Whytes (Adele Hughes), Woolley and Wallis (Ed Beer), Charles Miller Auctions Ltd (Charles Miller, Sara Sturgess), Andrew Bunce, Andrea Spurling, Victoria Ham, Louise Kosman, Poppy Stothert, Barry Trice, Paul Liss and Harry Moore-Gwyn.

Kimberley Ahmet from the Artists' Collecting Society helped me make contact with Ihlee's heirs and Gabrielle Abbott from the Baker Perkins Historical Society provided useful information about his wartime work in Peterborough. Dorothee Gerkens from the Museumslandschaft Hessen Kassel told me about Ihlee's great-uncle, the German painter Johann Ihlée. Thanks also to my editors at Lund Humphries, Lucy Clark, Anna Norman and Rochelle Roberts, and to my wife, Natalie, and children, Katie and Tom, for more or less tolerating incessant talk about Ihlee on family walks.

Index

Page numbers in *italics* refer to illustrations.